IN LOVE WITH MOVIES

IN LOVE
WITH MOVIES

From New Yorker Films
to Lincoln Plaza Cinemas

DANIEL TALBOT
EDITED BY **TOBY TALBOT**
FOREWORD BY **WERNER HERZOG**

COLUMBIA UNIVERSITY PRESS
NEW YORK

Columbia University Press
Publishers Since 1893
New York   Chichester, West Sussex
cup.columbia.edu
Copyright © 2022 Columbia University Press
All rights reserved

Library of Congress Cataloging-in-Publication Data
Names: Talbot, Daniel, 1926–2017, author. | Talbot, Toby, editor.
Title: In love with movies : from New Yorker films to Lincoln Plaza cinemas /
Daniel Talbot ; edited by Toby Talbot
Description: New York : Columbia University Press, 2022. | Includes index.
Identifiers: LCCN 2021016371 (print) | LCCN 2021016372 (ebook) |
ISBN 9780231203142 (hardback) | ISBN 9780231203159 (trade paperback) |
ISBN 9780231554893 (ebook)
Subjects: LCSH: Talbot, Daniel, 1926–2017. | Distributors (Commerce)—
New York (State) —New York—Biography. | Motion picture theater owners—
New York (State) —New York—Biography. | Motion pictures—Distribution. |
Motion picture industry—Anecdotes.
Classification: LCC PN1998.3.T34235 A3 2022 (print) |
LCC PN1998.3.T34235 (ebook) | DDC 791.43092 [B]—dc23
LC record available at https://lccn.loc.gov/2021016371
LC ebook record available at https://lccn.loc.gov/2021016372

Columbia University Press books are printed on permanent and durable
acid-free paper.
Printed in the United States of America

Cover design: Chang Jae Lee
Cover image: Dan Talbot in the Lincoln Plaza Cinemas booth
(photographer unknown)

To the Lincoln Plaza Cinemas and our audiences

CONTENTS

FOREWORD

WERNER HERZOG

Dan Talbot marks an epoch that has vanished. These were glorious times for cinema. Dan started with the New Yorker Theater in March 1960, and he ran the Lincoln Plaza Cinemas until the end of 2017. In fact, he saw a film there and checked on the operations on December 22. A week later, on December 29, he died. The Lincoln Plaza lease was not renewed.

The art house theaters are gone, the films are gone, the audiences are gone, the reviewers are gone. Recently I asked a daughter of our friends, a fifteen-year-old, about her habits of going to the movies. Going to the movies? she asked, astonished. No, she and her friends would not go to the movies. Why? I asked. Because, she explained, it was dark there, and she would not know anyone around her. She would see films streamed on her plasma screen at home, but also on her cell phone, and if a film went too slowly, she would accelerate it to double the speed.

In his recent article published in *Harper's Magazine*, Martin Scorsese eloquently describes the scene in New York that had started around the late fifties. He evokes the wanderings of a young man—quite obviously a self-portrait—through Greenwich Village, passing all the cinemas with their competing programs: a Soviet film by Mikhail Kalatozov, *The Cranes Are Flying*, and John Cassavetes's *Shadows*; from there to *Ashes and Diamonds* by Andrzej Wajda, *Breathless* by Jean-Luc Godard, *La Dolce Vita* by Federico Fellini, *Pickpocket* by Robert Bresson, screenings of Andy Warhol movies, and avant-garde films by Kenneth Anger and Stan Brakhage. All this on a single stroll that is filled with excitement and expectations—his, and those of the audiences queuing up at the theaters. And, what is important, right at the beginning of his article he describes the young man: "*Under one arm, he's carrying books. In his other hand, a copy of* The Village Voice." Here he describes everyone, himself, Dan Talbot, me, and the audiences: we were all reading books, and we looked out for the latest reviews of films in the *Village Voice*, *New York Times*, and *New Yorker* magazine.

It is not just that film culture has almost vanished; the picture is much bigger than that. Hardly anyone reads books anymore, and this is a cultural trend that started long before the arrival of the internet, where much of the written discourse in the social media has degenerated into tweets, Facebook posts, and monosyllabic exchanges embellished with emojis. At universities, for example, even the departments of classics, where students read poetry, philosophy, and the tragedies of Greek and Roman antiquity, find it hard to make the students read at all. Through a friend who teaches classics at a renowned university, I have seen texts written by graduate students who can barely express a simple thought in a few coherent sentences. It is therefore no surprise to see statistics that tell us that today 40 percent of high school students are functionally illiterate. Yes, they can read, but they cannot understand the text or put it into context, like recognizing something as satire or as fake news.

Over the last decades, almost all print media have abolished their film critics. There are only a very few left who seriously write about cinema; all the rest have shifted to celebrity news. The last mammoths are gone: Roger Ebert, Amos Vogel, Lotte Eisner. And gone are the days when on prime-time TV Gore Vidal and Norman Mailer would fight their battles over the course of the Great American Novel. Scorsese correctly points out that "the art of cinema is being systematically devalued, sidelined, demeaned, and reduced to its lowest common denominator, 'content.'" The term "content" in the jargon of the film industry means the profitability of a streamlined, conformist, and safe product, and a screenplay is called not a screenplay but a "property."

Where are those days? Where is the new Dan Talbot? Why do we not have his New Yorker Theater any longer? I am not in the mood of mourning, or in the mood of complaint. We have to celebrate him and the culture, the collective excitement, that he fearlessly steered through cliffs, and storms, and treacherous whirlpools. I personally owe him the discovery and the release of all my early films. *Aguirre, the Wrath of God* opened at the Cinema Studio, and it was my breakthrough in the United States. Many of my other films followed, but I am indebted to him in particular for his appreciation of *Land of Silence and Darkness*, which held a very special place in his heart, as it does in mine.

The entire pantheon of films that were made in eternity and for eternity appeared on Dan's screens, where, as Bernardo Bertolucci phrased it, "there are no more national identities, no more classes . . . they are the Cathedrals of Collective Dreams." He helped revive Satyajit Ray's *The Apu Trilogy*, which had been dormant on shelves for a decade, and he wrote about these films in the most inspired terms. If there is anything that has greatness in cinema, it is this work, no matter what culture is yours, no matter what the intellectual trends may be, no matter to which age group you belong. There are films for which I would like to bow to Dan, and then hug him hard: *Pickpocket* by Bresson, *The Tree of Wooden Clogs* by Ermanno Olmi, *Tokyo Story* (and eleven other films) by Yasujiro Ozu; the films by the French New Wave, François Truffaut, Godard, Claude Chabrol, Jean Eustache; the films of the New German Cinema, Rainer Werner Fassbinder, Wim Wenders, Volker Schlöndorff, my own films; those of the Brazilian Cinema Novo, Glauber Rocha, Nelson Pereira dos Santos, Ruy Guerra; Iranian films by Abbas Kiarostami; *Shoah* by Claude Lanzmann. This film, nine hours long, was almost impossible to "market," but Dan showed it. It found almost universal praise by reviewers, and a rabbi came all the way from a small town in New Jersey and obstinately would not leave afterward, rocking in prayer against a wall, because he was blessing the theater. Only one voice was against the film, Pauline Kael, one of the really important critics. Dan immediately confronted her, and I loved him for this.

I have very fond personal memories of Dan. Our various meetings at the Cannes Film Festival in the 1970s; in Munich, where he and Toby, his wife, who edited this book, came to visit me (my first-born son was a toddler at that time). We became personally known to each other. Whenever I was in New York, I would drop by his distribution company, New Yorker Films, and simply walk in unannounced and grab a chair while he was in discussion with his staff about the next programs. Our deals were written as memos, less than a page long, like handshakes, and I never had to regret a single one of these contracts.

What can we, the filmmakers, do in a world that has shifted to the internet? Try to give it more depth? Fill it with content that challenges the "content" of the industry? I must clarify that I am not against the internet, I am very much for it, as long as we learn how to use it in a better way than in its present, early, chaotic days. Meanwhile, everything points in the direction of monopolies, as in late capitalism. We shall inevitably be a minority, but film culture will not die out. Even Scorsese sees clearly that his films that have had their run in theaters are alive and available on the internet. My films that New Yorker Films distributed are all present and reachable through the internet, on streaming platforms, and through my own production company. A young audience is articulating itself. Many of the emails that I receive come from very young people in obscure places, and they start to contact each other and point out the excitement of films I made when their parents were not even born yet. We should not battle the internet. We have to do everything to improve it. But it needs courage, long-range perspectives, and the spirit of men like Dan Talbot.

"Film distribution is not a normal, rational business. It is an ongoing craps game played by lunatics like me who are possessed by a love of cinema," remarks Dan in this book, and I am looking around as hard as I can, and there are no more lunatics. But he remains a point of orientation. I see him, the lighthouse that shows us the harbor in the dark. I embrace him. I miss him. And I will not stop singing his praise.

ACKNOWLEDGMENTS

I want to thank:

Jennifer Crewe, for her ongoing commitment to our work.

Cindi Rowell, dedicated all the way, from archival research to final proofs.

Diana Drumm, for sifting through the New Yorker guest books in the archive and for organizing the photos that appear in this book.

Leslie Kriesel, along with Cindi and Diana, for copyediting the manuscript.

Dana Isaacson, for early, valuable ideas in the shape of the text.

Aaron Cutler, for a meticulous indexing of Dan's personal files.

Matt Peterson, for his initial processing of the material now housed at Columbia University's Rare Book and Manuscript Library.

Our daughter Sarah Talbot, for her support from the start and for delving into her father's archive at Columbia and at home.

—Toby Talbot

INTRODUCTION

Fragments from the Dream World

Over the years, many people I've come in contact with have urged me to write my memoirs. They see my work as unusually exciting. I travel to foreign countries and participate in famous film festivals. I pick movies to distribute or play at my theater. I dine with movie directors, stars, and producers. I'm responsible for educating a large public with quality films. Occasionally journalists mention my name. I'm in the media. At parties, strangers compliment me for the movies I've shown at my various theaters on Manhattan's Upper West Side. I win awards and tributes. I have my Chevalier de l'Ordre des Arts et Lettres. I never wear the pin on my jacket and have given the medal itself to my wife, Toby, to wear as a necklace at parties. Occasionally I'm attacked for showing or distributing such-and-such film.

I enjoy reading other people's memoirs. Among my favorite books are the memoirs or reminiscences or diaries of Gerald Brenan, Thomas Mann, Ernest Hemingway, Thomas Bernhard, Edmund Wilson, Samuel Johnson. If you're in love with a person's work, you want to follow their trajectory. There may be some clue as to how to appropriate their endeavors and insights into the fine tuning of your own life. Great memoirs, fleeting as anybody's life may seem, often have the power to stop you in your tracks and steer you into profound contemplation. My soul came to a dead halt after reading Nadezhda Mandelstam's *Hope Abandoned*. My life compared to hers is that of a boring esthete. Can you imagine memorizing her husband's poems while in prison, since she was not allowed pen and paper, so that this rich legacy would live on? Most great fiction writers do not write memoirs. Their fiction is their memoir. The three great Jewish American writers—Bellow, Malamud, and Roth (whom Bellow referred to as the Hart, Schaffner, and Marx of American writers)—did not write their memoirs. They reveal more about themselves and the world around their selves than any memoirist. Memoirs are satisfactory only to the extent that the writing swings, the insights occasionally make the bulb light up, and there are some jokey or moving events as the person goes from A to B; the greatest writing remains fiction. My definition of a great writer is someone whose words make the reader want to write. At various periods, Proust, Miller, and Céline had this effect upon me; in recent times, Raymond Carver, Thomas Bernhard, José Saramago, Saul Bellow, Bernard Malamud, and Philip Roth have induced this desire.

I think: Who needs another book? Somewhere I read that fifty thousand titles are published annually in our country. My goodness. What a flood of pages, of words like machine-gun bullets spraying readers. I'm not "in literature," in the game. This gives me complexes. So, I say, let's do it for the fun of it, and see where it goes.

One day I bought a neatly lined journal, and over a period of ten years I wrote the short takes that now appear in this book. For years the journal rested in my study closet among travel books, maps of Europe, and issues of Robert Parker's *The Wine Advocate*, waiting patiently until I could organize my random thoughts into sentences I might come to trust. Meanwhile, life swirled around me: the jangle of New York City culture, family pursuits, my work as a film programmer and film distributor.

Some of my descriptions of things may not be entirely accurate. They may border on fiction. Some are outright fictitious. The stuff of my days had centered around running two businesses with fifty-five people on my payroll; doing complicated business deals, much as I've always wanted to simplify them; using my brain to make rapid decisions on what films to show or distribute; raising three powerful girls; ever striving to be a nurturing and loving mate; tending to my mother before she died; dealing with my in-laws, both professional gamblers whom I often had to bail out from financial disaster; chatting with or seeing my eighty-five-year-old aunt once a week so that she wouldn't feel abandoned; handling occasionally troublesome employees.

Often I wish I could make sense of my life. It's the silences, the insights that flash and quickly vanish like blips on an electronic screen, the failures to do such and such, the unrequited sexual and work ambitions, the rich fantasies that come and go like automobile travel on the Long Island Expressway—these desiderata that never make it to the page, more vital in life than in a paragraph in a book. Life itself and the attempt to memorialize it are mutually antagonistic. Those who pull it off have earned their right to be among the great ones.

IN LOVE WITH MOVIES

PART 1

EARLY YEARS

NUEVA YORK

In the days of my youth, I had two basic theatergoing experiences. One was in the Bronx, where entire weekends were spent at our local movie house. My mother packed huge brown paper bags full of sandwiches, pickles, apples, and pies early on Saturday mornings. I didn't return until late at night, my eyes dangerously bloodshot. It was the same story on Sundays. Having absorbed on those weekends every conceivable gesture, line, action, and plot turn, my friends and I would spend the remainder of the week practicing our repertoire on street corners and in schoolyards. We became masters of the hip draw, the death fall, ferocious jaw clouting, barroom dialect, wise-guyism, cool casualness, clowning, and swooning. Little did we then realize what a fantastic influence movies would have on our lives: our ethics, public behavior, clothes, and even our food.

The other experience was at Radio City or the Roxy. It meant getting up at five a.m. after a restless night, putting on a neatly pressed navy-blue suit, taking a one-hour IRT train ride, and having lunch or dinner at Gluckstern's or Lindy's. At times this was so formidable a family affair that it included several cousins and aunts and uncles from all over the Bronx and Queens. I can still recall going to bed at the end of the evening with my brain spinning so hard that I had to rest the entire following day.

. . .

Years later, when Toby and I began dating, it seemed only natural to go to the movies. We gorged on British films and Italian neorealism. Though an ardent moviegoer, I always preferred not to investigate the literature on a particular film or read the serious critics. I knew what I liked in a movie and had developed my own ideas as to what constituted artistry.

Curiosity arose and later I began rummaging through hundreds of books and articles, eventually struck by the existence of a vital body of writing on film. It had attracted some of the finest minds. Hence the genesis of my book *Film: An Anthology*. I quote from the preface of that 1959 edition, published by Simon & Schuster:

> Erwin Panofsky notes . . . that if suddenly all the "serious lyrical poets, composers, painters and sculptors" stopped creating, their work would scarcely be missed, whereas if films came to an abrupt halt, the result would be "catastrophic." . . . What painting and sculpture set out to do the movies complete: a heightened anthropomorphic vision, a continuous flowing of objects and people jammed together in moments of tenderness, spleen, melancholy, profanation, divination. A novelist often spends as much as twenty-five pages setting up an action that can take place in a second on the screen. This is the breath-taking economy that is the marvel of art.

As early as 1920, art historian Élie Faure, bored by the static limitations of theater, was among the first critics to hail film in an exciting way. He saw its inherent plastic and architectural possibilities:

> The revelation of what the cinema of the future can be came to me one day; I retain an exact memory of it, of the commotion that I experienced when I observed, in a flash, the magnificence there was in the relationship of a piece of black clothing to the gray wall of an inn. . . . These new plastic poems . . . transport us in three seconds from the wooded banks of a river that elephants cross, leaving a long track of foam, to the heart of wild mountains where distant horsemen pursue one another through the smoke of their rifle shots, and from evil taverns where powerful shadows bend over a deathbed in mysterious lights, to the weird half-light of submarine waters where fish wind through grottos of coral. . . . The cinema incorporates time and space. More than this, through the cinema time really becomes a dimension of space. We shall be able

to see dust rising, spreading, dissipating, a thousand years after it has spurted up from the road under the hoofs of a horse; we shall be able to see for a thousand years the smoke of a cigarette condensing and then entering the ether—and this in a frame of space under our very eyes.

Yes, I was hooked, having experienced the same "commotion" as Élie Faure.

■ ■ ■

Among the happier days of my life were those in the early 1950s. Toby and I got married in 1951. In fact, we'd grown up a few subway stops apart in the Bronx during the Depression, but only met by chance. After a few false starts, we finally hitched up and knew it was for keeps. We found an apartment in a block of three-story row houses in Sunnyside, Queens, a stone's throw from the Queensborough Bridge. We could walk into Manhattan.

Much has been written about how cheap it was to live in New York at the time—it's all true. Our rent was fifty dollars a month. It was a one-bedroom apartment. There was a spacious living room right off an ample kitchen, with plenty of room for our books, along with a hutch with two white rabbits.

In those years, Toby was developing her culinary magic. Some feminists get their backs up when I speak about these culinary achievements. They prefer to talk about her as a writer, translator, and professor. At one point, when making a plan with a travel agent, we requested a house rental with a kitchen. "I never travel without my cook," I told the travel agent, putting her on. She frowned. She didn't get it.

We also ate around town. One of our favorite restaurants was Joe's, a fish place right under the Third Avenue El in the Fifties. It had red-checkered gingham tablecloths and sawdust on the ancient wooden floors. The fish was simply prepared, grilled to our taste, served with french fries and a small paper cup of capered mayonnaise. With beer or white wine, there was no way to go wrong. When I sold my first anthology (*Thirteen Great Stories*), $1,000 advance in hand, we began our spending spree with a powerhouse dinner at Gallaghers: grilled porterhouse surrounded by the works.

Those were wonderful days. We had good health, good looks, the love of our parents, no children, our brains racing like the Concorde, and we did some of the things that well-educated, starry-eyed lovers like to do: read good books, listened to music, made a ton of love, and, of course, went to the movies.

■ ■ ■

We put in a lot of time at the Little Carnegie Theatre on Fifty-Seventh Street between Broadway and Sixth Avenue. And at the Normandie, a few doors down from the Little Carnegie, we saw *Symphonie Pastorale*, and Luis Buñuel's *Viridiana* at the Fine Arts in the Fifties off Park Avenue. Our favorite movie house was the Beverly on Third Avenue in the Fifties, near Joe's. The Third Avenue El hurtled over the theater, making a racket that intruded on the soundtracks of all the great British films shown at this marvelous theater. Going there in a comfortable sweater after work was an unforgettable joy.

At the Beverly, we first saw David Lean's *Brief Encounter*, one of my favorite movies. I thought that movies were invented for the sole purpose of David Lean making this masterpiece. It may well be the most perfect movie ever made. The essence of movie dreamland. We also saw Noël Coward in his moving *In Which We Serve*, and *The Life and Death of Colonel Blimp*, *Stairway to Heaven*, *Tight Little Island*, *The Man in the White Suit*, *The Ladykillers*, and so many other wonderful films of that period.

A year after Toby and I married, we changed our last name from Distenfeld to Talbot. I was looking for a job in publishing, and in those days few Jews were being hired. We plucked Talbot out of the telephone book. There was a saying in those days: "Look British, think Yiddish." Many years later I deeply regret what I did, ashamed by my failure of nerve, by my cowardice. The fact that millions of Jews have resorted to this tactic over the centuries doesn't diminish my discomfort. Oftentimes I'd say to myself in the company of others: *phony*. On the other hand, I've never adulterated my Bronx Jewish accent, my Jewish linguistic slant, or my Jewish way of thinking. I understand Yiddish, speak a bit of it, and *kvell* in its sound.

■ ■ ■

I was unemployed for some time and pounded the streets in search of work in book publishing. At an employment agency, I met a Belgian Jew. His name was

André. We'd hang out in Bryant Park, spinning our dreams to each other, bemoaning our difficulties in finding work. Since both of us were film buffs, we went to the movies every day, mostly at the Apollo, Lyric, and Victory, grungy houses on Forty-Second Street off Times Square. Often we were among a few stray souls who came in from the cold and didn't much care what was on the screen. Could be a gangster film, a cheesy girly flick, a decent move-over from another theater, or some good foreign film. It was an active audience, they talked to the screen. One of them, like some Pirandello character, might warn a hoodlum in the movie not to walk into a trap. "Don't do it!" he shouted.

That reminds me of a wonderful story Toby and I recently read aloud by Delmore Schwartz, "In Dreams Begin Responsibilities." In it, a young man dreams that he's in an old-fashioned movie house. While watching the film—shot in shaky black and white—he decides it's about his parents' courtship. Drawn in, he gets to the point of yelling at the screen, warning them against that perilous nuptial "I do," and he keeps shouting even when it seems they may break up. The audience thinks he's nuts, and finally some ushers drag him from the theater. Ultimately, the character wakes from his dream and observes that it's the snowy morning of his twenty-first birthday.

Well, André was away from home Monday through Friday from eight a.m. to six p.m. He lived in Great Neck and gave his wife the impression that he had a full-time job. Since he had ample cash squirreled away, given to him by his rich Belgian parents, he'd hand his wife spending money as if it were the proceeds of his weekly paycheck. She was never suspicious. He was one smooth fellow. Told his wife stories about his heroic activities at the office, acting out how nudniks were threatening his position.

I had no such luck. Neither Toby nor I had rich parents. We were flat broke. I depended upon her earnings as a teacher and translator. Not entrepreneurial, at least in those days, I fantasized about how easy it would be to rob a bank. It looked easy in the movies, didn't it?

I also thought a lot about the wonders of WASP life. Admired that cool WASP look: jutting jaw, casual optimism, world ownership. I liked their uniforms: charcoal-gray suits, navy-blue pinstripes, or glen plaids; button-down Brooks Brothers oxford shirts; rep ties with red or green stripes.

They took care of each other. If Paul lost his job at Macmillan, a musical chair awaited him at Houghton Mifflin. Jonathan would leave Lippincott to take Paul's job at Macmillan, Scribner's, G. P. Putnam's Sons, William Morrow, or W. W. Norton.

■ ■ ■

Finally I got a job as an editor with Gold Medal Books. These were the early days of paperback publishing in America. I copyedited suspense novels by Cornell Woolrich, David Goodis, and Jim Thompson, who were much admired by the French literary establishment and later became icons among the French New Wave filmmakers.

My salary was fifty-five dollars per week. Toby worked as a reporter and cultural editor of *El Diario de Nueva York*, a well-written paper in *New York Times* broadsheet format. While she was ankling around town, reporting and writing literary essays (her salary twenty-five dollars a week), I was also writing film criticism for the *Progressive* magazine. All and all, we lived well on eighty dollars a week.

At first I found my book publishing job exciting. I loved literature and good writing, and if the writers whose manuscripts I read weren't big guns, at least they wrote good, lean, energetic prose along the Hemingway line. I liked the feel of manuscripts and page proofs. Got high on the smell of print, and it was fun writing blurbs. It was even amusing, at least at first, having three-martini lunches with agents and writers. I was in my early twenties and felt as if I'd arrived upon a scene I'd always dreamed about while growing up in the Bronx. Eventually I got caught up in office politics at Gold Medal Books, all of which I found boring, wasteful, consuming. It discouraged me and affected my work, and within a year I was fired.

In short order, I got a job with Avon Books. Bill Meyers, the publisher, had been a post office clerk who drifted into comic book and girlie magazine publishing. He also reprinted public domain classics by such nineteenth-century writers as J.-K. Huysmans and Pierre Louÿs, all of which had some exploitable sex angle. Then he started publishing a line of original novels—essentially cock novels, ably written silly stories that made him a fortune. He moved his office to Madison Avenue and Fifty-Seventh Street, decking out its walls with Currier & Ives lithographs. I was hired to start a new line of class-act books. Having made so much money in crap, he thought he could make even more in legitimate stuff. Meyers took a shine to me and provided an acquisition budget of

$100,000—tall money at that time—and told me to publish whatever I wanted, but it had to be good. A dream!

My first book was a reprint of Jean-Paul Sartre's *The Wall and Other Stories*. Then I met with Philip Rahv and Catharine Carver and commissioned them to do the first *Partisan Review Reader*. We published pseudonymous novels by Calder Willingham and Chandler Brossard, both of whom were with other publishers under their real names. After a year or so I became restless, edgy, hemmed in by the nine-to-five routine. My work was going downhill. Again, I was fired.

■ ■ ■

I felt liberated. Able now to do what I often dreamed about: read whatever I wanted all day long. I was a fast reader, had inherited my passion for books from my father, and, from the time I studied languages with him in back of Jean's Variety Store, my mother's shop in the Bronx, had developed a mad love for books. I read on the subway, hand dangling from a strap, back and forth from classes at City College. I read on the beach, in moving or stationary cars, in office building lobbies, at the circus, in the zoo, while walking in the streets, under trees, by lakes, on hills, in my bathtub, at the breakfast table. I was seized by an obsession to learn everything known to man. Naturally I was delighted when I lost my job. Vowed never to be employed by someone else.

I'd saved up a little money, was getting unemployment insurance, and Toby was teaching. We had no kids or parental obligations. So, for three years I read in Room 315 of the New York Public Library on Fifth Avenue. I read books by Sigmund Freud, Harry Stack Sullivan, C. G. Jung, Geoffrey Gorer. I reread virtually all of Hemingway, Faulkner, and Sherwood Anderson. I discovered Isaac Babel, Louis-Ferdinand Céline, Henry Miller. I reread Marcel Proust, James Joyce, Joseph Conrad, Henry James, and Virginia Woolf.

In Room 306, where many art books were kept behind locked glass doors of walnut bookshelves, I read Heinrich Wölfflin, Charles Baudelaire, Wilhelm Worringer, Erwin Panofsky. I discovered Otto Rank's masterpiece, *Art and Artist*, one of the best books ever written about the artistic impulse. Back in 315, I ran into the works of Francis Mott, the forerunner of psychobiology, and the works of Georg Groddeck, whose *The Book of the It* was acknowledged by Freud as the model for his history of the id.

Groddeck must have asked the first question pertaining to the unconscious. When visiting a patient in the hospital who had broken his leg by slipping on a banana peel, Groddeck cursorily examined his patient's leg and then asked, "*Why* did you slip on the banana peel?"

In that period I published three anthologies. *A Treasury of Mountain Stories* covered an obstetrician's bill, though I never had climbed a mountain, and was in fact fearful of heights. *Thirteen Great Stories* was a labor of love. It included stories by James Joyce, F. Scott Fitzgerald, Katherine Anne Porter, James Agee, Saul Bellow, William Goyen, Isaac Babel (one of my favorites), and some lesser-known authors.

In 1959, *Film: An Anthology* was published; it included essays by James Agee, Manny Farber, V. I. Pudovkin, Jean Cocteau, Siegfried Kracauer, and Henry Miller. It was the first highbrow anthology dealing with the aesthetics, theory, and history of cinema. The project stemmed from those years of delicious reading in Room 315 of the Forty-Second Street library and at the Museum of Modern Art. I feel a memory rush as I try now to recall, decades later, the hundreds of books I read in the library, rummaging through the card catalogue, plucking titles as if they were delicious berries. The joys experienced in this period of my life were the closest thing to good sex. If I could have figured out how to make love to a book, I would have done so.

THE NEW YORKER THEATER

I n the early 1960s, the Upper West Side was a dangerous place, heroin the drug of choice. The DMZ began at Ninety-First Street and Broadway. Pimps, hookers, pushers, and heroin addicts operated out of dope dens in brownstones between West End Avenue and Riverside Drive and on the side streets off Amsterdam and Columbus avenues. Some of these addicts worked as doormen and porters in the nearby apartment buildings.

They hung out at Benny's, a hole-in-the-wall luncheonette. Benny served lousy coffee, Sabrett hot dogs cradled in spongy rolls, and greasy hamburgers. The cops also hung around Benny's. There was a tacit link between the cops, the hookers, the pushers, and the small-time criminals, held together by a busy message center—an early version of email—at Benny's counter. With hands cupped over their mouths, fences sold stolen goods through this center. There was never any evidence of the goods; these were stashed away in building basements nearby. Supers would take a cut on each transaction. Also, at Benny's, a $35 parking ticket could be settled for $17.50. Benny never took a commission on a fixed ticket. For him, it was an accommodation, goodwill. It brought traffic and color to his whirling joint. With all this Benya Krik stuff in progress, a few doors down on Broadway and Eighty-Ninth Street, I ran the New Yorker Theater from 1960 to 1973. Originally, some of the idea behind the name had to do with salvaging the "York" part of the marquee of the previous theater, the Yorktown, since changing a neon section of a marquee is expensive. Henry Rosenberg, my accountant, owned a string of Spanish movie houses throughout the city and was about to convert the Yorktown, a move-over house of

Hollywood pictures, into another Spanish theater, for there were many Hispanics living in the neighborhood at that time. I urged him to turn it into a repertory house. Henry agreed. Flat broke at the time, needing work, with a wife and kids to support, I became its manager and programmer. My salary: $125 a week. The ticket price was $1.25 for adults, for kids maybe fifty cents. The concept of senior citizen admission had not yet emerged.

By and large it was a joy, but there were always so many things to worry about: correct screen ratios, best lenses, density of projection light, noise levels in the auditorium, program notes. I bought a cot and often slept in the back of the theater. Working only two blocks from the apartment with my wife and three daughters meant I could spend more time with my girls as they were growing up. Most men are running to their offices at the crack of dawn, clutching their shiny briefcases filled with—what? Boring documents meant to be transformed into money?—while I was diapering my kids, feeding them farina, talking to them, reveling in their charming expressions.

So went the days—my world enveloped in two short blocks, home and theater, theater and home. I consider myself incredibly lucky for having had that experience, all the more so for having created it myself.

I had a wonderful toy to play with: a nine-hundred-seat repertory theater! I knew nothing about managing and programming a movie house. I learned by *doing*, making mistakes, heeding an urge to make it fresh. And, flashing back to boyhood Roxy days, we purchased hundreds of its red velvet seats when that theater closed.

The New Yorker Theater opened on March 9, 1960. Our first program was *Henry V* and *The Red Balloon*. A huge success. From that first day, the place had an electric atmosphere, virtually all the customers young, with a genuine hunger for film—and not satisfied with run-of-the-mill junk. All the shows ended with applause.

THEATER DIARY: 1960

May 5. Opening night of *Pull My Daisy*, the American theatrical premiere at six p.m. We had a very slow matinee, phone not buzzing. Are we going to die with this show? I'm enchanted by Jack Kerouac's line in the film, "You better act real on behavior thar."

As I walk across the front lobby, a customer pursues me, demanding her money back. "What kind of a crazy movie house is this?" she asks. "You have a hell of a nerve showing pictures like this." $1.25 down the drain.

A Vespa pulls up in front. A hippie couple disembark. Beard has trouble digging coins out of his tight dungaree pocket. Meanwhile, girl cases framed poster advertising our next attraction. I study her reaction to the ad, hoping to get a clue as to whether we'll do anything with the next show. No reaction. She's either high on tea or simply has the Ice Age look.

I go next door to Murray's for a sturgeon-lox-onions-cream cheese sandwich on a bialy. Since we've created extra business for him with our lines, he charges me just thirty-five cents for this blockbuster sandwich.

Back inside the lobby, I punch the Pepsi-Cola button for a drink. I had to move all the vending machines from inside the orchestra to the outer lobby where their noise wouldn't be heard. In our first few weeks, we'd received several hundred complaints about the racket they were making. Our guestbook was filled with threats like: "Move those goddamn machines out or you'll never see me in this theater again!" "You show wonderful pictures here, I haven't missed any of your programs, but if you insist upon creaming each show with that candy machine, you will fail!"

From my office, I buzz the cashier and ask her if the pickpocket is in. She says no. This bastard has been coming in for a month now. He knows that we know, etc., etc., but insists on coming. I've had a pair of detectives in the house watching him. Unfortunately, he's not a pickpocket previously caught by police. If he were, all he'd have to do is jostle somebody, and he gets the rap. The detectives are miffed by him. They say he doesn't operate like the usual ones. He's eccentric. A young fellow. Looks like a Harvard man. Operates with an overcoat. Throws it over the seat next to him with a woman's purse and goes to work. He's scored a few times.

I make a note in my datebook to call the French Film Office for a screening print of Robert Bresson's *Pickpocket*. At this point, there don't seem to be any takers for the film in America. Like Carl Theodor Dreyer's work, Bresson's is super-Art. Death at the box office.

"Slow" as it is, I was drawn into Bresson's *A Man Escaped* for its odd mystical qualities. I doubt that I'll ever get out of my image warehouse all the devoted labor performed by the prisoner on his cell door. I'd been less enthusiastic about *Diary of a Country Priest*, its austerity (austere as Bresson himself), but on second viewing, could "feel" its devoutness and the torment of that young priest.

Wham! A huge line outside for *Pull My Daisy*. It seems that everyone has crawled out of their holes and converged on the theater. Right then and there I estimate that the bill will go two weeks. A bet I make with myself.

■ ■ ■

July. I had just made the deal for *Sunset Boulevard*, my brain dented after all the jockeying for reasonable terms, when in comes a fire inspector. I feel like smashing in his face. He looks hungry, like the rest of them.

He starts off buddy-buddy with, "Doing any business these days?" A nervous cough-laugh, thyroidic glance.

I say to myself, *Cut it, Jack, let's go and look over the goddamn fire escapes and all the other jazz in the theater.* As we tour the theater, I keep thinking of the day, some months back, when two fire engines pulled up in front and spilled a battalion chief and twelve firemen. They went over every inch of the place. The chief, with a fresh crewcut, was carrying a five-hundred-page book of department regulations (the Bible), with as many violation possibilities per sentence as the Dow Jones Average. That day, I got hit with thirty-two fire violations of the most idiotic kind imaginable. Since I refuse to give any money to these creeps, I contested half the violations (like hanging red buckets of sand and water on hooks). It took me six weeks of annoying surveillance and about $1,000 in equipment and labor to clear them up.

Today, my boy scares up three minor violations, insinuates that he's giving me a break (read: "That'll be a fine, kid"), gives me ten days to comply, and leaves. I need about three minutes of silence and yoga discipline to get the lint out of my psyche and go on.

Sunset Boulevard! I begin estimating what we'll do the first week—six G's? Eight? Ten? Twelve? The picture is a powerhouse, no doubt about it.

Suddenly I have the urge to read. I go home to stretch out with a volume of one of my favorite writers: Joseph Conrad—*Under Western Eyes*. But that's a no go. I've got the flicks bug today. Instead, I read *Sight & Sound*. As a result, I come up with three new pictures to book for the theater.

THE IDEAL MOVIE HOUSE

One's mood on heading to the theater is terribly relevant. Films not previously cared for may change when watched in a different setting. I never enjoy a film in a screening room, unless I'm there alone or with Toby, since I know most of the critics and film people who attend these screenings, feel their presence, and cannot properly watch the film. On the other hand, I can catch a bill in anonymity at a neighborhood house in an old sweater and enjoy this immensely. But even there, the setup within the house is important; noise, lights, production, etc., all have a tremendous influence upon how a film is viewed.

Most of the older baroque houses still in existence were really not designed for viewing films seriously. Since their purpose was to be a destination—"a place to go to"—there are too many distractions. Still, I've spent hours studying the chandeliers, marble staircases, Persian rugs, and statues in these theaters—they have the concept of enshrinement.

Our newer viewing cages are antiseptic, with a tendency toward controlled warmth (deep-pile rugs, pastel paint, flowers, good electronic equipment) and are more nearly suited to viewing films—no longer "a place to go to." They have about as much identity as a Madison Avenue cubicle. Therefore, a cinemagoer's predisposed mood is key. You go to see a film at these modern places as a psychic cultural event.

■ ■ ■

On entering a movie house, we harbor an expectation of communing with moving characters and landscapes on a canvas of images. What we see is an extension of our dream life. No brusque invasion must divert our attention. Audiences justifiably take for granted a smooth show. As Bernardo Bertolucci said: "In the darkness of movie theaters, there are no national identities. There are no more classes. Maybe I'm an idealist, but I still see movie theaters as big cathedrals, where people come to dream the same dream together."

My ideal theater would have an old-time baroque setting, with any number of architectural marvels to be taken in before or after the show. But there should be comfortable seats, excellent sight lines to the screen (raised screen, staggered seats), a minimum of personnel hanging around (I prefer picking my own seat), an ample supply of candy and soda, and as little noise as possible. Good projection goes without saying, although in the earlier days that might be difficult because of the way unions were set up. I hunt for good projectionists like wild game.

As to films, why not try everything? American, foreign, classics, new ones, westerns, comedies, musicals, private dick plots, etc., put together in illogical combinations, with only one thought in mind: the picture's the thing.

OTHER SIDE OF THE TRACKS

The Upper West Side was regarded by Upper East Side residents as the "wrong side of the tracks." Mothers on the UES were reluctant to have their kids cross town for play dates. But it was like our little shtetl, where we could bump into friends—Linda and Aaron Asher, Jack and Carol Gelber, or Judy and Jules Feiffer. Peter Bogdanovich lived right across the street, at 175 Riverside Drive, and we saw each other virtually every day.

And then there was Susan Sontag up at nearby Columbia University, where she was teaching. One week after the New Yorker opened, Susan, with young son David in tow, approached and declared, "I'd like to have"—or did she say, "I *want* to have?"—"a permanent guest pass to your theater." And I gave it to her!

■ ■ ■

I found myself musing on others linked to this arcane trade of running a movie house. Carl Theodor Dreyer was able to pursue his art by managing the Dagmor in Copenhagen. James Joyce struggled to stay afloat while writing and living in near poverty in Trieste when someone suggested that he might import skyrockets, a trade he found too dangerous, whereupon he revived an old plan of becoming the agent for Irish tweeds, but this too never came to pass. Then he hit upon the idea of opening a movie house in Dublin. The year was 1909, with no movie theaters in Ireland. So he followed up with a circuit around the country and, aided by several businessmen from Trieste, went about buying a building in Dublin and transforming it into a movie house. His opening show got a good review, but as the days passed, the numbers went south, and he abandoned the theater. Lucky for us that Joyce failed, otherwise we might not be reading *Ulysses* today.

■ ■ ■

I was lucky, had a good staff, and was especially close to David, one of my ushers, a Puerto Rican who spoke little English. His winning smile invariably shone through an acne face. One day when he came to work with a small pistol tucked in his belt, I questioned him. He'd learned through Benny's message center that Tony, a gimlet-eyed dope addict whom I'd fired several weeks before for stealing money from the box office, was going to bump me off. David had appointed himself my bodyguard.

I became angry and depressed. It was difficult enough booking this theater and keeping it in good shape. I didn't need little punks—menaces to society— threatening to kill me. *Lock them all up*, I thought.

But then I got so busy looking for films to book and putting together some interesting programs that I mostly forgot that my life was at stake. In due course, Tony muffed a stickup at a newsstand, and the bastard got thrown into the slammer.

■ ■ ■

In 1963, three years after the New Yorker opened, I received a three a.m. phone call at home from the cops. "There's been a break-in at your theater. Come on down." When I got there, I saw that the soda machine had been jimmied open and the coin box smashed. There were six cops in the lobby. The thief was a short, stocky Black guy in his early twenties. Two Black policemen were pummeling him with their fists, while the other cops—all white—looked on. "Nigger motherfucker. Take that!" a Black cop shouted. *Bam! Slam! Whack!* I couldn't stomach the police brutality, intervened, and made them stop hitting the fellow.

Some twenty-five years later, at our New Yorker Films distribution offices at 16 West Sixty-First Street, I was in the elevator when this short, stocky Black guy—that very same robber—entered on the sixth floor. He was working for the New York City Police Department, which occupied five floors in the building.

His eyes met mine. Instant recognition. The air froze. You could cut the tension with a knife. What would this guy do? What would I do? Would he, on second meeting, show contrition? Or beat me up?

Should I approach and say, "No hard feelings?" That I wouldn't reveal anything about the past to his superiors in the police department? We both got off on the ground floor and headed in different directions.

WHAT TO PLAY

Obviously, programming is at the very heart of the enterprise. Most exhibitors in America are sheep. They know nothing whatsoever about films. They never have to suffer the financial losses that creative experimentation entails. It's analogous to investing in the stock market. By and large, the people who lose in the market are those who watch the daily quotations. The winners rarely speculate. They maintain well-ordered portfolios that appreciate over the years. Similarly, all that an exhibitor has to do is stick to the proven winners, and if their theater is in a well-trafficked neighborhood and they keep expenses down, they earn a lot of money.

But earning money this way is boring. Therefore, breaking out of the traditional mold, risky as it is, is unquestionably worthwhile, for within the framework of experimentation there is ample room for the kill. One simply stumbles by accident upon a whole group of pictures that are big draws, and inevitably these pictures suggest other similar pictures. Put together in interesting combinations, they appear to our sophisticated city audience as very hip stuff. For example, *Forbidden Games* and *Beat the Devil*, as unlikely a combination as you will find in a theater, was very big at the New Yorker—in fun and in draw.

My idea of programming then varied, with a tendency toward fragmentation. Typically, in most places, shows are thematic—an all Gary Cooper show, two horror pix, a big laff show, a Jimmy Dean show, etc., etc. Generally, I consider this—with rare exceptions—unsatisfactory. I can see two Bogart or Hitchcock pictures on one bill, since both combine humor, raffishness, unintentionally serious pop-culture comment, lots of blitzing, and unbelievable fantasy satisfaction. Fragmenting a bill, however, offers lots of entertainment in three hours.

I'd come up with the New Yorker Film Society right from the start. Monday nights being traditionally slow, why not stage a special event and call it a society? It would be fun ferreting out interesting films, otherwise ignored.

Our first series was extremely successful. We played a wide range of films, among them *Greed*, *Freaks*, and *The Cabinet of Dr. Caligari*. Our first showing in the series was *Triumph of the Will*. The response was unbelievable. It was the New York theatrical premiere of its full-length version. The Museum of Modern Art had shown an edited version in 1943 and 1946. We had ticket-buyer lines three blocks long. Over three thousand people showed up. We turned away hundreds and eventually held shows until three in the morning. And who were they? Mostly Jewish kids in their twenties who'd heard about Hitler but had never seen any films about him. We thought that there was going to be some rioting or people accusing us of being neo-Nazis, but there was none of that. People were plain curious, fascinated. No other show drew quite like this one, though attendance was generally substantial.

Among our audiences were "regular" moviegoers, film buffs, and cinephiles, plus burgeoning critics like Morris Dickstein, Gary Crowdus, Leonard Maltin, and Phillip Lopate and full-fledged critics such as Vincent Canby, Pauline Kael, Stanley Kauffmann, Manny Farber, Jonas Mekas, Dwight Macdonald, Richard Schickel, Herman G. Weinberg, and Parker Tyler.

Back in 1947, the first film society in New York City, Cinema 16, was founded by Amos Vogel and his wife, Marcia. It was modeled on European cine-clubs and meant to show "films you cannot see elsewhere." It didn't take long for the film society movement to spread around the city. It has gotten very arty-smarty at times, an occasional good classic but often precious cinepoems about skin pores, stanchions, lots of angled railway work, and IRT fevers—I understand the stuff is even catching on in Long Island and Westchester. Back to Fred Astaire for me!

When we showed *Gold Diggers of 1933* in our second series, there was a big fistfight. Somebody had taken the film seriously and was put out by the laughter at this brassy, deliciously vulgar musical. He insulted someone's sister in a nearby seat, and before the evening was over I had to pull apart ten people, slugging it out. Once peace was restored, I realized yet again that each moviegoer views a film through his own lens. Sure, *Gold Diggers* dazzles with its kaleidoscopic Busby Berkeley numbers, but "Ole Man Depression" appears in the very opening number, "We're in the Money," and most poignantly in "Remember My Forgotten Man." Our irate viewer and his followers couldn't swallow *Gold Diggers* as sheer entertainment, unable to dismiss it from the dire economic reality on our very doorsteps.

■ ■ ■

Hooked on programming, I found myself sometimes staying up all night out of an inner necessity, working up programs. At three in the morning, I thought of such diversity as a triple bill of rock 'n' roll movies, and a combination of *Room Service* with *A Man Escaped*—as wild a bill as had occurred to me in months.

What riches to choose from! Murnau, Eisenstein, Griffith, Lubitsch, and Renoir. Keaton, Chaplin, and Fields. Josef von Sternberg's *The Blue Angel*, Vittorio De Sica's *Shoeshine*, Alfred Hitchcock's *Strangers on a Train*, Stanley Kubrick's *Paths of Glory,* Orson Welles's *Touch of Evil*, Jacques Becker's *Casque d'Or*. By dawn, I was in a frenzy of excitement.

Has it ever occurred to moviegoers what's behind programming? Pleasure, necessity, Home, Mother, that internal desire to placate. Anyone who has ever taken the slightest interest in movies will at the drop of a hat suggest a picture to play. I've gotten into the habit of analyzing people simply on the basis of the intensity or lack of intensity of the request, even the request per se.

Movies are so much a reflection of what happens in the culture that to overlook them as possibilities for sheer pleasure and analysis of our society is utterly obtuse. I sometimes get so confused that I don't quite know what to look for in movies: a Work of Art; a Work of Pop Culture; Mood at Movie Attendance; an avatar of Everyman's fantasy life.

■ ■ ■

In the early days of the New Yorker, my brain was spinning with program ideas. The regular, daylong programs had films I myself wanted to see, in some cases revisit but many I'd never seen, and hopefully what my friends would want to see. My primary interest at that time was in American repertory, the period of the thirties and forties, and for about five or six years I pretty much went through a broad swath of those films. This worked well, but I never booked a program where I thought in advance, *Gee, this is going to make a lot of money*, or something like that. I just wanted to see this film.

I also got tips from Pauline Kael, whose essay "Movies, the Desperate Art" had been included in my 1959 *Film: An Anthology*. At the time we opened the New Yorker, she was operating a twin theater in Berkeley, and we would exchange a lot of information, namely tracking down prints. I might discover bills of lading indicating that an old nitrate print was languishing at some forgotten railroad siding somewhere in deepest Texas, so I'd call the studio to inform them that, contrary to their belief, they in fact had a print of such and such film. Or Pauline might phone and say, "Hey, I know there's a 35mm print of *Sunset Boulevard* in Los Angeles," whereupon I'd confront Paramount in New York with that information.

Our theater also had kiddie shows on Saturday matinees. Toby went downtown to obtain a matron's license, which consisted of an official New York City certificate (indicating that she was tuberculosis free!) and a large white plastic disk with MATRON inscribed on it that she had to display prominently on her person while hosting these screenings.

For several years, we had a two-week Forgotten Films series. Peter Bogdanovich was the impresario of these delightful shows. The daily double bills included such abandoned works as Howard Hawks's *The Crowd Roars*, William Wyler's *The Letter*, Robert Milton's *Outward Bound*, Roberto Rossellini's *Journey to Italy*, Hawks's *Ceiling Zero*, Frank Borzage's *Flirtation Walk*, Raoul Walsh's *White Heat*, John Huston's *Across the Pacific*, and John Ford's *Wagon Master*. Peter programmed these films with my easy approval. He also did the show times and organized newspaper ads, program notes, and the letters on the marquee.

These programs became popular with film buffs, less so with the general audience. Our request book in the lobby was crammed with titles suggested by our patrons, who would sometimes talk to each other via the book. At one point, I received a letter from one of our regulars, David Vaughan, a dancer with the City Ballet, who complained about our selections. So I invited him to make the selections for a series.

Perhaps our most ambitious series was the Monday Night series of classics. These programs were organized by Marshall Lewis (then assistant manager of our theater, who eventually did all the fine programming at the Bleecker Street

Cinema) and his friend Rudy Franchi, who ran a film magazine. They made selections with my approval. We scheduled two evening performances. Arthur Kleiner, pianist for the Museum of Modern Art silent films, played his scores for the films we showed.

I involved film critics and literary figures to write program notes (later reproduced in Toby's book). Chandler Brossard wrote those for Cavalcanti's *Dead of Night*, which he entitled "Problems of Being the Real Me." Bogdanovich was in charge of getting these program notes in print. Jack Kerouac—whom I knew from his pre–*On the Road* days, when he and Allen Ginsberg had just graduated from Columbia University and Kerouac was about to hit the road—did the notes for F. W. Murnau's *Nosferatu*. He came to the screening of the film smashed, already an alcoholic. Bob Brustein (whom I met through our friend Judy Sheftel, later to marry Jules Feiffer) was teaching at Columbia University and wrote on *Never Give a Sucker an Even Break*. Bob was in the early stages of his long career as a writer and one of America's foremost drama critics, while running his repertory theater at Yale University and then the American Repertory Theater at Harvard. He became an intimate friend.

Co-founder of the *Paris Review* and novelist of note Harold ("Doc") Humes did the text on Murnau's *The Last Laugh*. It was an ordeal to get him to write the notes; Peter hounded him day and night. In those days, Doc was up to his ears as self-appointed ombudsman on behalf of Black victims of police brutality in Harlem. He, his wife Marylou, and their kids were living in a large apartment on Ninety-Fourth Street off Broadway (the building in which Norman Mailer stabbed his wife Adele). Tough young Blacks streamed into Doc's apartment all day long, spilling horrific tales. Doc was planning to sue the city on behalf of these victims, some of whom smelled a dollar and showed up with a phony story. Harold's activities made the front page of the *New York Times*.

In those days, Jonas Mekas was one of the champions of the New American Cinema. Publisher of *Film Culture* and, subsequently, founder of Anthology Film Archives, Mekas wrote on Aleksandr Dovzhenko's *Shors*. I'd become a close friend of Andrew Sarris and of Eugene Archer, second-string film critic at the *New York Times*. Archer did a note on Alfred Hitchcock's *The Woman Alone* (released here as *Sabotage*). In a subsequent Monday Night series, Andrew Sarris wrote the program notes for Hitchcock's *The 39 Steps* and *Foreign*

Correspondent. Other close friends wrote on Erich von Stroheim's *Foolish Wives* (Jack Gelber) and Mervyn LeRoy's *Gold Diggers of 1933* (Jules Feiffer).

This all-star cast of American writers doing film program notes was rounded out with Terry Southern on William Wellman's *A Star Is Born* and Herb Gold on Robert Flaherty's *Nanook of the North.* My notion was to hire serious American writers who'd grown up on movies and continued to discuss some of these classics in a nonacademic writerly manner. These notes were distributed free at each program and seemed to turn audiences on.

BELLA AND THE CRITIC

Ours was a family store: Toby's parents, Bella and Joe Tolpen, worked at the New Yorker Theater, Bella behind the candy counter and Joe prowling the auditorium, on the lookout for mashers or pickpockets, or—since he was a retired window cleaner—he polished the glass.

Bella ran a tight ship. Her days were taken up with not only neatly stacking candy bars, keeping the glass-cage popcorn warmer filled almost to the top, and maintaining a spotless counter but also dispensing homegrown counseling to the lost souls who sought her wisdom.

In the sixties, there were many such lost souls. College graduates in physics and communications were flocking to the hills with their looms and potter's wheels. The air was rank with cannabis fumes. Skinny skeins of love beads, small thin-wired glasses that once graced the nose bridge of the likes of Ben Franklin, antique granny dresses reaching to the floor, leather accoutrements that looked like soldier uniforms: these were among the emblems of that age. Bella was not judgmental. The strays all had mothers, and as long as the sense of *a mama's kint* had a niche in her heart, she'd listen carefully.

In our scheme of things, we often use the phrase *a mama's kint*, a mother's child, sympathizing with someone who's fallen through the cracks. I was introduced to the use of it in Toby's haunting memoir, *A Book About My Mother*, mourning her death. If a lame person or a beggar or someone depressed came across Bella's path, she'd say, "*Nebbich, a mama's kint.*" This beautiful utterance is the beginning of folk wisdom, a first law perhaps when it comes to reaching out for the gift of life.

I quote from a letter a former manager at the New Yorker sent to Toby when her mother died: "Bella had a habit at the New Yorker, at once charming and disarming: She would hold my hand over the candy counter as we talked. She did it to you as well as to Dan, your sister, daughters, our manager Jose, the ushers and the cashiers and not a few customers. Everyone she knew. Those hands of hers come so easily to mind: warm, soft and altogether wonderful. I used to think she handed out her medals only to me. Just imagine, that sly one was handing them out to others as well at the same time!"

■ ■ ■

Bella's wits served her listeners. "Do what's good for you" was a major piece of advice. "Try this . . . try that . . . something will work out." She felt a kinship with one of our porters, Durwood Wilkerson, whose favorite line, imported from "Twenty-Fifth Street" (as 125th Street was known in Harlem) was "Everything is everything."

Bella liked that. It summed up the transcendental experience. She didn't know from words like "transcendental," but she could spot it when it came down the pike.

In that period, Manny Farber was a regular at the theater. His essays on American movies had become cult classics among the cognoscenti. He did for Howard Hawks and Raoul Walsh what André Bazin did for Jean Renoir and Jean Vigo. Manny didn't care for most foreign movies. He characterized many of them as "deep dish," and since America was an action-oriented continent, complex psychological environments were—in his view—against the grain of our society. Little did he realize that years later he'd be writing about and preaching the gospel according to Jean-Marie Straub and Danièle Huillet, the Schoenbergs of modern cinema.

Manny hung around Bella's counter. He'd duck in and out to catch a particular scene in *Red River*, *Scarface*, *High Sierra*, *They Drive by Night*, or *White Heat*. Or sit in the theater, watching a foreign movie just to confirm his lack of interest in *cinemah*, then dip out after twenty minutes to converse with Bella.

"Why are you so restless?" she'd ask. "Go back. Give it a chance."

He dedicated his book *Negative Space* to the New Yorker and to "Toby's mother."

■ ■ ■

Bella became a film buff. Yasujiro Ozu and Robert Bresson were her favorites. In another life in Dynów, Poland, she was orphaned, with a stepmother she hated. At age seventeen, without a future in that shtetl, she came to America. Lived with relatives in Buffalo, saw Niagara Falls, and eventually floated down to the Bronx, married, and raised two charming girls, one of whom I married. Bella was unlettered.

Her husband, Joe, a scholarly window cleaner, read the print off daily newspapers. After they went broke as a result of him chasing Canadian mining penny stocks on the Nasdaq, I gave them jobs at the New Yorker. Joe too became a film buff—his specialties were W. C. Fields and the Marx Brothers. He knew every line in the Fields movies. He also kept his eye out for gonifs trying to sneak in free, cashiers with fast fingers, and ushers who ransacked the candy machines, running their nimble fingers up and down the candy bars like Vladimir Horowitz.

■ ■ ■

Meanwhile, Manny Farber got in trouble. Separated from his wife, the critic fell behind in child support payments. On top of that, he was a certified scofflaw. With an imminently collapsing jalopy—a Red Grooms contraption always parked in the wrong place at the wrong time—Manny ran up over a hundred tickets. He couldn't even afford to pay the 50 percent discount that Benny had worked out with the cops who hung around his corner luncheonette. Not one to give up, Benny had certain connections. In mustard-flecked white apron and argyle socks, he asked Manny, "Should I try for a bigger discount?"

Manny was also having trouble meeting deadlines at the *New Leader* for his film column. He'd deliver text at the last minute to the printers, still making changes as Sol Levitas, editor of the magazine, was poring over the prose with his thick lead pencil. I knew Sol through his son Mitchell ("Mike"), a brilliant rising star in New York City journalism.

Sol reached his rope's end with Manny. He couldn't take it anymore and asked me to suggest a reliable film critic. At first, out of loyalty to Manny I refused, but on seeing that the situation was virtually hopeless, I sent over Peter Bogdanovich. Sol was desperate, the magazine in permanent deficit. He looked Peter over and offered the kid $17.50 per article.

Peter wanted thirty-five bucks. "Too much," said Sol. "You can come to the office and write your article here. We'll give you a pastrami sandwich." It didn't work out. Sol continued his sufferance with Manny.

CHANDLER BROSSARD

Years back, one of our closest friends was Chandler Brossard. A young man from Idaho, largely self-educated, he found a job as an editor at the *New Yorker* magazine. We met in the early fifties, when he'd just written *Who Walk in Darkness*. Published by New Directions, it caused a stir. Certain characters were based on friends of his: William Gaddis, Milton Klonsky, and Anatole Broyard, to name a few.

Broyard had particular reason to complain: Chandler not only characterized him as a phony, amoral womanizer but also revealed Broyard's secret—"People said Henry Porter was a 'passed' Negro," the novel originally began. Broyard threatened to sue, so New Directions rephrased the first line to read, "People said Henry Porter was an illegitimate." Chandler used *The Sun Also Rises* as his model in theme and prose style. Broyard eventually took revenge when he reviewed Chandler's novel *Wake Up. We're Almost There*.

Around the time that we met, Chandler was the editor of the *American Mercury*. The literary folks in our group included Seymour Krim, David Bazelon, Bernard Wolfe, Herb and Willie Poster, and, at times, Christopher Lazare, a brilliant writer whose career never took off. On Friday evenings, we would meet to talk about—what else? Books.

When I'd been working at Avon Books, I was Chandler's editor on a novel, published under the pseudonym of Daniel Harper. Also, we were partners in a beat-up old Chevrolet, bought for seventy-five dollars. On weekends we'd sit in the car, drink beer, tell stories and jokes.

In 1962 I was given the opportunity to purchase the lease of the New Yorker Theater but didn't have a dime. Seeking funds, I approached Chandler, among others, including my father, uncle, and mother-in-law. Chandler and I walked over to his bank. This frugal fellow, on the spot, withdrew all his money (six thousand bucks) and lent it to me. I paid him back within a year.

Years later, we stopped seeing Chandler. Not given his due attention in the New York literary firmament, he became nasty and contentious, despite his ability to charm rattlesnakes. A monologist, he went on and on about this and that until you gave up trying to get a word in edgewise. Monologists are compulsives, showbiz performers. God forbid one of them should ask, "How are you doing, kid?" In earlier years, he hadn't always been like that.

It sometimes bothered me that as time passed, we were no longer friends. He continued to write. In the countercultural ethos of the times, he wrote what he called "visionary" fiction, got involved in the antiwar movement of the sixties and seventies, and became an increasingly angry man at not getting what he regarded as proper recognition.

As his wife Maria put it, "You may be unaware, but half an hour around Chandler can be very exhausting." And he himself acknowledged, "I've never been comfortable at all with other people." Chandler died of cancer in a hospice in 1993. He was seventy-one.

PART 2

THOSE WHO MADE ME LAUGH

MAE WEST AND W. C. FIELDS

It's impossible to be neutral about either Mae West or W. C. Fields, but I'll try. The cult worship of these two gargoyles of sex and misanthropy has reached such proportions that critical attitudes have been frozen in a pro-and-con rigidity that tolerates no gradations of response.

For example, Henri Langlois of the Cinémathèque Française declared in an interview that Mae West was *the* outstanding personality of the American cinema, and more than one Fields champion has ranked *their* man the best of cinematic clowns.

If I'm not yet ready to concede on Garbo and Chaplin, I can at least appreciate some of the perverse enthusiasm inspired by West and Fields. There is no nonsense about either of them. No one has ever matched Mae West in running off an IBM calculation of a man's sexual potentialities with a single discerning glance. And who else but Fields could thumb his nose so vigorously at gentility? Although West and Fields both have style of high order, I suspect that their appeal lies instead in their nihilistic attitudes.

They are a strong antidote to the bogus sentimentality one associates with Hollywood. The cynicism of Preston Sturges and Billy Wilder operates in much the same way, and this is all to the good. However, too strong an addiction to vinegar breeds an oddball attitude toward cinema. Nothing is serious. Nothing is important. Nothing is moving. Nonsense! There is a place in film for emotion, for romanticism, for passion, indeed a very exalted place not even the antics of West and Fields can discredit.

Both are very verbal. It's difficult to conceive of Fields being a success in silent films like Gregory La Cava's *Running Wild*, but apparently he was. In any case, when we recall the funniest moments of the West–Fields repertory, it's in the way a line is delivered with appropriate body language.

Unfortunately, *My Little Chickadee*—despite these two stars working in tandem for the first and only time, despite their collaboration on the script—has few memorably comic moments. West and Fields are basically soloists to whom the world is a stooge. There's an air of anticipation on the screen when they come out at the bell jabbing each other with their unique inflections, but they never add to each other, and quite often distract. They seem to have different interests, which they pursue with equal ruthlessness. Except for George Cukor's *David Copperfield*, Fields never appeared in a film that would have had any interest without Fields, and it's impossible to imagine a Mae West film whose sole raison d'être was not Mae West. This is star cinema of a certain sort. Perhaps not the best cinema for historians, but one can forgive a great deal when W. C. Fields observes that he's stepping on "pussy cat fur" in Mae West's boudoir, or when Miss West wiggles her shoulder at an admirer with the comment "I don't give out samples." At those moments, the demarcation line between one star vehicle and another becomes blurred by a consistent stream of personality, for Mae West and W. C. Fields compress every film they ever made into one bubble of laughter.

I'm a huge W. C. Fields fan. *It's a Gift* is one of my favorites. It chronicles the day-to-day challenges faced by Mr. Bissonette, owner of a general store. In a scene leading to chaos, one of his customers is a blind man, whose flailing cane wrecks the place into a war zone—making me think of Fields himself, a one-time juggler. Anyhow, it's one madcap thing after another.

Bissonette dreams of planting an orange grove on a plot of land he has acquired in California, whereupon he and his dubious family head there in a jalopy. Then, lo and behold, the Holy Grail materializes. And in the last shots we see his now happy tribe driving off in their new car, leaving the lord of the manor contentedly pouring booze into a flask of orange juice.

Toby claims that if ever she went looking for me at the New Yorker Theater while a Fields movie was playing, she could invariably spot me in the audience by my outbursts of laughter.

In China, I'm told, there are Laughing Clubs, where groups seeking to heal themselves—or simply feel better—gather and laugh! My father-in-law, Joe, our unofficial sentry in the lobby, was also a W. C. Fieldser, except that his laughs were—well, not exactly guffaws but little inner explosions. As he was afflicted with Parkinson's disease and its concomitant quiver of hands, hopefully those surges of pleasure were therapeutic. Between the two of us, we had a considerable repertoire of W. C. Fieldsisms to exchange at the candy stand where Bella officiated.

What is the appeal of that henpecked drunk with blotches on his face, a confirmed misanthrope with drawling voice? What drew us law-abiding citizens, moderate drinkers, measured in our lives, to W. C.? As Montaigne wrote in his essay "On Solitude": "There is scarcely less trouble in governing a family than in governing an entire state. Whatever the mind is wrapped up in, it is all wrapped up in it, and domestic occupations are no less important for being less important." Fields was the Don Quixote of domestic life. A victim of "Home Sweet Home." Dandling baby on his knees, he voiced what others dared not: the shackles of life are infinite, and the best we can do is turn it into a comedy.

THE MARX BROTHERS

I like to think that a tiny part of my brain is labeled "Marx Brothers," and rattling around in that merry pocket is Groucho himself. I grew up on Groucho, spending thousands of street-corner evenings imitating him, even once thinking he might serve as a model for my future life. God knows how many ribs he cracked in movie houses around the world.

As a grown-up, I detected the darker dimension of his nihilistic comedy, dished out in verbal gags. A flow of funny bits, none of which had any relation to the others: "Love flies out the door when money comes innuendo." Or, a detective suddenly tells him, "The table is set for six," whereupon Groucho replies, "Yes, I know, but the clock is set for ten." These gags virtually became mainstays in the glossary of gags.

Groucho blitzed through his stories, a one-man hallucination who could suddenly swing out of a funny screen conversation and speak *directly* to movie viewers with a *different* joke. His scenes with the long-suffering Margaret Dumont—lounging on recamiers, framed by rubber plants, or at huge banquet tables—are among the high moments of screen comedy. Groucho claims to fight for her honor, "Which is more than she ever did!" And what physical destruction he wrought—of rooms, boats, hotels, opera houses, racetracks, colleges, and whatnot! All done with such gusto that we, the audience, feel it's all on behalf of service to the community.

W. C. Fields apparently bore the Marx Brothers a lifelong grudge. When they were playing vaudeville together in the twenties, Fields seems to have always followed the Marx Brothers onstage. Naturally those brothers wrecked the stage, and when Fields came out, he had to perform on a floor of chaos.

Intrigued by Groucho—the man offstage—I unearthed a copy of letters exchanged between him and T. S. Eliot from 1961 to 1964. Despite Eliot's notorious anti-Semitism, he was an avid Groucho fan and wrote to him in 1961, requesting an autographed photo. The astonished Groucho sent him a studio shot.

But that was not what Mr. Eliot wanted. He wanted a likeness of the *screen* Groucho with jutting cigar, painted moustache, and dense eyebrows. Groucho complied, and soon that photo joined W. B. Yeats and Paul Valéry on Eliot's mantelpiece, and Eliot reciprocated with one of himself as Groucho requested. A delicious exchange followed with Eliot inviting Groucho and Mrs. Groucho to visit, and each informing the other of their current state of health. Midway through, Groucho ceased addressing his letters to Mr. Eliot, but rather to Tom. When Eliot claimed not to recognize that name, Groucho refreshes:

November 1, 1963

Dear Tom:

Since you are actually an early American, [*sic*] (I don't mean that you're an old piece of furniture, but a fugitive from St. Louis), you should have heard of Tom Gibbons. For your edification, Tom Gibbons was a native of St. Paul, Minnesota, which is only a stone's throw from Missouri. That is, if the stone is encased in a missile. Tom was, at one time, the light heavyweight champion of the world, and, although outweighed by twenty pounds by Jack Dempsey, he fought him to a standstill in Shelby, Montana.

The name Tom fits many things. There was once a famous Jewish actor named Thomashevsky. All male cats are named Tom—unless they have been fixed. In that case they are just neutral and, as the upheaval in Saigon has proved, there is no place anymore for neutrals.

There is an old nursery rhyme that begins "Tom, Tom, the piper's son," etc. The third President of the United States['] first name was Tom . . . in case you've forgotten Jefferson.

So, when I call you Tom, this means that you are a mixture of a heavyweight prizefighter, a male alley cat and the third President of the United States.

I have just finished my latest opus, "Memoirs of a Mangy Lover." Most of it is autobiographical and very little of it is fiction. I doubt whether it will live through the ages, but if you are in a sexy mood the night you read it, it may stimulate you beyond recognition and rekindle memories that you haven't recalled in years.

Sex, as an industry, is big business in this country, as it is in England. It's something everyone is deeply interested in even if only theoretically. I suppose it's always been this way, but I believe that in the old days it was discussed and practiced in a more surreptitious manner. However, the new school of writers have finally brought the bedroom and the lavatory out into the open for everyone to see. You can blame the whole thing on Havelock Ellis, Krafft-Ebing and Brill, Jung and Freud. (Now there's a trio for you!) Plus, of course, the late Mr. Kinsey who, not satisfied with hearsay, trundled from house to house, sticking his nose in where angels have always feared to tread.

However, I would be interested in reading your views on sex, so don't hesitate. Confide in me. Though admittedly unreliable, I can be trusted with matters as important as that.

If there is any possibility of my being in New York in December, I will certainly try to make it and will let you know in time.

My best to you and Mrs. Tom.

Yours,
Groucho

In subsequent correspondence, T. S. in fact signed off as Tom, and that meeting took place in New York.

PART 3

UNSUNG FILM PIONEERS

COLLECTORS

I came across the following entry in an old journal, a quote from Hermann Broch's *The Sleepwalkers*: "Certainly Elisabeth did not know that every collector hopes with the never-attained, never-attainable and yet inexorably striven-for absolute completeness of his collection to pass beyond the assembled things themselves, to pass over into infinity, and entirely subsumed in his collection, to attain his own consummation and the suspension of death."

Film distributors, curators, editors, agents, and importers of fine art exhibit many of the characteristics of the collector. Some of these folks are would-be artists who want to participate themselves in the mysteries of art. They collect and purvey art as if it were their own work. The collector takes the service road to immortality. As a vicarious artist, the collector sometimes feels humiliated, often envious of the artists whose work they handle. Thus, they take refuge in the work itself, visiting it often, absorbing it, selling it, repackaging it, talking about it at cocktail parties, making a living off it. Meanwhile, the artist is busy with his next work. He has long forgotten his past work. He doesn't have the luxury of the collector, who is partly in the world through a total immersion in a work he did not create.

From the outset, I resisted any impulse to distribute films. But it was the collector's high that kicked in when I first saw Bernardo Bertolucci's *Before the Revolution*. I immediately wrote to the Italian producer, saying that I wanted to launch it at the New Yorker Theater.

He wrote back, "No, I'm not interested in a single exhibition of the film, but if you want to buy the distribution rights, that's another matter."

"All right, I'll buy distribution rights and we'll see what happens." With a $500 advance, I got the film. *Before the Revolution* was a disaster. Fantastic critical success, but nobody came to see it.

As I got more interested in what was being done abroad, I started bringing in other films. Within a year's time, I had about a dozen—and suddenly realized that I was a distributor. I developed a small network of people who were running repertory houses across the country—Max Laemmle's Los Feliz in Los Angeles, Mel Novikoff's Surf Theatre in San Francisco, Art Carduner's Bandbox in Philadelphia, Cy Harvey's Brattle Theatre in Boston. I also made a deal with the *New York Review of Books* to handle all my 16mm nontheatrical distribution—reaching sites like college campuses, where all the action was initially.

Variety, at the time, wrote that it costs a minimum of $35,000 to open a commercial film in New York, and even then, a distributor never expects to make money on its New York run. He does it for the reviews, in order to sell it to exhibitors around the country. In film, more than any other art, the iron will of the "Big Apple" prevailed: our programs at the New Yorker often appeared in art houses nationwide.

EARLY DISTRIBUTORS

Right after World War II, Arthur Mayer and Joseph Burstyn joined hands to distribute *Paisan, Rome Open City,* and *The Miracle.* These pioneer films paved the way for the French New Wave. They received much attention in the press, drew audiences, and the so-called "art film" came into being. I've always hated this term, often used as shorthand so as not to interrupt conversations.

Should we say that John Ford or Alfred Hitchcock, Orson Welles, John Huston, Preston Sturges, or Martin Scorsese *didn't* make "art films"? The term came about because many Americans have a foggy notion that only Europeans and Japanese are capable of making artistic films while Americans make only . . . well, what? Crap?

For a long while, the favorite American auteur in France was Jerry Lewis. His spastic movements and imbecilic speech appealed to the French. Why? Perhaps they regarded Lewis as the epitome of the American personality.

As to Russian cinema, "art film" also seems off. Classic Russian cinema—Pudovkin, Dovzhenko, Eisenstein—was more in the vein of action cinema, urgent news of the history and state of the Soviet Revolution. These magnificent films were distributed here by an American couple, Sam and Rosa Madell, under the flag of Artkino. They had a lock on Russian films in the United States, a reward for being loyal members of the Communist Party. The films were shown in a Russian-sponsored theater, the Stanley on Manhattan's Irving Place, where my own education in Russian cinema took place.

When that theater lease expired, they moved uptown to Eighth Avenue, off Forty-Second. Years later, the building got triplexed into a porno house.

Russian films then played at the 55th Street Playhouse off Seventh Avenue, until that became a gay porno theater in the seventies.

In the fifties and sixties, a cluster of distributors and exhibitors in New York City handled all foreign films in America. No Hollywood studio would touch them with a ten-foot pole.

After Burstyn and Mayer, there was Ilya Lopert: a Russian émigré, he was an executive with United Artists in Paris and quit his job to form Lopert Pictures. He took a long-term lease on the Plaza Theatre on Fifty-Eighth Street between Park and Madison. In those pre–Don Rugoff days, the Plaza, Paris, Fine Arts, and Little Carnegie were the class houses of New York—all showing only foreign films.

Another great distributor was Cy Harvey. Operating at first out of Cambridge, Massachusetts, he began the Brattle Theatre, which prompted him to go into film distribution. He cofounded Janus Films and imported all the great films of Ingmar Bergman, François Truffaut, and Ermanno Olmi, among others.

Harvey appeared to be successful: he bought the lease to the 55th Street Playhouse in New York and screened Janus Films titles there. As he got deeper into distribution, however, the costs of making a go of it defeated him. He sold his company to Bill Becker and Saul Turell, who assumed his debts but gave Harvey no cash. Years later, Becker's and Turell's sons became the operators of the Criterion Collection, so the good news is that Cy Harvey's work survives.

■ ■ ■

There are others we must not forget. A dapper gent from Manhattan's East Side, Ed Kingsley, brought *Viridiana* and other assorted glories to this country. And Irvin Shapiro managed the Little Carnegie Theatre on West Fifty-Seventh Street, smack up against the Russian Tea Room. Back in 1929, he showed Carl Theodor Dreyer's *The Passion of Joan of Arc*—yes, thank you, it was a big hit! Shapiro went on to bring *Breathless* to the United States, and for this alone he'll be a legend. And then there was Tom Brandon, who introduced Kurosawa, Mizoguchi, and Kinoshita to this country, as well as some of the early works of Pasolini.

The Fine Arts, on Forty-Eighth Street off Park Avenue, was owned by Richard Davis. His wife, Olga Baclanova, one of the stars in Tod Browning's *Freaks*, was the theater's cashier. Davis imported some European films, none of any distinction. Along the way, he hit a few home runs, sold his business, and ran off with a young Chinese woman with whom he lived in the Hôtel George V in Paris.

When that story came to an end, Davis returned to New York, having spent most of his money in Paris. With the little left, he bought a soft-shoe Italian film that got renamed *Come Have Coffee with Us*. After having screened it, I advised him to open at the Paris Theater. He begged me, certain of a big hit. The film was borderline—not so good, not so bad—and I wound up showing it. My excuse for this, which happened infrequently, is that if a film wasn't offensive to an audience, some moviegoers might enjoy it. *Coffee* got decent reviews and ran four weeks, not a successful run, and on it, Davis lost the rest of his money.

Alone and broke, he disappeared into the woodwork. Not an uncommon story in our trade. The history of distributors is rife with people of goodwill, as well as con artists and ditzy speculators. (Read on!) Occasionally a distributor who hits the jackpot will quit and retire in comfort in Florida. Most of the others have sad endings.

■ ■ ■

The point of these minitales is that distribution is not so much a business as a casino. And in this casino, the independent filmmaker must spend 90 percent of his time looking for money to make his film. Would they be as lucky as Wayne Wang, who made *Chan Is Missing* for $420,000, or Jonathan Caouette, who assembled *Tarnation* for $231? But such stories are rare.

Years ago, I wrote an editorial for the *New York Times* Op-Ed page ["Use Junk to Bankroll Art," January 17, 1994] suggesting a system of film subsidies based on the Centre National du Cinéma operation in France. Simply put, if the Independent Filmmaker Project or some offshoot of IFP lobbied for a setup that would accumulate money out of box office receipts, the boring, stupid, and deadening search for independent film financing could appreciatively change. If just ten cents on each ticket sold could go into a pot, sufficiently large, based for example on one billion or five hundred million tickets sold in one year, there would be enough money to finance at least 140 films with reasonable budgets. Of course, this would not guarantee good films, but it would encourage filmmakers to think more about their art and not what will work at the box office.

ED HARRISON'S INDIAN IDOL

E d Harrison was the American who brought Satyajit Ray to our shores. Ed was a dreamer, possibly delusional. He talked day and night about *The Apu Trilogy* (*Pather Panchali*, *Aparajito*, and *The World of Apu*), three Indian films that are monuments in the history of cinema. He phoned exhibitors at all hours, even while they were asleep, cajoling them, exhorting them, accusing them of being rotten philistines unless they gave him a theater for his Satyajit Ray films. Ed's mission in life was to get every single American to see the numerous Ray films he handled, including *The Music Room*.

When we met, he was in his late fifties. I never knew where in America he came from nor what he did before becoming a distributor. He simply appeared on the scene in the late 1950s and struck a deal with Don Rugoff to open his Ray films at the Fifth Avenue Playhouse off Thirteenth Street.

Ed was a tall, stout man. He wore double-breasted gray worsted suits, polka-dot Sulka ties, and plain round-tipped black shoes. Also, a gray fedora hat with a black grosgrain band. That hat never left his head. He worked with his older brother Jack, who did the financials, and a secretary in a small office in the Brill Building.

Ever on his black pole-style phone, which looked like a weapon, haranguing exhibitors over their cowardice, he always looked haunted and hungry—a hunger that could only be appeased when he found a timid exhibitor in the sticks who would become a Satyajit Ray convert. Ed never spoke to them about money or deals, the oil of the business. It was always, "This Indian fellow from

Calcutta, do you have any idea what a great artist he is? You, you, you, do you only dream of picking oranges from a tree in California?"

He eagerly sought to show Ray's films in my New Yorker Theater. In fact, I very much myself wanted to have these films in my burgeoning New Yorker Films distribution company.

A visit to Ed in the Brill Building was like a scene from Woody Allen's *Broadway Danny Rose*. There were marble floors in the vestibule, air vents and ceiling lights surrounded by gold-plated metal covers in art nouveau style, troupes of performers marching to the elevators to see their agents. Dwarfs with leather cases carrying gong sticks for their xylophones; tightrope walkers; tall men with lace-frilled shirts; twelve-year-old twin girl singers in black pumps accompanied by their dowdy, paranoid mother; a couple with a large suitcase containing glass jar instruments that made wow-wow noises not unlike Theremin's music machine.

If Satyajit Ray were an American filmmaker living in New York, every one of these characters would be in some movie of his. These people early in life avoided normal occupations; for that reason, Ray would have found them interesting as possessed souls. Satyajit Ray was an original, unlike any other director in the history of cinema, and it was this that drew Ed Harrison to his films.

Before becoming a distributor, Ed might have been a shoe salesman or a high school administrator, and then one day—yes, one day, as in the life of Sherwood Anderson, who walked out of his paint factory to become a great American writer—Mr. Harrison saw *Pather Panchali* and became a distributor.

After ten years of Ray madness, he gave up. America wasn't buying. His work was over. With the little money he had left, Ed went to India, where he died a pauper and lies buried, I know not where.

The Apu Trilogy traces Apu's childhood in a small impoverished Brahmin family in a Bengali village, to separation and youth in Benares, and finally to adulthood in Calcutta. I reviewed *The World of Apu* in the March 1960 issue of the *Progressive* magazine:

> I haven't been moved by a film so profoundly since *Bicycle Thief*. . . . [Satyajit Ray] emerges, in my opinion, as the outstanding film artist of the new generation. He is a humanist, a poet, a realist, unsentimental but majestically romantic. He knows more about people in simple and complicated human situations than any director I can think of. He does not advance his

perceptions by logic, but by some well-ordered, intuitive process, convinces the beholder of their absolute truth. . . . The plaintive Indian musical score [on the sitar] is used perfectly, and the photography has that apocalyptic quality of catching trees, rooms, people as we configurate them in their most vital forms. Every inch of celluloid is the work of an inspired man.

Pather Panchali was dismissed as primitive when first screened at the 1956 Cannes Film Festival, but the great French critic André Bazin championed it behind the scenes and the Cannes jury gave it a special award. It had been unavailable in the United States for over a decade when Merchant Ivory Productions assisted in its restoration, and we played the entire trilogy at the Lincoln Plaza Cinemas in 1995.

One morning I looked at *Pather Panchali* during that run. I'd seen the film more than once and remembered it quite well, but one scene had left a powerful impression, which was when the father returns from the city, laden with gifts for his family, and learns that in his absence his daughter has died. The sari brought for the girl drops to the ground. He is utterly shattered, as was I—also a father. But the film earns its emotion, and just think: this was Ray's first film.

In that same *Progressive* issue, I wrote: "I am sure that any artistically intentioned American filmmaker seeing these films will walk out of the movie house with heartburn, a migraine headache, and funny stomach noises—not, mind you, the result of disliking them but because he cannot be making similar films in the United States."

MEL NOVIKOFF

West Coast Perfectionist

Toby and I met Mel Novikoff in 1961 in San Francisco, shortly after he opened the Surf Theatre on the outskirts of the city. Mel was a genial man, with warm eyes and burning enthusiasm, attentive to all the details of programming and managing a theater.

He seemed awed by us because we came from the Big Apple. New York City was Mel's ultimate test for gauging the potential of a film in San Francisco. "Well, you know San Francisco is *not* New York," he'd say in that agitated voice of his—meaning you couldn't, after all, expect our films to do so well in San Francisco. He may have been right about the numbers, but if numbers were all that mattered to him, he might as well have been a stock trader. Mel had the impulses of an artist, and it showed in everything he touched. Those who lived in San Francisco couldn't imagine how privileged they were to see movies in his beautiful movie house: their mansion for communing with screen souls.

When Mel booked a show, the first thing he inquired about was the quality of the print. He took great pains about the noise levels in his auditorium, the density of projection light, and the possibly unruly characters in the audience who could spoil a show. He took great pains to use the correct screen ratios and the best lenses. He worried about everything! Mel had an international reputation for worrying, for his goal was perfection. He worried about the adequacy of his program notes, about the intelligence and panache of posters and trailers. So many things to worry about—such is the life of a culture worker. Mel schooled himself in the presentation of a movie. Yet there had never been a school for this endeavor. Only strange cats like Mel Novikoff, Tom Luddy, Peter

Scarlet, Edith Kramer, Albert Johnson, Pauline Kael, Gary Meyer, and others got mixed up in this peculiar vocation.

In 1988, at the San Francisco International Film Festival, I received the first Mel Novikoff Award, given to someone who has significantly enhanced the appreciation of film. That ceremony, held in the landmarked Castro Theatre, was accompanied by a screening of Robert Bresson's *Pickpocket*. We had premiered that great film at the New Yorker Theater and then distributed it. What could be more exquisite than receiving this award in that magnificent movie palace?

PRESENTING DON RUGOFF

Manhattan Exhibitor Like No Other

Don Rugoff inherited a string of premiere houses in New York from his father, an exhibitor in the thirties and forties (the Rugoff & Becker chain). Don went to Harvard, studied literature, wanted to be a writer, but never got that off the ground. He was not a film scholar, nor had impeccable taste in selection of films, yet never has there been anybody like him in our business.

He ran spectacular theaters in a grand way, visited them daily, checking everything out. He operated the Beekman, the Paris, the Sutton, the Murray Hill, Cinema I & II (which he built), followed by III, the Gramercy (previously owned by Arthur Mayer), the Fifth Avenue Playhouse, and the Austin in Queens. All were high-quality halls. He shoehorned Cinema III into an impossible space in the Plaza Hotel, and it came out a beauty. Each theater had its own identity, separate and apart from the others, for Don liked to experiment with color, fabric, wall design, lighting, floor covering, bathroom fixtures, door handles, the box office.

He took huge risks; Don's roulette wheel was the size of the Rose Bowl. You could spot a Don Rugoff newspaper ad or poster one hundred miles away—it was elegant, powerful, seductive, probably better than the film, but invariably pulled in audiences. He fought the studios, often barred their pictures from his theaters. Hollered at critics. Threatened exhibitors if they wouldn't play his films under the conditions he laid out. It was cartoon time.

Don locked horns with me many times. Once he made me so furious that it provoked me, when no longer in exhibition, into going back into it. Another time, he called me at midnight at home, rattling off sentences in spritz fashion like a character in a Céline novel.

"Hey, Tiger," (he addressed everyone, including women, as "Tiger") "I need a picture . . . in two days . . . at the Plaza. I hear you own some Fassbinders . . . Whatdya say, Tiger? Come to my office . . . Nine in the morning." *Bang.*

Among the films he himself distributed were Costa-Gavras's *Z* and Robert Downey's *Putney Swope*. He was known as a distributor for his stew of unpredictability and showmanship. Once he staged a $35,000 party for Dušan Makavejev at the Plaza Hotel for the opening of Makavejev's brilliant movie *WR: Mysteries of the Organism*. He liked doing things on the spur of the moment.

"Yeah, let's rent a boat tomorrow and stack it with flags announcing our new film. Call Glorious Foods to cater. Get a steeplejack who'll climb up the sails. We'll circle Manhattan two times. Invite Norman Mailer and Andy Warhol."

Don had an inoperable benign brain tumor, the pressure of which caused him to nod off during screenings. It also produced a splenetic temperament, with speech often slurred. When he ate, food would spill on his shirt. He married a woman named Evangeline and had two sons with her, neither of whom was interested in the distribution and exhibition business. Evangeline couldn't keep up with Don's obsessional behavior. The marriage broke up. He was totally consumed, day and night, night and day, with his theaters and his distribution company, Cinema 5 (*The Garden of the Finzi-Continis, State of Siege, The Sorrow and the Pity, Scenes from a Marriage*, etc.).

As an exhibitor, Don visited his theaters daily. He'd catch ushers picking their noses and yell at them, check the bathrooms, hold long conversations with the projectionist and manager, scowl at the slightest misframe or sudden drop in the sound level.

Don was a master at opening films in seventy-two hours. Nobody could duplicate him. Normally it would take four to six weeks to open one. More recently, with the endless cascade of films on the market, it takes three to four months to open a film.

Once I was with him in his office when he'd just bought a picture that he slept through for one million bucks. With an empty yellow-lined pad by the telephone, sporting ten names of exhibitors around the country, he swung into action. He called Mel Novikoff, the class-act exhibitor in San Francisco—of the Clay, the Lumiere, the Castro.

"Hey, Tiger, it's Don Rugoff. Just bought this Italian film for a million bucks. I want you to open it. Send me an advance of one hundred thou."

When Mel wavered, Don responded, "Listen, Tiger, if you don't tool up the bread, I'm going to take the next plane to San Francisco and open a theater across the street from the Clay."

That was Don's way. Insatiable. Driving. A cyclone.

After his marriage with Evangeline broke up, he married Suzy Child, half his age. Suzy's father was aghast that she would marry this nut, a corpulent man weighing over 250 pounds. But Suzy loved Don and stuck with him until the end. She was always at his side.

"Suzy, follow Fran to the bathroom. See how much time she spends there."

Fran Spielman was his theatrical sales manager, then seventy years old, a great-grandmother. Once Don took a whole-page ad in *Variety* with a picture of Fran wearing a feathered Native American headdress, holding a tomahawk, announcing a new Cinema 5 picture.

He expected employees to keep long hours like himself. Besides building and booking his theaters and traveling to Paris to buy new pictures—like retail merchants going to Rivington Street to buy *schmatas*—he scrutinized and paid every invoice himself; interviewed cashiers, ushers, and porters, never trusting managers to do this. So, what was the function of his office staff? To be there long hours, available to him for whatever.

Don was unsure about me. I detected envy. I was an airy fellow, a *luftmensch*, never following rules if I could help it, distrustful of professionals, taking on impossible films, a history of dippy programming. He couldn't get a handle on me. Often he'd invite me to his office just to hang around. I could see that he was studying me sideways, looking for some key, some clue as to what made me tick, some way to cut in on my jib.

At one point he needed tons of money to run his operation and buy more films. Hired people at fancy salaries, overpaid for films he took on, overspent on advertising campaigns. He was a master promoter, his ads the best in the history of movie ads. They were postmodern—large Lichtenstein-like images with dots, huge *Citizen Kane*–like typography.

Before their prices became stratospheric, Don collected artwork by Warhol, Rauschenberg, Johns, Rosenquist. He had pictures by these fellows hanging all over the office. They influenced his ads. When opening a film, he might reject as many as ten ads prepared by his agency, Diener/Hauser/Greenthal.

As he was getting deeper into money troubles, a step away from tap city, he went public: creating Cinema 5, he sold over 65 percent of his stock to the public.

Along the way, Don insulted William R. Forman, one of the wealthiest exhibitors in America. In addition to the Pacific Theatres chain of several hundred theaters, Forman owned large blocks of real estate in Honolulu, hotels, casinos. A tall, well-built man, muscular, aggressive, and combative, Forman once socked a Frenchman on the Champs-Élysées who had called him a filthy American—the man nearly died. Libidinous to a fault, he provoked fear in others. As a result of Don's insult, Forman began buying Cinema 5 stock on the open market.

In short order, with the help of some of Don's friends who owned large blocks of stock in the company and betrayed Don out of greed, Forman accumulated enough stock to take control of the company. One day he kicked Don out of the office.

Don contacted other exhibitors in the city, offering his services as an advertising consultant. He went around town with Suzy, who carried a large black leather portfolio of ads. It was no soap with the exhibitors. They knew what a madman Don was and didn't want any part of him.

His health declined. The tumor got worse. His speech became more affected; he slurred words more often. He was confined to a wheelchair. This once powerful magnate appeared to be eating crow.

But that was not the case, for his spirits remained high. He and Suzy abandoned their apartment on Second Avenue and Sixty-Sixth Street and moved to Edgartown, on Martha's Vineyard. There he struck a deal with the owner of a large café, formerly a church, with one hundred wooden chairs. On the spot he put up a screen and ran a film society there. Immediately he contacted me. Wouldn't deal with our booker. He wanted me. By then I had a large library of films.

"Hey, Tiger, I want to play *Aguirre, the Wrath of God*. What are you going to charge me?" My dilemma was to avoid making him look like a charity case, yet not charge him book price, for then he'd lose money. I arrived at a face-saving formula, and he was able to operate his one-hundred-seat theater mostly with my films, Suzy doing all the administrative work.

When no longer getting "Hey, Tiger" phone calls from this master showman, I wondered what was up. Then one day I read a one-paragraph obituary

in the *New York Times*. Don was buried in a pauper's grave on Martha's Vineyard. I was so angry at this inadequate obituary that I phoned Vincent Canby
and complained. Vincent told me to write something about Don and he would
shepherd it into the Arts and Leisure pages, which I did ["Donald Rugoff: In
Memory of a 'Wild Genius,'" May 21, 1989].

■ ■ ■

None of these fellows here described was delicate. They clearly understood how
to get their beloved object, their beautiful film, to a cultivated, expectant audience, weaving in and out of all the intricate cogs of the system: agents, producers, stars, exhibitors, critics. Distributors ask themselves: Will Judy or Vincent
or Sheila like my film? Will the producer think I'm a cheapskate for not pro-
moting his film enough? Will the star complain about the small size of the type
in the ad and where his or her name appears? And so on . . .

In the end, the *real* distributor is the *film itself*. A film that succeeds almost
always has something inside itself, an It, God's blessing, what's known in Yiddish as the *rozhinkel* (that exquisite raisin), a magical edge that bespeaks HIT.
And once that occurs, there's only one thing I have to say to my colleagues: Stay
behind the film, watch it, and lead it to audiences. Stick with it—and whatever
else, don't tread on it with your clumsy feet. Leave the ad campaign and pro-
motion work alone, just run to the rooftops and shout the glories of the work.

PART 4

ACQUISITIONS

EMILE DE ANTONIO AND THE MAKING OF *POINT OF ORDER*

Walking down Broadway every day, my eyes oblivious to the surroundings, I thought only about films to show. In the early 1960s, one of my ideas was to get hold of the Army–McCarthy Hearings and play the entire 187 hours uncut over thirty-four days (the way they ran it on television in 1954), and charge customers by the hour. This idea eventually became the documentary *Point of Order*. At the time of the hearings, I'd been happily out of work. For those three months, I'd watched them daily. It had been the biggest show in town. People stood in front of radio-television stores, glued to TV sets in the windows. They also watched the hearings in barbershops, candy stores, bars. Having vividly remembered all this, I wanted to revive in some format that spectacle six years later.

I met Emile de Antonio in 1960 when he began distributing films. His first was a short by Dan Drasin called *Sunday*. He also had Alfred Leslie and Robert Frank's *Pull My Daisy*, which I had shown at the theater with *The Magnificent Ambersons*.

De Antonio was a charming, charismatic fellow. He had an infectious laugh and a raffish smile. Women were all over him. He said funny things, often grotesque. He lived with his teenage son in a small office in a two-story taxpayer building on Sixth Avenue and Fifty-Third Street. Painted on the side of the building was a wall poster of *The Naked City* and *Brute Force*, a Warner Brothers combo in the forties. We called it the Brute Force Building.

Besides distributing films, de Antonio represented painters, among them Andy Warhol, Jasper Johns, and Robert Rauschenberg. Warhol was doing shoe drawings for Bendel's. De Antonio urged him to quit this work and try his hand at silk-screen paintings. De Antonio also hung around with John Cage, Merce Cunningham, and other avant-garde artists of that feverish art scene. Knowing some of these artists resulted years later in his fine film *Painters Painting*.

De Antonio was struck by my Army–McCarthy idea. After much discussion, we discarded the one-hour format and decided to make a feature documentary out of the hearings. De Antonio, who also knew his way around the rich liberal-left set, went about raising the money we needed to buy the kinescopes in order to make the film.

We screened this material in my Riverside Drive apartment near the New Yorker Theater, each making notes of sequences we wanted to use. We labored together agreeably. We could only work part time. It took over two years to organize our selections, find an editor, and put the film to bed. I had originally wanted Orson Welles to do a voice-over. This never came to pass.

Some journalists recited de Antonio's account of how he and I were at "cross-purposes" over how to make a feature from almost two hundred hours of footage—a conflict de Antonio characterized as "war," stating that he "booted out the staffers working with Talbot." This makes groovy newspaper copy, but believe me, it's fantasy. We worked together extremely well, and I don't know what "staffers" he was talking about, unless he meant my mother-in-law, Bella, whom I loved and often consulted on life matters. She knew a lot about Hitler, but I doubt that she was an expert on Joe McCarthy.

What grabbed de Antonio and me about McCarthy was his anarchic spirit. We thought of him as a stand-in for W. C. Fields. Politics was less on our minds than making a good show out of this stuff. Yes, we both had strong lefty political points of view—whatever that amounts to in our beguilingly complex society. As one wag of those days said: "Karl Marx won't get you a five-cent cup of coffee on the Hoboken Tubes."

De Antonio and I differed on only one point: the film's ending. We resolved our differences with a toss of the coin. De Antonio won, and we used his ending, which I'm happy to say was probably much better than what I wanted. It ended with lawyer Joseph Welch asking McCarthy, "Have you no sense of decency, sir, at long last? Have you no sense of decency?" Whereupon the room empties, McCarthy blustering to himself.

■ ■ ■

We shared the producer credit, and de Antonio became "editorial director." (In one version, this morphed into "directed" [*sic!*] by Emile de Antonio.) As a salve, I was given "From an idea by Daniel Talbot." It was fine with me—knowing that once the film was finished, I wouldn't dream of embarking on another. This had been a harrowing financial burden. We'd run out of money in the final editing stages. Our lab would process footage only on a cash basis. For several months, I went there to get the footage with weekend New Yorker Theater box office receipts.

I was a straight-arrow fellow with a wife and three kids and a theater to run; future film projects were the last thing on my mind. Except for the ending, the shape of the film was an entirely mutually agreed-upon venture. Once we knew what we wanted, we hired an editor to put it together. Neither of us had ever seen a moviola before.

One of our first editors was Paul Falkenberg, a director of films on art who had worked with Fritz Lang on *M* and G. W. Pabst on *Diary of a Lost Girl*. Paul was further to the left of de Antonio and me. At one of our periodic viewings of his edit, we found that he had inserted a scene of a May Day parade in Moscow to make an "ironic" point on communist infiltration in the army that McCarthy ranted about in the hearings. We fired Falkenberg. De Antonio later said slanderous things about him in a *Harvard Lampoon* interview. Falkenberg sued de Antonio. It was settled out of court.

We flew in Irving Lerner from Los Angeles for an interview. He spent a weekend with de Antonio and me in the East Hampton house of a real estate broker whom de Antonio was dating. We drank and ate a lot and got into a high-stakes poker game with Irving, who dropped $2,000. At other moments we watched de Antonio, who liked guns, shoot at rabbits in his girlfriend's flower garden. We decided not to hire Lerner. Eventually we hired a young production editor, Robert Duncan, who worked closely with us on the final edit. We were pleased with the result.

■ ■ ■

The first person for whom we screened the finished film was McCarthy's sidekick, the ruthless lawyer Roy Cohn. We showed him *Point of Order* one morning at the New Yorker before the theater opened. We wanted his take on the film. When it was over, Cohn said, "I'm going to sue you guys."

"Why?" I asked.

"I don't like what you did with my role in the hearings," he declared, as if we'd been directing Cohn "live" instead of using raw footage.

I opened my big mouth: "Go ahead, sue, we've got insurance."

Cohn called *Variety* and reported the conversation. As soon as the story appeared, we received a telegram from our insurance carrier announcing that they were canceling our insurance. Fortunately, de Antonio knew George Plimpton, whose father was on the board of directors of our carrier. Our insurance was reinstated.

With a finished film in the can, we flew to Washington, DC, to screen *Point of Order* for many senators and congressmen, an obvious audience who could serve as "mouths." To organize this event, we'd hired David Bazelon, a friend of mine and a nephew of Judge Bazelon, a famous judge on the DC federal court. A swinging intellectual, David wrote a brilliant book on how power operates in America. Through his uncle, he knew his way around political corridors.

In DC, the film screening was enthusiastically received by all. The only hitch was, unbeknownst to me, my name had been removed from the closing credits by de Antonio. Outside the hall on the sidewalk, I confronted him.

His face turned red. No explanation. *Fuck you, Jack*, is what he must have been thinking when he put scissors to film. This was my introduction to a side of de Antonio's personality that would surface again. Years later, for example, he also removed Robert Duncan's credit as editor.

My credit restored, I said nothing further. We had much work to do to get our film launched. Since de Antonio had ideas for other films he wanted to make, and knowing I'd never again produce films, I stuffed any resentment in my craw. The credit had no practical meaning for me. It was connected with vanity, to the accomplishment of having a finished film, to a vague notion of being in Show Business Heaven.

We launched *Point of Order* ourselves in 1964 at the Beekman Theater, part of Don Rugoff's chain. The reviews were unanimously terrific. Numerous editorial writers—like James Wechsler of the *New York Post*—wrote about the importance of this work; Susan Sontag and Dwight Macdonald applauded it. The film worked well at the Beekman. But, deep in debt, we decided to sell it to Continental, the Walter Reade Organization's distribution subsidiary. The large advance helped us defray much of our debt as well as fulfill obligations to our investors. It took many years before we became whole.

■ ■ ■

De Antonio went on to become a full-fledged documentary filmmaker. His next film was *Rush to Judgment*, based on a book by Mark Lane. Not one of his better films, it played off the madcap notions of the conspiracy mavens.

I returned to my work as an exhibitor. In 1965, I founded New Yorker Films. After I became de Antonio's American distributor, he invited me to discuss the rough assemblies of several of his films, including *Millhouse: A White Comedy* and *In the Year of the Pig*, which we would show at the New Yorker. *Millhouse* got us both on Nixon's enemies list, a badge of honor in the eyes of our radical friends who were jealous of not making the list.

We had been named on cheap little memos on White House stationery by Dean and Erlichmann. One stated that "Talbot has no criminal record." Another guardedly danced with the notion of an IRS audit of me and my theater, but they held back, deeming it too unsophisticated.

Around that time, I had several visitors in our shabby one-room New Yorker Films office in the taxpayer building. "Ya know, Mr. Talbot," one of them said, "we don't know anything about the fil-um business, perhaps you could enlighten us."

This visitor was a New York City gumshoe, and I asked him to hang out in the theater for a while, since I couldn't see him right away. At the time we were showing Robert Bresson's *Pickpocket*. A bevy of pickpockets showed up—not to steal but to study the techniques of the Algerian masters in that famous pick-pocketing ballet sequence. And guess what? The gumshoe's pocket got picked! He ran into my office, shouting, "Hey, what kind of a theater are you running?!"

I was somewhat sanguine in those days about these strange events. Sufficiently patriotic not to be too alarmed, since I've always believed that we live in a sophisticated, complex democracy where things sort themselves out. These days, I'm not so sure about it.

As the years went on, de Antonio became cranky, angrier than ever. Felt that he wasn't being taken seriously enough. He wanted to be regarded as an artist, not merely a political documentary filmmaker.

When he made *Underground*, about which I had mixed feelings, he asked me for a $50,000 upfront guarantee, which I refused. This made him sore. After all, I distributed all his films, why not *Underground*?

We no longer spoke to each other. He'd send me several letters a week, written in a manic telegraph style, commanding me, asking why I didn't do this, do that—why aren't you showing my films in your theater?—on and on. He was drinking heavily.

Then one day I received a nasty letter from him, in which he called me a "sausage merchant." I rang him up and told him to send a messenger forthwith to pick up all his prints; I would have nothing further to do with him and gave up my distribution rights to his films, except for *Point of Order*, which we owned jointly.

He died several years later of a heart attack, an angry man. As the years passed, I often thought about him and remembered the good times we had together, even though he continued doing his crazy numbers, such as moving the negatives of *Point of Order* to the University of Wisconsin without telling me. Fortunately, I discovered a pristine duplicate negative elsewhere.

De Antonio was not a cinephile. He rarely went to movies. He was a dyspeptic intellectual who loved women and booze, was unmarried for years. After his son was grown, he lived in a one-bedroom apartment in the East Sixties, tatami mat on the bedroom floor. No furniture. A busy assignation pad.

He made several wonderful films. Few walk the hallowed halls of art. De Antonio was certainly not the artist he wanted to be thought of as, but I'm equally convinced that his best films—*Point of Order* (with me included), *Millhouse*, *In the Year of the Pig*, and *Painters Painting*—will stand strong for many years to come.

NEW YORKER FILMS

Distributing foreign and independent films makes little sense. The work is mainly tedious, if not downright boring, and at times nasty. It demands enormous patience, for it's a hit-driven business and not unusual to wait as long as five years before your ship comes in. I watch over 350 films annually, sitting in dark, stuffy screening rooms all year long. When my mother first learned that I was looking at movies in the morning, she said, "Oh, so that's how you make a living!"

Many films I click off after ten minutes. Those that I watch in their entirety, if not beauties, often require concentrated attention. That is, they may be interesting and worthy of our time but lack the magic and density of the really good ones. They deserve a window—passing two hours pleasantly or even interestingly, yet not becoming transcendental experiences. We'll take a chance on them. Who knows? Perhaps the director's next film will impinge upon our lives.

In my journal, I note the day's screenings: director, story, the "look" of it. "A television movie," I may grouse, half an hour in—Toby has heard this aplenty.

My friend Andrew Sarris once said to me, "Can you imagine a fourteen-year-old, when asked what he or she wants to do upon becoming an adult, saying, 'A foreign film distributor'?"

Precisely. There are no schools or classes that teach this trade. Distributors are by and large distrusted, if not hated, by many people. They're usually perceived to be fat, middle-aged, balding, beady-eyed men with a thick cigar jutting out of thick lips, forever looking for an angle, snaking about for an "opportunity." They're also perceived as a band of crooks—inventors of tangolike accounting, often simply no-pay guys. ("Go ahead, sue me, your legal bill will be bigger than the money I owe you!") Once the decision to take on a film is made, negotiations begin between the distributor and the producer's representative—sometimes a high-powered lawyer whose wealth derives from the art of ball-breaking. Some people find this process challenging, if not sexy. They dance around numbers, percentages, prohibitions, and punishments. I loathe the process. When I fall in love with a film, I'm in love with the film-maker as well and prefer to make my deals with that person. Invariably, these deals are quick, fair, simple.

Yes, I distribute and show films for a living—sometimes precariously. But when I "discover" a new director, I want to sing out to everyone that something new has come along—a work of art that is fresh, different, exciting. The really good stuff makes me want to grab passersby by the collar, like a barker, and rave about my "offspring."

MY DINNER WITH ANDRÉ

One day in 1981, Louis Malle came to my office with a script in hand, somewhat dubious. It was *My Dinner with André*, an almost two-hour dinner conversation between playwright and actor Wallace Shawn, who wrote the script, and André Gregory. The latter, an avant-garde theater director who had disappeared in the early seventies, was rumored to be seeking enlightenment in Tibet, finding ecstasy in a remote Polish forest, and eating sand in the Sahara.

I went home and read the manuscript in one sitting. The writing was magnetic. I told Malle to make the film straightaway, and arranged to procure production money from Gaumont, with whom at the time I was partners in distribution.

In the film, a grave waiter calmly doles out pâté and pours wine at an Upper West Side restaurant across the way from our office, while two writers, playing themselves, discuss Jerzi Grotowski, electric blankets, money, mortality, despair, and love. According to Gregory, Malle's single direction was "Talk faster."

I launched the film in the United States at the Cinema Studio on one screen. We nursed the run at moderate grosses until it took off after the eleventh week. By then, it had reached the magic number of spectators—eight thousand—a number quoted to me by French intellectual Daniel Toscan du Plantier as a landmark for word of mouth to kick in. It ran for fifty-three weeks, grossed $5 million theatrically, and became a sensation at our theater, playing to a packed house for a solid year—the biggest grossing film in the history of our company.

My Dinner with André is funny, quixotic, confessional, moving, and—like life—suffused with melancholy and joy. But not gloomy. It was a long shot. A gift.

RULES OF THE GAME

I wrote my own contracts for distributing the works of directors Rainer Werner Fassbinder, Werner Herzog, and Alain Tanner, which consisted of one page of lay prose stating our arrangement. Many years later, as the business became more complex and it was no longer possible to deal directly with directors, I was urged to have my lawyer, Bob Montgomery, draft longer and more formal contracts.

When I showed my one-pager to Bob, a decent and brilliant man, he winced at first, then smiled. "These are Dead Sea Scrolls," he said, likewise true and accurate. Bob followed my mandate and came up with a three-pager, simply written.

Still and all, I would like to propose a new form of contract: a photograph of two hands shaking, the owners of these hands portrayed on top by two oval head shots, and two signatures below, alongside the name of the film and the parties. And, directly below: "It is understood among both parties that a willful, malicious break of the contract is punishable by death."

Many of the films I distributed early on were without advances, for I didn't have the cash. This I didn't like, since I think an advance is a sign of commitment, but due to the type of distribution I wanted to pursue, I was at times forced to proceed this way. The usual token advance was only something like $1,000, but it had a symbolic value—the distributor is not getting something for nothing—and I was usually able to manage it.

At one point, later on, I made a trip to Paris and acquired about fifteen or twenty films. I went with a bit of cash in my pocket and handed out advances to a lot of directors. I even gave Jean-Marie Straub a $1,000 advance for a hopelessly uncommercial short film. He was very happy. When I had less money, I was unable to do this, but by then I'd already built up relationships with filmmakers such as Bertolucci, Herzog, and Fassbinder.

By dealing directly with filmmakers rather than producers and giving exposure to new works at the New Yorker and then at the Cinema Studio, our distribution company successfully eliminated barriers between filmmakers and their audience. By 1980, our catalogue had grown to two hundred entries, ranging from Mizoguchi, Ozu, and Oshima to Rossellini and Rivette. It was a labor of love. How I managed to survive all those years with zero interest in the business end of things is a mystery to me. Ultimately, I did not have a magic touch. There is something undefinable inside successful films that makes them work. The ultimate aim of the distributor is to get behind them.

Once a film is taken on board, there's the business of getting prints, anxiety that scratches or sound defects may be on the film, gathering publicity material, preparing for its release, complicated decisions of when and where to premiere the film, how much to spend on advertising, and, of course, additional anxiety over the critical response. In the course of time I launched more than four hundred films, and yet, each time I prepared myself for failure (despite high expectations of success) and would die another small death.

I'm never cynical or cool about opening a film. But there are so many walls to hurdle: producer's representatives, critics, tough exhibitors—as well as audiences who are by and large unadventurous, passive, waiting for journalists, spinmeisters, and critics to tell them what to see and what not to see. For twenty-four hours, my body is tense and thoughts dance in my brain.

I'm angry, threaten to quit, have had it up to here. I decide that I'll buy all of Western Europe, maybe Eastern Europe as well. I hate. I love. I become a total *meshugana*. The upside is that as the years pass, the works of many great directors, shunned when first presented, become certified in the pantheon. And that includes *The Rules of the Game*.

PART 5

DIRECTORS IN MY LIFE

YASUJIRO OZU

In 1969, Donald Richie, then film curator of the Museum of Modern Art, screened *Tokyo Story*, a Japanese film made in 1952 by Yasujiro Ozu, for us. Toby and I were knocked out by this simple story: black and white; camera three feet off the ground, like someone seated on a tatami mat and barely moving; short on plot, long on wisdom.

An elderly provincial couple eagerly prepare to visit their son and daughter in Tokyo. But the offspring, busy with their lives, dispatch their parents to a hot-springs resort to get them out of the way. At a certain point, husband and wife, seated on a parapet, gaze at a passing train. Nothing is said. Nothing needs to be said. Their daughter-in-law, young widow of their son who died in the war, says at one point, "Life is disappointing, isn't it?" Who could disagree? A universal truth, told quietly.

We opened *Tokyo Story* in 1973. It ran for eight weeks. Now, each year on a Sunday morning, Toby and I screen it alone in our theater as a kind of ritual. From time to time, one of us quotes an Ozu title. On a windy day in the swimming pool, fallen leaves and greenery dot the water, and in between strokes, Toby looks up: "*A Story of Floating Weeds*," she says, and away she swims. It's our private language, our secret code that evokes images. Donald Richie tells us that "floating weeds, drifting down the leisurely river of our lives" is a favored metaphor in Japanese prose and poetry. And viewed as emblematic of our own lives.

At some harried moment, I come up with "*I Was Born, But . . .*" And Toby nods in inner accord.

■ ■ ■

Our first catalogue listed *Late Spring*, one of Ozu's greatest works. It was made in 1949 but never had a commercial run in Japan—it was to have its New York premiere twenty-four years later. Again, a small story: a widowed father and daughter, living together, must gracefully separate. Eventually New Yorker Films distributed almost a dozen Ozu films, among them *Early Spring*, *Early Summer*, and *Late Autumn*. Seasonal titles, the human journey.

When Ozu died in December 1963, leaving behind more than fifty films made from 1923 until his death, he was little known here—a comment on the film gap between the United States and many overseas sources. By 1975, we published a catalogue devoted solely to Ozu's films. Its cover, bright red, simply read "The Major Works of Yasujiro Ozu," with an introduction from Richie's splendid book *Ozu: His Life and Films*, first published by the University of California Press in 1974. Below is an excerpt:

> Yasujiro Ozu, the man whom his kinsmen consider the most Japanese of all film directors, had but one major subject, the Japanese family, and but one major theme, its dissolution. . . . Ozu's films are a kind of home drama. . . . As Ozu himself said, during the publicity campaign of his last film, *An Autumn Afternoon*, "I always tell people that I don't make anything besides *tofu* . . . and that is because I am strictly a *tofu*-dealer."
>
> Not only did Ozu often use the same actor in the same kind of role, playing, generally, the same kind of character (Setsuko Hara and Chishu Ryu are notable examples), he also used the same story line in various films.

Seemingly simple, his stories struck a universal chord.

NAGISA OSHIMA

I'd like to show you a short film by a director very different than Ozu," Donald Richie told us one evening at Lattanzi, a favorite Italian restaurant of his in the west Forties, where he always ordered his favorite little artichokes *alla giudia*. He'd come to New York to deliver one of his lectures on Japanese culture. Next morning, in the small screening room of our office, we screened *Diary of a Yunbogi Boy*, a twenty-eight-minute collage film made in 1965 by Nagisa Oshima, a name then unknown to us, but that would subsequently figure prominently in our growing library. The film consists of diary entries of a six-year-old orphaned Korean street boy, accompanied by still photographs and voice-over. Unlike Ozu's family stories, this is a highly political tale, epitomizing Japan's involvement in Korea and the mess it created during the occupation. Spare as it is, this "small film" packs a wallop and is all the more poignant for being about the predicament of a child.

Our New Yorker Films distribution catalogue listed ten films by Oshima, subsequently regarded as the most important figure in Japanese cinema since the classical era of Ozu, Mizoguchi, and Kurosawa. An angry, outspoken critic of traditional Japanese society, Oshima merges politics, violence, eroticism, and dazzling camera work. *Death by Hanging*, a damning satire on capital punishment, describes in detail the execution of a young Korean worker found guilty of rape. *The Ceremony*, perhaps his masterpiece, chronicles the downfall of a family ruled by an autocrat whose life is pledged to the supremacy of the emperor. The film that gained him the most notoriety, *In the Realm of the Senses*, provoked censorship and controversy for its explicit depiction of sexual obsession, treating the body with ultimate directness.

OUSMANE SEMBÈNE

I met Ousmane Sembène in Paris a year before the 1968 uprising. I was a fledgling distributor at the time, with no more than twenty or thirty films under my belt, among them works by Rossellini, Bertolucci, Marker, Godard, and Bresson, and with few dollars in my pocket. One of my ideas about leading a sane life was to seek out and acquire only films that spoke to my soul. And since I never had a problem with taking on films deemed by my fellow distributors to be money losers, I was free to pursue those by filmmakers who possessed a truthful and poetic purchase on life. Sembène fell into that category, and then some.

My wanderings that year in Paris—the best city at that point in which to see new work—were abetted by Louis Marcorelles, a champion of the New Cinema. Both on the same track, we became friends. Years later, he became the chief film critic of *Le Monde*. Among the directors he singled out as worthy of my attention was Ousmane Sembène.

Marcorelles organized a screening for me at Club 70, 16 *bis* Rue Lauriston, of *Borom Sarret*, an eighteen-minute short about a man with a cart, driving around and picking up people, who carries the burdens of his race on his squat shoulders, and *Black Girl*, a sixty-minute feature about a young Senegalese woman hired as a domestic by a French colonial family, who treat her as a slave. It is a heartbreaking story and a savage attack on neocolonialism.

To say that I fell in love with these films is an understatement. I was simply shattered. I remember sitting alone after the screening in that small, dimly lit auditorium, a room where over the years I'd screened Godard's *2 or 3 Things I Know About Her*, *Les Carabiniers*, and more than a few Chabrols.

Thus began a relationship between Sembène and myself that kept going strong for forty years. In my catalogue, I have every film he ever made. He was a firebrand, a humanist who worried about the tragedies of modern life. Our business dealings were swift, simple, mutually satisfactory.

There's fresh air between us in the occasional short letters we write. He offers to have me stay at his seaside cottage outside of Dakar. I invite him to stay with us in New York. He asks to have his royalty checks sent to his son Alain, who's studying engineering at a college in Pennsylvania. We meet from time to time in Paris or during the Cannes Film Festival. We dine and discuss family matters, books we've recently read (he'd read Saul Bellow, Bernard Malamud, and Philip Roth), and both complain about how hard it has become to pursue the cinema we respect in an increasingly unbearable economic climate.

Ousmane Sembène's films became the matrix of our deeply felt relationship, long before he was called the father of African cinema. A self-educated Senegalese, one-time docksman and union organizer, he became one of Africa's leading novelists before turning to cinema as a means of reaching a wider audience. To that end, he went to study in Russia and was a student of Mark Donskoi.

His work often centers on identity problems encountered by Africans caught between Africa and Europe, tradition and modernization. His second feature film, *Mandabi*, adapted from Sembène's own novella, is the first film shot in the Wolof language. It is a satire on bureaucratic difficulties in cashing a foreign money order. *Emitaï* is about the confrontation between a Senegalese tribe and French soldiers. *Moolaadé*, one of his most devastating films, deals with female circumcision and women in a tiny village who revolt against this ancient barbarous practice.

As to his style, I can compare him to Jean Renoir. Both loved telling stories populated by eccentric characters, ever challenging the petit-bourgeois moral order and on the lookout for truths that rattle the soul. I see affinities between *Xala* and *The Rules of the Game*; *Camp de Thiaroye* and *Grand Illusion*; *Mandabi* and *Boudu Saved from Drowning*.

Sembène wasn't too fond of experimental filmmaking. We once screened together, at a film festival, a Jean-Luc Godard film from his post-*Weekend* period. Sembène winced at the disjunctive narrative and discordant quotations, to the exclusion of a real story with real people about real-life matters.

He himself would bicycle from one village to another, presenting his work on a makeshift screen. His films were made on a level for Africans with no formal education, yet with Marxist underpinnings that audiences all over the world might relate to. At the core of his work is a profound humanism. He deplored crippling customs, religious fakery, demeaning poverty and ignorance, the arrogance of the rich and powerful. I suspect that his appearance as a character in some of his films was devised as a ruse so that certain players didn't pull the wool over the eyes of others.

Sembène shot all his films on 35mm. He was strong, alert, and wily, wary of many of the new technologies. For years I begged him to allow me to put his films on DVD. Jonathan Rosenbaum, a film critic of the *Chicago Reader* and a great admirer of Sembène's films, attacked me for not getting them a wider distribution on DVD, not knowing that I was handicapped by Sembène, who finally relented. For starters, we put out *Borom Sarret, Black Girl, Mandabi,* and *Xala*. Sembène's work will endure as long as there is a film culture.

The last time we saw him was at Cannes in 2005. He looked terrific and was seeking money for a new film—perhaps *Samori*, about which he often spoke to me over the years, a large-budget work about a heroic African who battled French colonialism. Sembène was then eighty-two going on sixty-two. I imagine he was one of those who avoided doctors. What a pity. He died of colon cancer—if detected early on, it could have been cured. But this was not his way; he never complained to me once about his health. Too busy cooking up stories, challenging received ideas, piercing holes in hot-air balloons.

ROBERTO ROSSELLINI

Roberto Rossellini and I met in the late sixties and became friends at once. He'd retained the rights to *Paisan*, *Journey to Italy*, and *The Miracle*, and without lawyers we made a distribution deal for these films. Rossellini was a hard bargainer. No matter; I was prepared to give the father of modern cinema anything.

Rome Open City and *Paisan* introduced audiences and a generation of film directors to neorealism: films shot on location, often with nonprofessionals, and freed of studio-type shooting. Roberto was the precursor of the French New Wave. Jean-Luc Godard wrote: "He is the only one to have a true and total vision of things. Thus, he films in the only way possible. No one could film a scenario by Rossellini. His vision of the world is so exact that his vision of detail, formal or not, is also exact. For him a shot is beautiful because it is true, for others a shot becomes beautiful by being true."

Roberto had a breathtaking intelligence and imagination. His mind cut through history and ideas like a high-speed electric saw. He could relate an incident during the Renaissance to the mismanagement of the Communist Party congress in Bologna in 1964.

In later years he went on to make film essays on historical subjects. *Socrates*, the first, establishes the period by noting simple details of everyday life: Socrates buying octopus at the market, Socrates extracting a coin from his mouth (clothes of that period were without pockets). The film covers the time from the Spartan conquest of Athens in 404 BC to the death of Socrates in 399 BC. Long excerpts from Plato's *Dialogues* give dialectic examples of Socrates's mode of reasoning and present his ideas on madness, eloquence, death, justice, politics, rhetoric, beauty, knowledge, and the immortality of the soul. It is a lesson in history presented on a human scale. Rossellini continued this approach in *Blaise Pascal* and *Cartesius*.

Whenever he came to town for a few days, we'd have lunch with him and his teenage daughter Isabella. We always ate at the same restaurant: La Scala, on Fifty-Fourth Street between Sixth and Seventh avenues. He always ordered the same meal, which Isabella told me he had each day 365 days a year: pasta, salad, espresso coffee.

For a director of his international fame, he was simple and unpretentious. He bridled whenever someone referred to him as an artist. He saw himself as a carrier of ideas, nothing more. We rarely spoke about cinema. He spoke about the world we live in, about historical events. I listened carefully. I considered him my teacher. It was Roberto who taught me to look for new film styles and ideas as well as the truth. It's no accident that the first film that launched New Yorker Films as a distribution company was Bernardo Bertolucci's *Before the Revolution*, in which our dear friend Gianni Amico urged Fabrizio to "always remember Rossellini." The metal can in which that film lives is labeled number one. And that's how I'll always remember Rossellini.

The other side of him that I admired was his love of women. He hid nothing, had lovers all over the world. His lovers knew about the others, and apparently there was never any confusion or sense of betrayal. Roberto was obviously blessed with the capacity to make love well.

Perhaps the film very close to his artistic vision, one that became an icon for the French New Wave, was *Journey to Italy* with Ingrid Bergman and George Sanders. It's about a marriage on the rocks. The couple genuinely love each other, but their union is mysteriously in disintegration, due perhaps to something sinister in the air of Europe. I viewed it as Rossellini projecting a future landscape filled with depressed, anxiety-ridden souls, victims of narcissism, sexual obsession, and role confusion, a new breed floundering in tentative relationships.

■ ■ ■

Years later, whenever Toby and I were in Paris, we stayed in what used to be Roberto's suite at the Hôtel Raphaël on the Avenue Kléber. We felt his presence in our small apartment, bedecked with heavy burgundy and satin drapes, kelly-green felt on the walls, and lithographs of Italian Renaissance faces and street scenes. We often dined with our friend and business partner Daniel Toscan du Plantier, the general manager of Gaumont at the time, and spoke with deep feeling about our cinema hero, Roberto Rossellini.

In 1991 in Cannes I was honored and moved to be given the Rossellini Award. "If I have been working in cinema all these years," I said, "it is only because of Roberto Rossellini." I vividly remembered having seen *Rome Open City* and *Paisan* as a very young man. At that point I had no doubt that I would have something to do with cinema. I dreamt a great deal about these two films and have never stopped dreaming about them.

JEAN-LUC GODARD

I met Jean-Luc Godard in Paris in 1969. My friend Claude Nedjar, who worked with him on *See You at Mao*, made the introduction. Claude, for several years, oversaw Louis Malle's production company, theaters, and distribution company in Paris and Munich. Occasionally he produced a film on his own.

At the time we met Godard, he was living with Anna Karina in a duplex apartment in Montparnasse. When we arrived at his place on a hot June day, he was writing on a grid-lined pad with a felt-tip pen that made scratchy noises. Short, well built, he was dressed in a salt-and-pepper tweed suit with cuffed trousers, a red woolen tie, and dark-tinted glasses. He had a powerful handshake, which somehow surprised me, since for some strange reason I never associated serious movie people with powerful handshakes. He spoke softly, a slight rasp in his voice, solemn and to the point. When he smiled, his cheeks dimpled, all boyish charm.

He knew that I had distributed two of his early works (*Les Carabiniers, Le Petit Soldat*). That was okay by him but didn't get a rise. He worked for a fee and didn't own the negatives to most of his films. Moreover, what he had done in the past was absolutely of no interest to him. Unlike some filmmakers, especially those who've made only a handful of films, he was not one to indulge in narcissistic, nostalgic accounts of every wart and pimple on past productions or dwell on the historical status of the films.

Jean-Luc was always ten miles in front of everyone else, his eyes on the next project and the one after that. He never spoke with me about the problems of narrative or the manner in which he worked with his collective. Ever since I've known Jean-Luc, we've never exchanged one word about filmmaking. We are friends who feel an affinity toward each other and never have to say so. I like this quiet friendship.

In those days, we spoke about money (about which he knows a good deal), Havana cigars, and airline travel. Occasionally we talked about tennis. Our relationship developed after Grove Press branched out from book publishing and started distributing films. Just as Barney Rosset's press was always on the cutting edge in book publishing, so he proceeded on the film front. And what better director to start with than Jean-Luc Godard? Barney and I were friends, and I acted as point man between Godard, Nedjar, and him. He picked up a few of Jean-Luc's films of the Dziga Vertov period, I acting as the go-between on a no-fee basis. Jean-Luc later rewarded me with *Tout Va Bien*, *Letter to Jane*, and *2 or 3 Things I Know About Her*. We signed our usual one-page document.

In the 1980s, when I was in partnership with Gaumont in the States and handled *Every Man for Himself*, *Passion*, and *Hail Mary*, Jean-Luc would come to New York to work with us on the ads, posters, and trailers. He was very easy to work with: precise, firm, knowledgeable. Always knew what he wanted. It was a pleasure being with him, although most people I know were very intimidated, terrified by his cold, detached manner.

Eventually he became interested in video. It was cheap, easy to handle, and lent itself to the kind of filmmaking that Alexandre Astruc wrote about in the forties in his famous essay, "La Caméra-Stylo": filmmaking as though writing with a pen, without the mammoth machinery of large-scale 35mm production.

Jean-Luc asked me to accrue his royalties. From time to time he'd call from his home in Rolle, Switzerland, and read me his video shopping list, instructing me on how to deploy his royalty money, purchasing equipment from 47th Street Photo.

He also asked me to handle some of the video films he made, but much as I admired them, I had to turn him down. Not having accepted video technology, I could not honorably distribute these films. As a theater person, I was too accustomed to the look, texture, and power of the 35mm image. For me, video was not only coarse but untrue to the magical art of cinema.

He appreciated my feelings, and I said I'd act as his agent at no fee, making an arrangement with a small video distribution company that had expressed interest in those videos. Jean-Luc insisted that this company work through me during the license period. I got an advance for him, listed the offering of his twenty-six-hour video film in our catalogue, and referred clients to the distributor, Electronic Arts Intermix (EAI). Money passed from EAI to me to Jean-Luc. If a question arose that required his approval, I was designated to make the sole decision, while he kept 100 percent of the revenue. I enjoyed doing this for him, indebted for the pleasure given me by his seminal works. It's not often that a filmmaker of his incredible stature comes down the pike.

RAINER WERNER FASSBINDER

Sometime in the early 1970s, I was having dinner in Rotterdam with film critic Louis Marcorelles when he whispered into my ear that an article was about to be published by a well-known savant on the front page of a big French newspaper with the headline THE END OF CINEMA. I wondered what this was all about. Chic, provocative journalism? Some strange ax to grind? The fact is, European cinema was in good shape at that time. It was the heyday of the French New Wave, Ingmar Bergman and Luis Buñuel were turning out masterpieces, and England and Italy had a good run of films. Despite the strength of cinema during that period, the idea of the article put me in a funk.

Some months later, in the fall of 1972, I saw my first film by Rainer Werner Fassbinder, *The Merchant of Four Seasons*, at the New York Film Festival. Bells and whistles went off in my head. I was trembling with excitement. Fassbinder's fusion of social dysfunction with soap opera melodrama, Brechtian distancing, and a riveting narrative drive kept me at the edge of my seat. Not since Jean-Luc Godard's *Breathless* had I seen a film that spoke to me with such originality. During the next several years, in my role as distributor and exhibitor of foreign films, I screened *Katzelmacher, The American Soldier, Fox and His Friends, The Bitter Tears of Petra von Kant, Why Does Herr R. Run Amok?, Chinese Roulette, Beware of a Holy Whore, Gods of the Plague, Effi Briest*, and *Ali: Fear Eats the Soul*.

At that point my distribution company, New Yorker Films, was moving into high gear. I saw most of Fassbinder's films at the New York Film Festival and in private screenings in Munich. It was clear to me that a great director was in our midst; his films looked like no others I had seen. They had all the wonderful things you expect in great films—superb acting, stylishly crafted narratives, sharp political and social commentary, an inner truth—and then some. (At one point in my immersion in Fassbinder's work, I called Louis Marcorelles in Paris to check whether the article he mentioned was ever published. Unfortunately, as of then it hadn't seen print. A juicy scandal down the drain.)

I met Fassbinder in the mid-seventies. At that time, New Yorker Films was in the Sofia Moving and Warehouse building on Sixty-First Street off Broadway. He was brought to our office by Klaus and Francine Brucher-Herpel, who were managing Filmverlag der Autoren, a film cooperative in Munich that handled the world sales and German domestic distribution of the New German Cinema: films not only by Fassbinder but also by Werner Herzog, Wim Wenders, Volker Schlöndorff, Reinhard Hauff, and Margarethe von Trotta. In Germany the Nazi period had produced a disruption in artistic continuity from the period of F. W. Murnau, Ernst Lubitsch, G. W. Pabst, and Fritz Lang until the arrival of these new directors. Fatherless for over forty years, these post–World War II German directors looked elsewhere for inspiration: John Ford, Billy Wilder, Alfred Hitchcock, Roberto Rossellini, and, in Fassbinder's case, Douglas Sirk, Jean-Luc Godard, and Claude Chabrol.

I had just signed a contract to distribute thirteen films by Fassbinder. I collected his films like rugs. Didn't give a hoot if the cost of distributing them would send my small company into bankruptcy. I'd been on the edge so many times before that I'd become immune to the fear of going under. Film distribution is not a normal, rational business. It is an ongoing craps game, played by lunatics like me who are possessed by a love of cinema.

Fassbinder strode into my office with Klaus and Francine, in the company of his friend Peter Chatel, one of the stars of *Fox and His Friends*. He had an aggressive look on his face, as if about to throw a punch at me. He was in black leather head to toe, jacket belt and buckles swinging. He didn't say hello. He grunted. He hated businesspeople, and distributors were in the businesspeople category. For Fassbinder, distributors and producers were crooks, beady-eyed fat guys chomping down on thick cigars, whose only purpose in life was to wheel in the bread on large trays so that he might continue to make films rapidly— two, three, four a year. (See the scene in *Beware of a Holy Whore* wherein the director of a stalled film is on the phone in a roadside booth, his face red with anger, clamoring to the producer to fork over more money so that the film can proceed.)

We walked a few blocks to the Ginger Man for lunch, Rainer's leather-armor crunching away. He came on as a tough hombre, no wimp, this big gay guy. Tall, well built, Tartar mustache and flinty eyes that didn't meet yours, he always seemed to be on the cusp of anger and insult. At the table he was silent, bored, bugged. The cheeseburger and Coke arrived. He took one big bite of his burger, stood up, and wordlessly walked out of the restaurant with Peter Chatel in tow. Francine and Klaus explained that this was often Rainer's way, pay no attention to it. I found his behavior, to say the least, very strange. Years later I learned that he spoke of his personality as manic-depressive. The size of his body of work—forty-four films in sixteen years—makes one realize that he functioned mainly in the manic way. His encounter with me was a distraction from his work, and it depressed him.

For several years I struggled to get his films opened in New York and around the country. Except for the annual outings at the New York Film Festival, continuously programmed by Richard Roud, whose support of Fassbinder made it easier for me to "discover" him, Fassbinder was virtually unknown in the United States. It was the enthusiasm of Andrew Sarris and Vincent Canby that helped put his films on the map here. The films they wrote about were the ones I had seen in New York and Munich and subsequently signed up. These were all "small" films, without wide commercial appeal.

Fassbinder's commercial breakthrough came with *The Marriage of Maria Braun*, his first big-budget film. The reviews were unanimously enthusiastic. I opened the film in my theater, the Cinema Studio, in 1979. Nobody can ever explain why a film catches on and becomes a hit; we leave these musings to Monday morning quarterbacks and ecumenical wise men. My way of divining a hit is that something ineffable and unexplainable exists within the film. The film ran for fifty-three weeks. Fassbinder had become an international star.

His films were hand grenades thrown at his native land, a country in the midst of growing prosperity but with a recent past so unspeakable as to overshadow any period of cruelty previously known. Here was the new Brecht, using similar themes and stylistic devices. In *The Merchant of Four Seasons*, a fruit peddler goes berserk, a victim of middle-class conformity. *Ali: Fear Eats the Soul* and *Katzelmacher* are portraits of German xenophobia. In *Fox and His Friends*, Fassbinder does the ritzy gay scene. A sharpie picks up Fox in a public toilet

("I like it front and back, Jack") and introduces him to a circle of rich gays, one of whom bilks him after his lottery ticket hits the jackpot. In *Mother Küsters Goes to Heaven*, he portrays the bankruptcy of left-wing politics and the thin line between political journalism and showbiz.

Fassbinder was a complex man with love-hate feelings toward his country. He spoke about emigrating to the United States. He kept an apartment in Paris and did some of his writing there. His films attacked both the conservative and liberal pieties that prevailed in Germany, with the underlying suggestion that fascism was around the bend.

We saw each other whenever he came to New York to defend his films at the New York Film Festival. Once he visited our apartment and became friendly with my mother-in-law, Bella. My wife, Toby, in her memoir, *A Book About My Mother*, writes: "Fassbinder stood up to say good night. He approached my mother, who was still seated, took her hand, kissed it, and told her how happy he was to meet her. . . . The next morning, he called my husband to say how touched he was to have been invited into the 'heart of your family.' Seldom did he come into people's homes, meet their children and mothers."

The last time I saw him was in New York in 1979. *The Marriage of Maria Braun* was the closing-night film at the New York Film Festival. I complained about the color of the print, which I had ordered from the negative in Germany. He muttered "gangster" under his breath. I couldn't tell whether he meant the producer or the laboratory. By then he had become more attentive to the quality of his films. His early films were made quickly (one- to three-week shoots) on very low budgets (in the low six figures and some much less). Now, at the height of his career, he was more relaxed, given to a good deal of high spirits and comfort with others. He thanked me for my work in getting his films shown here. There were no grunts now, only charming smiles. The lion was tame.

Since he worked quickly, enjoying the making more than the finished film itself, often going with only one take, his films do not have the polish and intricacy of a Resnais or an Antonioni film. He was not interested in making masterpieces. He was more interested in the next film than in discussing a past work. In this, he resembled Godard. His dream was to be in an ongoing utopia, working with people he liked, spinning works from the loom of his anarchic imagination. He once said: "I would like to build a house with my films. Some are the cellar, others the walls, still others the windows. But I hope in the end it will be a house."

WIM WENDERS

Wim Wenders is one of the most imaginative and prolific directors to have emerged in the German cinema of the 1970s. My first memory of him is associated with music. Toby and I were in Munich, having met with Werner Herzog, and now about to meet Wim. As we climbed the stairs to his loft, we heard American jazz emanating from above. Having seen *The Goalie's Anxiety at the Penalty Kick* and *Kings of the Road*, I was eager to meet him. This tall, rangy fellow—who could've been the hero in a western movie—greeted us halfway down the steps and ushered us into a bright space lined with shelves of music albums. Thus began our lively friendship.

The American Friend established Wenders, alongside Fassbinder and Herzog, in the first rank of the resurgent German cinema. New Yorker Films took it on for distribution and it opened at the Cinema Studio to excellent reviews. A film still of Bruno Ganz and Dennis Hopper appeared on the cover of our 1978 New Yorker Films catalogue. Based on Patricia Highsmith's thriller *Ripley's Game*, it's about a young Hamburg picture framer, happily married and with a young son—in other words, quite an ordinary man—who learns that he's suffering from a rare, ultimately fatal blood disease. Out of the blue, he's approached by an insistent Frenchman who promises to pay him handsomely, help him obtain special treatment, and assure his widow of security. All he has to do is assassinate a Mafia figure, through the manipulation of a mysterious American in Paris (Dennis Hopper). One thing leads to another in this predicament. American director Nicholas Ray, by then in failing health, is in the cast as well, as is Samuel Fuller. Soon after, Wenders and Ray co-directed *Lightning Over Water* (also known as *Nick's Film*), about the last days of Ray's life.

In 1988, we opened *Wings of Desire* at the Cinema Studio. In it, an angel (played by the great Bruno Ganz), growing frustrated at his inability to affect the people of Berlin over whom he watches, decides to leave the heavens and enter the world of earthly delights. And there he falls in love. Cinematographer Henri Alekan, whose credits include Jean Cocteau's *Beauty and the Beast*, William Wyler's *Roman Holiday*, and Abel Gance's *The Battle of Austerlitz*, blends rich black-and-white photography with bright bursts of color to contrast the dilapidated, glum Berlin of yesterday to a new and vital city.

In 1999, we opened *Buena Vista Social Club* at the Lincoln Plaza Cinemas. It had one of the longest runs of any documentary and returned a second time around. The film follows guitarist Ry Cooder and his son as they travel to Cuba and bring a group of the finest musicians from pre-revolution Cuba out of retirement to record an album. Among them are Ibrahim Ferrer and pianist Rubén González. Present-day shots of Havana enrich the film. Eventually the ensemble came to the United States and performed in front of a rapt audience, Toby and I among them. What a treat seeing them in person at the Beacon Theatre on the Upper West Side!

In 2014, we played *The Salt of the Earth*, a magnificent documentary by Wenders and Juliano Ribeiro Salgado, Sebastião Salgado's son. The film portrays the work of the great Brazilian photographer, who spent forty years and traveled over 120 countries, capturing images of men toiling in gold mines, oil fields, and the desert, as well as of war-devastated countries such as Rwanda. Salgado operated in black and white with images conveying the onslaught of modern society. Moreover, he and his wife, Leila, succeeded in planting two million trees in the Minas Gerais region of Brazil to preserve its forest. Wenders, a photographer himself, was the perfect director for this film.

One of the rewards Toby and I have in attending the Berlin Festival each year is an opportunity to see Wim. At one gathering, he introduced Toby's book *The New Yorker Theater and Other Scenes from a Life at the Movies*; at another, he paid tribute to Lia van Leer. This is a man forever cooking on all four burners!

WERNER HERZOG

On a flight to Berlin in 2014, I began reading *Werner Herzog: A Guide for the Perplexed: Conversations with Paul Cronin.* The book offers Herzog's observations on the art and craft of filmmaking as well as his descriptions of what occurred while making his films. His text on the making of *Fitzcarraldo* is mesmerizing: an account of the dangers and harrowing conditions of a visionary (played by no less than Klaus Kinski) intent on hauling a three-deck, 320-ton ship across rivers and up a small mountain to fulfill a dream of opening an opera house in a small city in the jungle, with Caruso singing. Any aspiring filmmaker would do well to read this book about obsessions and challenges.

I went to Munich to meet Herzog in the early 1970s. I wanted to take on whatever he made for my burgeoning distribution company, New Yorker Films. By the end of the decade, I'd made arrangements with him for at least six films. *Aguirre, the Wrath of God* gave him international notoriety, and it was one of our highest-grossing films when we opened it at the Cinema Studio. Who can forget that scene of the mad conquistador (again Klaus Kinski!), floating down the river on a raft, in quest of El Dorado, amid chattering monkeys?

Werner never went to film school. An autodidact, with enormous curiosity about strange places and strange folk, he has regularly shuttled between documentary and fiction. *The Great Ecstasy of the Sculptor Steiner* captures in beautiful slow motion the death-defying leaps of the world's greatest ski jumper. For *La Soufrière*, Herzog goes down to Guadalupe to film a volcano about to erupt—it never did. *How Much Wood Would a Woodchuck Chuck* is about a competition in Pennsylvania of mile-a-minute calls of livestock auctioneers. For me, one of his greatest films is *Land of Silence and Darkness*. The central character is Fini Straubinger, a remarkable fifty-six-year-old deaf-blind woman who travels all over Germany to act as a consultant and morale booster for her fellow inhabitants in the land of silence and darkness. It's a poetic documentary unlike any that has ever been made. I urge everyone to see this film. Herzog surely has a masterpiece or two more up his sleeve.

■ ■ ■

LETTER WITH OFFER FOR HERZOG'S *AGUIRRE, THE WRATH OF GOD*

December 24, 1975

Dear Werner:

The reason I have not written to you sooner is that I was waiting to screen *Aguirre, the Wrath of God*, which I was finally able to do. (I screened the 16mm. print which Goethe House had here for their showing—the English-dubbed version). Dubbing always turns me off and for the first ten minutes of the film I was a bit worried about the dubbing but once I got into the film, I did not mind it. In a word, the film is superb. You have every right to feel the way you do about this film. It has an utterly hypnotic quality to it, a tremendous sense of the primordial, of a subterranean dreamlife.

I would be very honored to distribute the film. Given the theatrical market in the States at this time, I do think it would be difficult. As to the university market, I have no doubts. I am sure it will work there over a period of time.

I am writing to you with a proposal, rather than Cine International, because I was a bit put off by the way they handled *Kaspar Hauser* here. (This is in confidence.) Also, believe it or not, Rugoff has still not seen *Aguirre*. He has been sitting with the 35mm. print for over six weeks. I have called him repeatedly and asked for the print after his screening and he keeps putting me off. I spoke with him this morning and I had to pretend that I did not see the film since I do not want to be put in the position where once he learns that I am interested in the film, he will want to take it on automatically just because I want it—even though he may not like it. You know that he does not like *Kaspar Hauser* and he was prevailed upon by Coppola, so can you imagine what he will think of *Aguirre*? I am writing this to you very openly and trust that you will keep all this confidential.

I should like to make a contract with you on *Aguirre*, using the same terms and conditions on all our other contracts, except that I would be willing to advance $2,000 as a guarantee on *Aguirre*. You understand that the real cost of distributing the film will be in prints and promotion. Would it be possible to get the German-language version with English subtitles? I think this would be better for our market.

In any case, do let me know what you think. Then, when I hear from you on this I will write to you about print preparation on all the other films we have together.

It really was both an honor and a pleasure to meet you. I do indeed admire your work. You are certainly among the most uncompromising filmmakers in the world today. And with such a special vision!

Warmly—
Daniel Talbot

PART 6

SHOAH

CLAUDE LANZMANN

I found *Shoah* through the *New York Times*. I'd heard mention of this documentary a year before from my friend Lia van Leer, director of the Jerusalem Cinematheque, when Claude Lanzmann was still working on it. I simply forgot about it, hoping it would eventually surface. On May 2, 1985, Richard Bernstein, the *Times* reporter in Paris, wrote a long, vivid article about the film and its maker.

As soon as Toby and I read this in the morning in bed, I turned to her and said, "We must fly to Paris immediately to see this film." She agreed. Although I'd never met Lanzmann, I knew about his relationship with Jean-Paul Sartre and especially with Simone de Beauvoir, with whom he had lived for seven years. I'd seen his first film, *Pourquoi Israel*, at the New York Film Festival and admired it but was unable to spring for it, in one of our periodic cash crunches at that time.

I called Lanzmann and asked if we might see the film right away and meet with him. Aware of our work, he was pleased to hear from us. I told him I'd call when we arrived in Paris the next day.

It was early morning when we got there. And hard to get a decent hotel in Paris on such short notice. We wound up at the Hôtel Solferino on the Rue de Lille, a small, modest place, which turned out to be pleasant, near the Seine and close to the Rue Jacob and Saint-Germain-des-Prés. We were tired and wanted to nap, but our room wasn't ready, so we left our bags in the lobby and went to a nearby café for a coffee. I called Lanzmann and he met us at the café within thirty minutes.

I recognized him from the photo in the *Times*. At age sixty he looked quite youthful, a rugged fellow, a cross between a boxer, movie star, and anxious intellectual, with an air of Willy Loman. He strode into the café with a plastic shopping bag full of *Shoah* reviews and began reading some of them; they were raves. He was eager for us to like the film and want it for distribution.

Lanzmann then drove us in his snappy red Rover to the Monte-Carlo theater on the Champs-Élysées. It was a typically gray Parisian day: chilly, overcast, and raw, yet nice to be there. Toby and I can never get over the physical beauty of the city.

At the theater showing *Shoah*, every patron was frisked at the door by detectives. A bomb had apparently been set off several weeks earlier at an Israeli film festival, and people were scared about more violence wherever the film played. The Monte-Carlo was one of the three theaters showing it in Paris. Inside, two plainclothes were monitoring the crowd, walkie-talkies pinned to their ears.

The film began, and in no time at all we fell into its skin. We saw and heard conversations with Mordechai Podchlebnik, one of two survivors out of four hundred thousand murdered at Chelmno, and others with Abraham Bomba and Filip Müller, who were forced to become *Sonderkommandos* at Auschwitz, escorting fellow Jews into the gas chambers. Franz Suchomel, the deputy commander of Treblinka, declared, "No, Herr Lanzmann, you are mistaken, we only processed twelve thousand a day, not fifteen." Polish peasants admonish Simon Srebnik, the other survivor of Chelmno: "You are paying for having sinned against Christ." Itzhak Zuckerman, who survived the destruction of the Warsaw ghetto, subsequently became an alcoholic and died of a damaged heart. Jan Karski, the aristocratic Pole, is brought to tears as he recounts his visit to the Warsaw ghetto as fires were destroying it. Listening to heroic Karski, on his futile mission, brought us to tears.

We were overwhelmed by what we'd seen of that first part of *Shoah*. Finding it difficult to discuss it with Lanzmann, we arranged to meet him later in the evening.

For a few hours Toby and I wandered Paris, agitated by what we'd seen. We walked to the Luxembourg Gardens, one of our favorite local haunts, and discussed the film. I recall how astonished we were at our staggering ignorance about the Holocaust. Over the years, we'd seen the same stock footage on television and theater screens: smokestacks at Birkenau emitting fumes, piles of corpses, starved prisoners in striped clothing, yellow stars. But now we realized how little we knew.

The next day, after we'd seen the entire film, Lanzmann told how it came about. After having seen *Pourquoi Israel*, some Israel friends suggested that he make a film on the Holocaust. At that time in 1972, Lanzmann was fed up with the anti-Israeli position of his friends on the Left. With that in mind, he was persuaded the time was ripe for a big Holocaust film. To start with, a meeting was arranged between him and Prime Minister Menachem Begin. He spent a half hour with Begin, who gave him the go-ahead. Thus, financing for the film was initiated with the State of Israel.

It took Lanzmann twelve years to make it. He recounted the stops and starts after having depleted the amount received from Israel; his round-the-globe travels tracking down and interviewing Holocaust survivors; the hundreds of hours of footage left on the cutting room floor, incredible material that didn't honorably fit into the narrative; the dangers he encountered (beaten to a pulp outside of Munich by a gang of neo-Nazi toughs, requiring a month in the hospital); and attempts to find completion money in America. At a private screening at the home of a well-known billionaire, who was well aware that it was intended as a one-on-one fundraiser, the host tuned out after twenty minutes and slept through four hours of film—and of course didn't give a dime.

■ ■ ■

One day in November 1985, a rabbi and his wife came to my theater, the Cinema Studio, to see Part I of Lanzmann's monumental *Shoah*. They had driven fifty-five miles from Livingston, New Jersey, to see it. I seriously doubt that the rabbi and his wife had ever seen a film before. The audience was not our typical cinema buffs. Many were here to see a film that was part of their lifetime, they themselves Holocaust survivors.

When the film ended, the rabbi lingered in the lower lobby, just outside the auditorium. Ushers were guiding people out of the theater. Once everybody was out, the ushers went in to clean the hall, in preparation for the next show. The usher politely asked the rabbi to leave.

When I saw the rabbi still there, I understood what was happening and told the usher to let him be.

The rabbi went back into the auditorium and facing a wall, his body rocking back and forth, he prayed. He was blessing the theater. Shortly thereafter, he and his wife left and went back to New Jersey. So moved was I by what I'd seen that I decided to track down the rabbi and offer tickets for Part II, which was playing in the adjoining hall.

By the time I located him, he'd already seen the second half. He understood that I was deprived of doing a mitzvah, so he spoke about his modest synagogue needing funds to stock their library with books. I sent him a check for $500 and received a written note from him about my "good Jewish soul."

I devoted one full year to the distribution of *Shoah*. I did all the launching, selling, and publicity by myself, wearing several hats that had been on a rack for a few years. The cost of distributing this film was staggering. Each subtitled print cost $15,000. We had six prints. When embarking on this project, little did I think about its commercial possibilities. I was prepared to personally guarantee all losses—I did not want to mix money and Holocaust work. For me, it was a moral undertaking.

To my surprise, this nine-and-a-half-hour film was a huge commercial success. Lanzmann was well taken care of by this success, much of his earnings going toward the reduction of his debts in making the film, the balance to live on so that he would not, as he put it, "die in misery." New Yorker Films profits from the film did not go into fur coats or champagne parties at Le Bernardin but were plowed back into a slate of new films. The whole lot went down the tube, so that one year after the release of *Shoah* I was back to square one. For me, the greatest reward was the national PBS airing of the film. More than ten million people saw it.

Presenting *Shoah*, as both exhibitor and distributor, was the most satisfying event of my work in film. It was also a profound emotional experience. While knowing the general outline of the Holocaust, I knew little or nothing about the specifics. The film put me on a track that I never left. I began reading extensively about this historical nightmare.

I'm still reading. It has become an obsession. I was seriously thinking of abandoning distribution about six months after opening *Shoah*, thinking there was no point in continuing, for everything after this film would be anticlimactic, trivial, depressingly boring. But the healthy, oceanic side of my spirit advised me to continue.

A MEMORY PROJECT

Our daughter Nina sought to memorialize her grandmother's birthplace, a village in Galicia, now part of Ukraine, from which she had emigrated at the age of seventeen. The rest of Bella's family perished. Jews were rounded up in June 1939, herded to the forest, and forced by the *Einsatzgruppen* to dig their own graves before being shot. Nina painted a series on Dynów, with portraits of Bella, her grandmother, other family members, and some present-day villagers. The main synagogue in that village had been burned down, but in the 2010s a study center was erected in its place, and Nina subsequently was commissioned to paint three wall-size murals depicting scenes from the Old Testament. She also helped to create a walled-in cemetery for the bodies of those slaughtered, with a plaque listing their names.

A small group of survivors from Dynów, now living in the United States, have published *Zakhor*, a memory book, with the following introduction: "This is a *conscious*, determined debt from our *conscience* to save that community from the claws of time. It tells of the life and existence of our congregation, there for more than twenty generations until its destruction in our own generation."

Of the two thousand settlements of Jews that once existed in Poland, only four hundred have succeeded in publishing a memory book. Nina's devotion to her grandmother, her viewing of *Shoah*, and hearing our conversations at home have served to help new generations remember lives that were lost.

PART 7

MORE DIRECTORS

AGNÈS VARDA

One afternoon director Agnès Varda phoned, having just landed in Manhattan, and invited herself to lunch at our apartment the next day. How to resist lunch with a good friend, the reputed godmother of the French New Wave?

"Agnès, c'est une vraie artiste," Bernardo Bertolucci had said in 1965, seated on our living room sofa. Yes, she was a true artist, her spontaneity beguiling in a town where social gatherings are planned well in advance.

"Quelque chose de léger," she instructed Toby. "Something light," in Manhattan-speak suggests a yogurt, simple salad, or sandwich on the run. Toby, opting for something a bit more substantial, added a few grilled shrimp to *une salade composée.*

Agnès arrived promptly at one p.m., dressed in one of those flowery tunics she'd unearthed in a flea market. We hugged, drifted to the living room window to admire the Hudson River and Soldiers' and Sailors' Monument, then headed to the kitchen. Scanning the windowsill of potted herbs and a column embedded with blue and golden Persian tiles, Agnès happily recalled it all from her previous visit.

Then out came the salad, a cluster of rosy shrimp perched on top like little banners. With typical gusto and concentration, Agnès dug in. No sooner was it gone, she gazed at Toby with the imploring expression of a baby having downed its bottle one-two-three, now asking for more.

Provident Toby headed for the fridge and returned with a Manchego, a Gruyère, and a Humboldt Fog. Immediately addressing herself to these,

Agnès complimented the Humboldt Fog from California, tasted for the first time.

But then again came that "What's next?" gaze.

Luckily, some brownies, gingerbread, and rugelach—from the Lincoln Plaza Cinemas—were at hand. At last, a sigh of satisfaction from Our Lady of Abundance, who always wanted More.

"Life is short," she said. "We must shoot the ephemeral."

■ ■ ■

Agnès's first feature, *La Pointe Courte*, from 1955, was often considered a forerunner of the French New Wave. It is beautifully shot in a Mediterranean village and follows the struggling lives of the fishermen, and of a youth returning with his Parisian wife in an attempt to save their marriage. It was shot on location with professional and nonprofessional actors. Alain Resnais worked as editor on the film.

Cléo from 5 to 7 (1962), her second feature, brought critical acclaim and was a success when we played it at the New Yorker Theater. It covers two hours in the life of a nightclub singer, awaiting the medical verdict on whether she has life-threatening cancer. She goes shopping with old friends, pops in on a short film, and wanders around in a park. The film is a vivid picture of Paris in the 1960s.

Les Créatures (1966) takes place on an island in Brittany. A writer (Michel Piccoli) is working on his novel; his beautiful young wife (Catherine Deneuve) is pregnant, and mute as the result of a car accident. The production of the novel parallels the birth of the baby. Beautifully shot, the film juggles illusion and reality, and the writer's story becomes the film's own plot. Though a critical and box office disaster, it was later regarded as one of Varda's most inventive and complex films.

Through the years, we played virtually all of her films. *Vagabond* (1985) was one of the most successful. It's about a fierce homeless young woman (Sandrine Bonnaire), a wanderer, flouting society's norms, and on the path to death. A road story; along the way she encounters "real" people, moved by their interactions with her. Quasi-fiction, quasi-documentary, Bonnaire the only professional actor.

Agnès moved between fiction and nonfiction films. Toby has screened all of the main documentaries in her class at the New School. *Daguerréotypes* (1975) visits the residents and merchants on the Rue Daguerre in Paris, the street where Agnès lives. We see the giggly wife of the local baker; the local barber and his wife, a beautician. We see two women, exchanging a bit of gossip on the sidewalk about a local marriage going noisily on the rocks. We see a housewife at the butcher shop, telling the butcher about her ailing husband: "They took an electrocardiogram," she tells him as he's removing fat from a beefsteak. "It's just the weather," he replies. A perfume maker rummages for a flask on his shelf, while his frail wife gazes out vacantly at the camera. Off camera, Varda, in one of her occasional comments on the soundtrack, says that she's fascinated by "the mysteries of daily trade."

"Who are they?" she asks. "Where do they come from? What do they dream about at night? Do we remember the faces of strangers who stood in line with us the last time we bought medicine? Unlikely, and they probably don't remember us. They vanish into obscurity." But somehow, as a viewer, it's hard to forget the bewildered and haunted gaze of the perfumer's wife.

The Gleaners and I (2000) calls to mind Millet's famous painting of three peasant women gathering stray stalks of wheat after the harvest, as well as Van Gogh's painting of potato gleaners. In this film, Agnès tells us that there are forty-six varieties of the humble potato: she identifies with the misshapen one, and with the gleaner rummaging in the ground. The film is about people in France who survive by gathering food forgotten or discarded. On excess and wastefulness. On scavenging and salvaging. "You pick ideas, you pick images, you pick emotions from other people, and then you make it into a film," says Agnès. And, at one point, she turns the camera on herself—gleaner of images— and holds her hand in front of the camera: a fan of bones laced with brown spots and blue veins.

In 1991, at the Cannes Film Festival, Agnès presented *Jacquot de Nantes*, about Jacques Demy, with whom she lived for thirty-three years and who's noted for *Lola* and the beautiful *Umbrellas of Cherbourg*. Agnès's film is a retelling of his life, shot exactly where he spent his childhood: in his father's garage, as well as in places where his later film sequences were shot. Jacques had recounted his memories to Agnès but refused to write the screenplay or dialogue; he wanted it to be *her* film. His health was failing, but he managed to visit the set locations and appear in a few scenes, and to see most of the rushes before he died.

In the film, three actors re-create Demy's life, starting in 1939, when at age eight he fiddles around with a hand-wound camera found in a junk shop. It ends with him on the beach, gazing out at the sea, with close-ups of the grains of sand running through his fingers. It isn't a sad film. It's about a boy lucky to discover how he wanted to spend his life, who managed to spend it that way. Both Agnès and the film got a standing ovation at that 1991 Cannes Film Festival.

JACQUES TATI

*M*onsieur Hulot's Holiday and Mon Oncle were on the Thalia's calendar every year. In my twenties, year in and year out, I made a point to see them. Life was smaller without these films. Years later, when *Jour de fête*, Tati's first film, was playing, I ran to see it. And when *Playtime* showed up, again I rushed to the theater like a thirsty man.

Tati must have learned from Chaplin the technique of using props to get a laugh. His trademarks: short trousers six inches above shoe top, a tight-fitting suit jacket ready to burst at the seams, a thin-brimmed fisherman's hat that made him look dumb, an umbrella unfurled like a sword and brandished when he was going through doors, that long-stepped gait trying to follow directions. All guaranteed to produce apoplexy in audiences. His sputtering cockroach car in *Monsieur Hulot's Holiday*, designed for a very short person and not for his 6-foot-3-inch frame, was one of the memorable automobiles of film history. A vacation in Tati's film was like a course in guerrilla warfare. Seaside resorts underwent mayhem.

Tati belongs to that small band of genius filmmakers who push all the right buttons in your soul. He makes you laugh at life. He made only five feature films; produced, directed, and starred in them all. Working slowly and painstakingly, always running short of cash; financing his films was always a problem. Unwilling to cede control, at one point he distributed them himself in Paris.

I met Tati in 1975. My lawyer, Bob Montgomery, got word that Tati's films, embalmed in bankruptcy for ten years, were being resurrected and might be available for distribution. A Swiss banker had paid off Tati's huge debts to banks and laboratories and now owned the negatives in part. But Tati retained the right to retrieve all his negatives once the banker's investment plus a handsome profit were paid back in full.

Toby and I flew to Paris to meet him. We had lunch with him and his wife in a pleasant restaurant near his office. He spoke English. His wife sat at the table quietly and patiently as we listened to his extended tales about himself, his films, his merchandising skills, what he would do when the films opened in New York.

Among other things, he offered to send hundreds of balloons into the air in front of the theater—anything to get people in. If need be, he'd stand naked in Times Square. Tati made masterpieces, and he wanted everybody on earth to see them. He didn't give a hoot about money for his lifestyle. He simply wanted it in order to make more films and preserve his work forever. Obsessed by those films, he may not have even known who Hitler was—too busy honing his shtick.

His wife: that poor suffering woman, hearing the same stories over and over again. It wouldn't have surprised me at the restaurant if, by chance asking his wife to corroborate some event in his life, he might not have remembered her name. He could always call her Tati. There's healthy narcissism and sick narcissism—Tati's had no category.

Only once did I encounter narcissism that approached his level, and that was in another film genius, Robert Bresson, whom I met when he was in his late seventies. He and his wife had no kids—thank God. Madame Bresson was another suffering patroness saint. I was told by my friend Louis Marcorelles that when Bresson's first wife died, someone present at that moment reported that Bresson, out on a shoot, did not cry or wince. Like a poker-faced character in one of his films, he said, "Oh, goodness! Who is going to take care of my accounts now?"

Madame Tati at the lunch table showed no displeasure or even annoyance at her husband's spidery monologue—only a vague smile, no change of expression. She made Joan of Arc look like a *jongleur*. Her face said, "Oui, there's my Jacques, my clever little boy, my genius companion."

The question is always whether great art is worth the suffering inflicted on a great artist's companion. Many times I've consulted with sages and until this day not heard any wisdom on this subject. The closest I came to an understanding was George Bernard Shaw's remark: "Men who have kids can't have ideas."

Tati organized five days of screenings for Toby and me at a theater near his Parisian office. They took place in the morning before regular screenings began. We sat alone in a large theater, watching in ecstasy the film that Tati showed each day. He would signal to the projectionist to begin. As the credits rolled on the screen and his name appeared, he clapped loudly, then left the theater, showing up again at the end of the film. Then, again, he clapped.

It was this way five mornings in a row. He didn't solicit our reactions. Not interested. Showing them was good enough: the first step in his ploy to get his hands into Uncle Sam's pocket.

I initiated conversations on U.S. distribution, quickly realizing that no matter what I proposed, there'd be no immediate deal making—that boring, ugly institution. With a man like Tati, it could only be a drawn-out process. No handshakes. No memos. The problem was how to stuff his pockets with lucre while simultaneously maintaining control.

When he came to New York, he described one of his merchandising techniques. On opening a new film in Paris, he'd hire twenty people to buy tickets and stand in line. After entering the theater, they would exit and then again buy tickets, and again stand in line, to display an ever-present line. Passersby, seeing it, would say to themselves, "Oh, there must be something good inside, let's buy tickets." Then, as the run continued, word of mouth would set in. As I mentioned previously, Daniel Toscan du Plantier said that the takeoff point of a film, as tongues wagged around town, was eight thousand spectators. Others calculated this tipping point number at ten thousand. Still others, twelve thousand.

We never struck up a deal.

GLAUBER ROCHA

W e met Glauber Rocha in 1962 at a SoHo loft. Short, thin, olive skin, jet-black hair, delicate face and hands; the Brazilian moviemaker had a deep resonant voice. Aside from his native Portuguese, he spoke French, English, Spanish, and Italian.

The occasion was a *feijoada*, named after Brazil's national dish, concocted with manioc, beans, and assorted unidentifiable parts of a hog and accompanied by chunks of peasant bread, whiskey, and pot. Across the loft space, a Black musician in African attire was playing the berimbau, a one-stringed musical bow derived from the hunting bow millennia ago.

So impressed was Toby with its sound, she straightaway went over and spoke to Nana, the player, and asked if they might make a documentary together. He agreed. The film was shot one morning on the balcony of the New Yorker and finished within months.

I set up a screening of Glauber's *Barravento* (*The Turning Wind*). Shot in gritty black and white and set in a village on the northeast coast of Bahia, the film is about exploited Black fishermen who worship gods and goddesses of the sea. For them, the modern world hardly exists. Peace gets shattered by the arrival of a young man who'd left for the city and returns now in a white suit with a suitcase of trinkets, hoping to sway the village from its primitive past into a viable present.

The film is distinctly ethnographic. We see an ever-circling chorus of village women; we see two men on the beach performing capoeira, a shadow dance of sorts. Low-angle shots under swirling skies with raging seas emphasize man's struggle against the forces of nature. This was Glauber's first film, clearly influenced by Rossellini's neorealism and operatic director Luchino Visconti (*La Terra Trema*).

Glauber was a spokesman for the Cinema Novo movement. The goal was to make authentic cinema quickly and cheaply, in a popular idiom, for a society with mass illiteracy. It was a total rejection of dubbed Hollywood movies and kitschy *chacadas* (musicals and soaps).

How to stir self-awareness against colonial exploitation and religious superstition? The rallying cry was "I want to hear the voice of man!" We opened *Barravento* at the New Yorker that year. It was the beginning of our long friendship with Glauber and vibrant Latin American films. Subsequently, we bought prints of *Black God, White Devil* and *Terra em Transe* (*Land in Anguish/ Earth Entranced*) and played them in our theaters. Operatic and apocalyptic, they reflected "the aesthetics of hunger and violence." I found them lyrical and haunting, yet uneven. Glauber wanted me to distribute them, but I hemmed and hawed, for there were complications. Several Brazilian producers claimed ownership of the films, including Luiz Carlos Barreto (producer subsequently of his son Bruno Barreto's *Dona Flor and Her Two Husbands*).

Glauber, an offspring of the sixties, was drawn to the French New Wave and the didactic films of Godard. Brazil was a mestizo and Black society, with whites firmly in control in the highest halls of government, and despite a growing middle class, the master-slave syndrome—delineated so clearly by Gilberto Freyre in *The Masters and the Slaves*—still prevailed.

New Yorker Films went on to distribute many Cinema Novo films. Nelson Pereira dos Santos's *Vidas Secas* (*Barren Lives*) was one of the earliest and strongest. It earned the Palme d'Or in Cannes in 1964. Based on a modernist novel by Graciliano Ramos, it traces the migration of an impoverished family—mother, father, son, daughter, and dog—from the drought-ridden *sertão* in the northeast all the way south to São Paolo in quest of work. Their hunger is desperate amid this bleached, dry landscape, and the story is told from the viewpoint of each character. Nelson continued making films, which we distributed into the nineties. Among them were *How Tasty Was My Little Frenchman, Hunger for Love, The Amulet of Ogum*, and *Tent of Miracles*.

Carlos Diegues's *Ganga Zumba*, Ruy Guerra's *Os Fuzis* (*The Guns*), Walter Lima Jr.'s *Plantation Boy*, Joaquim Pedro de Andrade's *The Priest and the Girl*, as well as other films exposed the political and social state in Latin America.

The Hour of the Furnaces, directed by Fernando Solanas and Octavio Getino, detailed the economic colonization of Argentina by the British, the ten-year reign of Perón, and the role of violence in the national liberation process. Premiered at the New Yorker, and in the zeitgeist of the sixties, these films drew enthusiastic audiences.

■ ■ ■

When Glauber and I first met, a military junta ruled Brazil, and it was imperative that he leave the country—kicked out or in self-exile. He was an articulate spokesman for change against decades of dictatorships, and widely known there not only as a filmmaker but also as a political figure, a defender of oppressed Indians, Blacks, and favela dwellers.

At one point he moved to Paris, where Toby and I would see him. Though he had made a few more films, his career was going nowhere. He missed Brazil but was unable to return, and was smoking pot day and night.

We subsequently learned that Glauber was living in Los Angeles, working on the script of a new movie and hoping to find a Hollywood producer (good luck!). About a year later, I was in San Francisco visiting my two good friends, Mel Novikoff, America's prime exhibitor of quality films, and Tom Luddy, programmer of the Pacific Film Archive. On my third day, Glauber called Tom. He was freaking out, sounded stoned, certain he had cancer. Thinking of returning to Brazil, he wanted help. Tom asked if I'd go to Los Angeles to see what was going on.

I spent the next two days with Glauber. He was happy to see me. Convinced that he had cancer, he wanted me to take him to a hospital so they could check out his liver. When I brought him there, he began raving, claiming there was a conspiracy against him. Who, what, where was never defined. The doctor examined him, found him physically fit, but Glauber didn't believe this and claimed that the doctor was killing him. Realizing it was time for him to return to Brazil, I bought a ticket and put him on a plane. Two months later I received word that he had denounced me in Rio de Janeiro as a CIA agent!

As time went by, Glauber stopped making films. He wrote a book on cinema and politics in which he paid me a few compliments. I began receiving affectionate letters from him. Brazil had rid itself of the junta and become a democracy with an elected president. As a journalist, Glauber wrote numerous articles on the political situation in Brazil and Latin America. He was thinking of running for president. Had he won, he would have been the first filmmaker to become president of a country. I tried to imagine Brazil as a film directed by Glauber Rocha—Antonio das Mortes in the *sertão*, fighting for justice, economic and political equality.

But tragedy struck. First, his sister, married to the filmmaker Walter Lima Jr., fell down an elevator shaft in a high-rise building and died. We never got the story behind this—whether she was pushed or stoned. A few years later, Glauber was hospitalized, this time indeed with cancer of the liver. He died shortly thereafter. I couldn't help thinking that his cancer paranoia in Los Angeles ten years earlier had been a premonition.

Glauber was indeed a prophet who brought the problems of Latin America to a wide audience and touched the lives of many Brazilians.

JEAN EUSTACHE

I met Jean Eustache in 1973, shortly after his film *The Mother and the Whore* won the Palme d'Or at Cannes. I was staying at a small, unpretentious hotel in the Sixth Arrondissement, and asked if he'd come over to discuss U.S. distribution of his film.

On arriving, he cased me as if to determine whether I was a real American, since real Americans could walk Paris streets with hefty bundles of cash. He had sandy hair that reached to his shoulders, lips permanently pursed, a cleft chin. If François Villon lived in our time, he would look like Jean Eustache.

I offered $35,000 to distribute his film and he accepted. There were numerous producers of *The Mother and the Whore*—Louis Malle, Éric Rohmer, Jean-Luc Godard, and Alain Vannier. But Eustache was the majority producer and could make the deal on his own. He was delighted. His work was unknown in the States.

While in Paris, I'd screened an earlier work of his, two fifty-minute films under the rubric of *Les Mauvaises Fréquentations*, which we eventually released as *Bad Company*. One of the pieces was *Robinson's Place*, about two teenagers who live in a *banlieue* and come to town to pick up girls. Raffish, with an off-the-cuff look and an aura of poetic realism, it was one of the early delights of the French New Wave.

Years later, I saw another early work of Eustache's: *The Virgin of Pessac*, about an annual festival in a dreary backwater town called Pessac (Eustache's hometown) in which the most virtuous (i.e., virginal) girl is chosen, as in a beauty contest. The winner gets rewarded with a crown of flowers, placed on her head by the mayor, who then proceeds to kiss her primly on the cheek. It was one of the best satires of small-town folkways I'd yet seen. Gentle, authentic, funny.

In order to buy *The Mother and the Whore,* I had to sell the carriage house in back of our main house in Water Mill. Since I didn't have the money to renovate this charming barn and now needed the cash for Jean's film, I sold it for $29,000. (Twenty years later, the barn fetched $750,000. I was probably the only chump in the Hamptons to lose money on a piece of real estate!)

To make matters worse, I lost a lot of money in the distribution of *The Mother and the Whore.* When the time came to launch it, I brought Eustache to the States to do publicity in New York, Washington, DC, and Boston. I quickly learned that he didn't give good interviews. A depressive, often sullen and sarcastic, lacking the gift of gab, he came across as a dolt, a cranky farm boy.

I flew down to Washington with him—in those days I never used publicity agents, couldn't afford them, did it myself. On the plane he carried an ancient, cracked brown leather satchel with two bottles of Jack Daniel's. During the entire trip, he sipped from them like a *clochard.*

When we arrived for the press interviews that I'd organized from New York, Eustache was smashed, and I got pissed at him. We were supposed to stay overnight for additional interviews, which I canceled, and we returned to New York after only one. He wasn't even contrite. As we headed for his hotel in a taxi, he asked me to get him some girls. I told him that that wasn't in my line of work. Dropped him off on Third Avenue in the heart of singles bar land and told him to hustle his own piece of tail. He smiled at me like a dunce.

Several years later, Eustache took his own life with a gunshot at the age of forty-two.

PART 8

CRITERIA

A young Dan Talbot with his parents

Dan and Toby Talbot on their honeymoon

A diverse collection of outstanding writing
on the film

Cover of Dan Talbot's *Film: An Anthology*
University of California Press, sixth paperback
printing, 1972; reproduced with permission

frankly,
we hope to
make money...

we've been imbued with the love of
it, and we revel in the image of shekels
pouring in at the box-office when
we light up our new marquee with the brand
new name ... THE NEW YORKER ...

Frankly,
we hope to be pointed out as a mecca
for the most discriminating moviegoer,
since we will be showing only the finest
films whose reputations have grown even
greater with the passing of time. Many will
be motion pictures not shown for many
years—the great masterpieces of cinema art.

And frankly,
we're a little snobbish about the fact
that they will be ours exclusively
in all New York.

the NEW YORKER

88th Street & Broadway

WATCH THURSDAY'S NEWSPAPER
FOR THE OPENING ANNOUNCEMENT

Teaser ad for New Yorker Theater opening

The New Yorker Theater marquee, May 1960; a large blowup of this image hung in Dan's New
Yorker Films office

Dan Talbot and Alfred Hitchcock in front of the New Yorker
marquee, January 13, 1965

Benny of Benny's Luncheonette, located on the same
Upper West Side block as the New Yorker Theater

Joe and Bella Tolpen, Toby's parents

the **film:**
summer
1960

*a retrospective exhibition
in 10 monday evening screenings
by the new yorker film society
at the air-conditioned
New Yorker Theatre,
broadway at 88th Street, n. y. city.*

EXCLUSIVE N. Y. SHOWING

JUNE 27—TRIUMPH OF THE WILL
(Reifenstahl, 1937)

Produced under Hitler's personal supervision, *Triumph* is the ideological film defined. Using the premise of a rally staged by Goebbels in 1934 Nuremberg where thousands of Nazi Germany's most militant were gathered, Leni Reifenstahl, working with a staff of over 120 technicians and thirty cameras, succeeded in documenting the carefully "staged" display of "national ecstasy" from every possible angle. The result is a film of fantastic pulsating emotional intensity . . . a Wagnerian world of martial grandeur with Hitler in the rôle of its iron-crossed Messiah. That Reifenstahl created all of this out of nothing is a tribute to her brilliant talent and technical mastery . . . truly a virtuoso performance to be repeated later in her *OLYMPIAD* where the reality was not forced solely for effect.

DACHAU . . . the film as witness to the truth, as members of the liberating French Army enter and photograph the nightmare world of the concentration camp. **Screenings: 7 and 9:30 P.M.**

EXCLUSIVE N. Y. SHOWING

JULY 11—THE MAN WHO KNEW TOO MUCH
(Hitchcock, 1935)

The original version of the B.C. — (Before Compromise) — Alfred Hitchcock thriller. A period piece to be sure, but *what* a period . . . the ending sequence, in particular, is a masterful ploy of tension and suspense in the former Britisher's greatest manner. Starring Peter Lorre, Leslie Banks and Pierre Fresnay.

WE ARE THE LAMBETH BOYS . . . The American premiere of Karel Reisz's (1958) filmic record of a week in the lives of a group of youths in one of London's worst slum areas, this unflinching documentary started a literal riot among critics at the Tours Film Festival—it was awarded first prize—and succeeded in further outraging conservative circles throughout Europe.

Screenings: 7 and 9:30 P.M.

JULY 18—THE PASSION OF JOAN OF ARC
(C. Th. Dreyer, 1929)

An immortal film . . . a cinematic tapestry of brilliant photography and superb technical accomplishment, *The Passion of Joan* is also one of the art form's greatest enigmas. The performance of Mme. Falconetti—an unknown discovered by Dreyer working in a cafe—in the title role is one of the screen's legends.

IMAGES MEDIEVALES . . . life in the Middle Ages as represented in miniature portfolios by 14th and 15th century artists found by William Novik at the Bibliothèque Nationale in Paris.

THE ROSE AND THE MIGNONNETTE . . . a quiet, truly beautiful testament to the universal dignity of Man. The text is a poem by Louis Aragon, translated by Stephen Spender and said by Emlyn Williams. Plus another film to be announced.

Screenings: 7 and 9:30 P.M.

EXCLUSIVE N. Y. SHOWING

JULY 25—FREAKS
(Browning, 1933)

One of the most unusual films in the history of the cinema, this heretofore long lost final work by Tod Browning is a classic of the bizarre and the macabre. Using a cast of authentic grotesques, the director sets his tale of a grisly murder plot by these creatures against a circus background . . . then drives his theme almost beyond the limits of the mind to rationalize and absorb horror. The resulting film is a chilling venture into terror and suspense.

DEMENTIA . . . John Parker's subjective journey to the middle of a schizophrenic's night, wherein a young woman's duplex psyche is probed and explored. With original music by the late George Antheil.

Screenings: 7 and 9:30 P.M.

AUGUST 1—OTHELLO
(Welles, 1955)

Six long years in production—(its director-star plagued almost from the first day's shooting by technical and budget problems)—Orson Welles's adaptation of Shakespeare's passionate tragedy opened to wide critical acclaim . . . and promptly died. No matter, we think the film brilliant and Welles at his finest.

DESORDRE . . . Jacques Baratier's artful impressionistic rendering of Left Bank Paris and the curious collection of those who dwell and visit therein. With the ubiquitous Welles, Cocteau, Juliette Greco and miscellaneous survivors of Sartrian Existentialism.

Screenings: 7 and 9:30 P.M.

AUGUST 8—GREED
(von Stroheim, 1925)

A classic in spite of itself, *Greed*, for all of Eric von Stroheim's "I-am-a-director-in-the-grand-tradition" passion for excess, is an American film of the upmost importance. A production truly years ahead of its time in its uncompromising surgical exposure of the power gold holds over men, *Greed*, as Paul Rotha in his *The Film Till Now* points out, ". . . is sheer, undiluted truth; the essence of reality expressed in the powerful terms of the cinema." To be presented with piano accompaniment by Arthur Kleiner.

Screenings: 6:45 and 9:30 P.M.

AUGUST 15—THE CABINET OF DR. CALIGARI
(Wiene, 1919)

The *alpha* of the psychological cinema, *Caligari* still retains the power to mystify, electrify and terrify its audiences. The film's decor, with its wild expressionistic flats, was designed to symbolize the interior of a madman's mind with the film itself to be his story. *Caligari*, for the first time in film history, forced its viewers into a reality beyond the limits of the seeming universal and thereby opened a new area for serious artistic experimentation. *To be presented in the original 1919 version.*

THE FALL OF THE HOUSE OF USHER . . . Made nine years after *Caligari*, Jean Epstein's famed impressionistic retelling of Poe's classic is an extraordinary accomplishment. Using the same effects invertedly in sets, lighting and photography as Wiene employed for his film, Epstein succeeded in creating his own brand of almost total subjective horror. **Screenings: 6:45 and 9:30 P.M.**

EXCLUSIVE N. Y. SHOWING

AUGUST 22—THE LAST WILL OF DR. MABUSE
(Lang, 1933)

At last in New York . . . the famed sound version of Fritz Lang's thriller of murder, hypnotism and psychoanalysis wherein a master-criminal seeks to plunge the world "into an abyss of terror," and whose successor almost succeeds in the attempt. Completed in France by an exiled Lang with a print smuggled to him from Germany—where Goebbels banned the film before final editing, *Mabuse* is a remarkable study of a man and nation in moral decline.

VIPERS . . . the American début of a brilliant first film. At times startling, amusing . . . yet always avoiding the standard pitfalls of the experimental, *Vipers* is a worthy introduction to the personal world of the hashish smoker and his surrealistic inner wanderings.

MOTHER'S DAY . . . James Broughton's wry dismissal of the universal symbol as scales are reduced and balances shattered.

Screenings: 7 and 9:30 P.M.

EXCLUSIVE N. Y. SHOWING

AUGUST 29—THE UNKNOWN SOLDIER
(Laine, 1956)

Set against the background of the Russo-Finnish campaign of World War II, Edvin Laine's violent protest against the chaos and annihilation of war has been a film ignored. Though at times almost revolting in its absolute faithfulness to the actual wherein the futility of self-destruction in the cause of national ideals is clearly expressed, *The Unknown Soldier* is a work of great passion, power and inner beauty . . . one of the finest "fugitive films" ever made.

Screenings: 6:45 and 9:20 P.M.

SEPTEMBER 12 AND 19—INTOLERANCE
(D. W. Griffith, 1916)

America's Greatest Film . . .

In order to present INTOLERANCE in its original full length—3¼ hours—there will be two successive single Monday evening screenings with each showing starting promptly at 8:00 P.M. Piano accompaniment will be by Arthur Kleiner.

For complete membership information see reverse side . . .

1960 Summer Series programming at the New Yorker Theater

Treasury of Ten Film Classics flyer

Dan Talbot and Alfred Hitchcock in the New Yorker Theater lobby during a promotional tour in 1965, looking at wall of director portraits

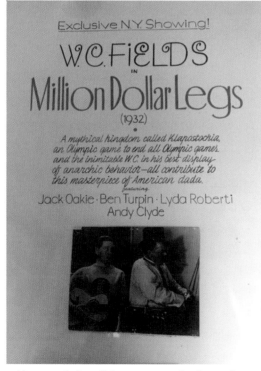

Lobby poster (22" x 28") for a screening of *Million Dollar Legs* (Edward F. Cline, 1932) at the New Yorker Theater

Jules Feiffer mural, created for the New Yorker Theater lobby

A sample of entries found in the New Yorker Theater guest books

Reprint of a full-page ad in the *New York Times* costing $5,000 in 1969

Ad for series of eight premieres at the New Yorker Theater on May 6, 1972; one journalist described it as a "last hurrah" for independently made foreign films

Cinema Studio marquee, Broadway and Sixty-Sixth Street; December 13–28, 1978, opening program

Cinema Studio 2 (185 seats) after the theater was twinned in 1978

Cinema Studio exterior sketch by unknown artist (Porter), c. 1990

Metro Theater, art deco interior refurbished by architect Peter Cohen, opening day, October 1, 1982

Metro Theater medallion; the façade was landmarked in 1989

The Lincoln Plaza Cinemas marquee, January 2018

The lobby at the Lincoln Plaza Cinemas
Photo: Richard J. Slote

The posters lining the hallway at Lincoln Plaza
Photo: Richard J. Slote

A *New Yorker* cartoon of the Lincoln Plaza lobby

Dan Talbot in the Lincoln Plaza Cinemas projection booth, c. 2007

New Yorker Films logo; this sign hung in the office entryway

Back cover of New Yorker Films catalogue, 1976–77

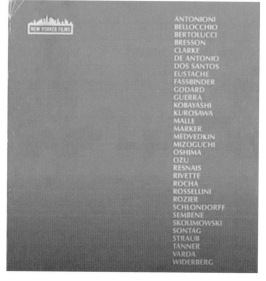

JEAN-LUC GODARD

HAIL MARY

Denounced by the Pope and the object of worldwide protests, this surprisingly serene and lyrical work is a journey through both recent European history and Godard's own filmic past. Centering on a grizzled film director who sets out to stage a play in the empty gas-station setting of *Weekend*, this film, with Mary as a basketball-playing gas-station attendant who receives the Annunciation by Jellinek. (Includes *The Book of Mary*, a companion film by Anne-Marie Mieville.)

France, 1985.
107 mins. Color.   Rental: 300

FOR EVER MOZART

This densely allusive work is a journey through both recent European history and Godard's own filmic past. Centering on a grizzled film director who sets out to stage a play in the empty gas-station setting of *Weekend*, this film, with Mary as a basketball-playing gas-station attendant who receives the Annunciation by Jellinek mixes fast-paced intellectual vaudeville with graceful philosophical reflections and startling moments of quiet beauty.

Switzerland/France, 1997.
85 mins. Color.   Rental: 350

IN PRAISE OF LOVE

An eloquently personal artistic testament structured into two parts. The first, set in Paris, where a young artist is developing a project on the nature of love, is shot in ravishing black-and-white celluloid. The second, set in Brittany, where the same artist interviews two Resistance veterans, is shot in supersaturated color video.

France/Switzerland, 2001.
98 mins. B&W and Color.   Rental: 450

(All films in French with English subtitles)

The films of
WERNER HERZOG

Werner Herzog is an original, an eccentric and a mystic. The main characters in his films have been dwarfs, deaf mutes, an autistic enigma, a demented conquistador, the world's greatest ski-jumper and the Sahara Desert. His locations have included an Aegean valley filled with hundreds of windmills, a God-forsaken Wisconsin truck stop, the rim of a volcano about to erupt, a remote rock of the Irish coast, and the heart of the Amazonian jungle. At all times Herzog is trying to push the boundaries of experience to their extremes, to the borderline between madness and genius.

FATA MORGANA

A hallucinatory meditation on the beauty of the Sahara Desert and the debris of civilization. The film begins as a near abstract fugue of traveling shots of sand dunes and shimmering mirages, but as the film progresses the landscape becomes increasingly sullied with abandoned cars, oil fires, and an absurdist parade of eccentric tourists.

Germany, 1971.
78 mins. Color.   Rental: 300

AGUIRRE, THE WRATH OF GOD

A stunningly photographed, spectacularly horrifying chronicle of imperialism gone amok, set in the mid-1500s. A large Spanish expedition searching the Amazon for the mythical lost city of El Dorado falls into the hands of Don Lope de Aguirre (a magnificently menacing Klaus Kinski), a power-driven lunatic who dreams of stealing an entire continent.

Germany, 1973.
94 mins. Color.   Rental: 350

THE MYSTERY OF KASPAR HAUSER

In 1828 a mysterious young man appeared in the town square of Nuremberg after having been kept in solitary confinement all his life. He became a nationwide sensation, only to be murdered five years later. Herzog confronts the mystery of Kaspar's brief existence with a fierce sarcasm and blunt, breathtaking lyricism.

Germany, 1975.
110 mins. Color.   Rental: 350

HEART OF GLASS

For this mixture of mysticism, apocalyptic grandeur and breath-takingly beautiful visions, Herzog hypnotized his actors to convey "an atmosphere of hallucination, of prophecy...and collective madness." The story, set in the pre-industrial past, tells of a small town that loses the secret of making its unique Ruby glass, and the townspeople who turn to murder and magic to recover it.

Germany, 1976.
93 mins. Color.   Rental: 275

STROSZEK

A lyrical, melancholy, bitterly funny tale of three oddly-assorted Berlin misfits who follow the American Dream to Wisconsin and find a bleak Eldorado of TV football, CB radio, truck stops and mobile homesteading. The title role is played by Bruno S., with Eva Mattes as a soulful whore and Clemens Scheitz as an eccentric old man conducting a homemade search for the secrets of "animal magnetism."

Germany, 1977.
108 mins. Color.   Rental: 300

WOYZECK

Herzog took Georg Büchner's extraordinary *Woyzeck*—a caustic tragedy of an ordinary man's plunge into madness and murder—and filmed it with a stunning clarity, punctuated by bursts of devastating lyricism. In the title role, Klaus Kinski delivers a harrowing and unforgettable performance, as sharp as the razor with which the hero carries out his chilling destiny.

Germany, 1978.
82 mins. Color.   Rental: 250

LAND OF SILENCE AND DARKNESS

This astonishing documentary about the world of the deaf-blind is neither morbid nor uplifting, but a mystical attempt to conceive the inconceivable. Through Fini Straubinger, a remarkable 56-year-old deaf and blind woman, Herzog immerses us in an existence so intense and abstract that at times it reaches great lyrical heights.

Germany, 1971.
90 mins. Color.   Rental: 250

THE GREAT ECSTASY OF THE SCULPTOR STEINER

This hypnotic documentary records, in amazing slow-motion photography, the splendid, terrifying isolation and ecstasy of Walter Steiner, a Swiss wood-carver who was also the world's greatest ski jumper. As Steiner confronts death at every leap, Herzog narrates the film in an awe-struck whisper.

Germany, 1975.
45 mins. Color.   Rental: 150

SIGNS OF LIFE

Herzog's first feature, which marked a turning point in the renaissance of German cinema, is an original mixture of Quixote and case history. The central character is a wounded German soldier sent to sit out the war in an isolated Mediterranean garrison. Unhinged by the torpid circularity of island life, he stages a lyrical, insane, one-man

EVEN DWARFS STARTED SMALL

An unforgettably nightmarish allegory of stunted humanity and frustrated revolt set in a correctional institute on a remote island peopled entirely by midgets. Herzog's Kafka-esque fable documents a day-long anarchistic uprising in which all manner of indignities are visited on and by the island's

New Yorker Films catalogue pages for Werner Herzog films

OSHIMA

According to Japanese Cinema expert Noël Burch, Nagisa Oshima (born 1932) is "by far the most important Japanese filmmaker of his generation." Best known in the West for his Brechtian tour de force *Death By Hanging*, his erotic masterpiece *In the Realm of the Senses* and for *Merry Christmas, Mr. Lawrence*, Nagisa Oshima is the most important figure in Japanese cinema since the classical era of Ozu, Mizoguchi and Kurosawa. Often compared to the luminaries of the French New Wave, and to Godard in particular, Oshima has in fact moved parallel to (and often been ahead of) European trends more than he has followed them. Complex, audacious and dynamic, mixing violence, eroticism, politics, self-reflexivity and dazzling camerawork, Oshima's style represents a seminal link between modernism and non-Western modes of perception.

CRUEL STORY OF YOUTH

The film that established Oshima's reputation in Japan, his first commercial hit and his first storm of controversy. The desperate nihilism and cruelty of a teenage couple who perform sexual shakedowns on middle-aged men is contrasted with the exhausted liberal idealism of the preceding generation.

1960. 96 MINS. COLOR.
SCOPE PRINTS ONLY.

THE SUN'S BURIAL

Oshima's most blatantly amoral and extravagantly violent version of the juvenile delinquent drama probes the underworld of Osaka's biggest slum, a hellhole where teenage gangs, prostitutes and an exquisitely cruel femme fatale vie for control of the area's most profitable business.

1960. 87 MINS. COLOR.
SCOPE PRINTS ONLY.

NIGHT AND FOG IN JAPAN

One of Oshima's most ingenious and radical films uses the wedding celebration of two young activists as the backdrop for a series of political confrontations shot with a dazzling theatricality, combining flashbacks, off-screen scenarios, black-outs, and balletic tracking shots.

1960. 107 MINS. COLOR.
SCOPE PRINTS ONLY.

DEATH BY HANGING

A notoriously daring and damning satire on capital punishment and Japanese justice. Oshima's early masterpiece describes, in detail, the execution of a young Korean worker found guilty of rape and the authorities' bizarre re-enactments of his crimes. A definitively stylish mix of documentary and hilarious black farce.

1968. 114 MINS. B&W.

THE MAN WHO LEFT HIS WILL ON FILM

A haunting, politically intriguing film set in 60s Tokyo. A young leftist finds the camera of a radical who has kept to his death while fleeing the police. The "will and testament" he discovers on film seems meaningless, but begins to obsess him as he retraces the filmmaker's political and erotic past.

1970. 91 MINS. B&W.

THE CEREMONY

An ambitious film which encompasses no less than the entire history of postwar Japan. *The Ceremony* chronicles the fortunes and the sorrows of the powerful Sakurada family from 1946 to the present. The story snowballs into the ripest of Jacobean dramas as well as forming an indictment of modern Japan.

1971. 122 MINS. COLOR.
SCOPE PRINTS ONLY.

DIARY OF A SHINJUKU THIEF

A romantic story of a violent, moody drop-out and a disaffected young woman becomes a powerful exploration of the world of the young Japanese radicals of 1968. Touching on such unlikely cultural icons as Henry Miller and Mohammed Ali, *Diary of a Shinjuku Thief* is distinguished by Oshima's dazzling hand-held camerawork.

1969. 94 MINS. B&W.

DEAR SUMMER SISTER

A lyrical history lesson that follows a miniskirted Tokyo teenager as she visits Okinawa to search for a half-brother she has never met. Oshima turns this simple story into a profound exploration of taboo themes such as incest, the guilt of war survivors and the colonial relationship between the island of Okinawa and the mainland of Japan.

1972. 96 MINS. COLOR.

BOY

A small boy is trained to throw himself against passing cars and to fake injury so that his parents can extort money from the confused drivers. The family wander from city to city, often only a step ahead of a suspicious victim. Oshima maintains a discreet distance between the boy's world and his family's cruelty with deft use of sound montage.

1969. 97 MINS. COLOR.
SCOPE PRINTS ONLY.

DIARY OF YUNBOGI BOY

A short film about the prejudice suffered by the vast number of Koreans living in Japan. Focussing on one abandoned Korean child living in the slums, Oshima's portrait is a fascinating collage of diary and stills.

1972. 24 MINS. B&W.

New Yorker Films catalogue pages for Nagisa Oshima films

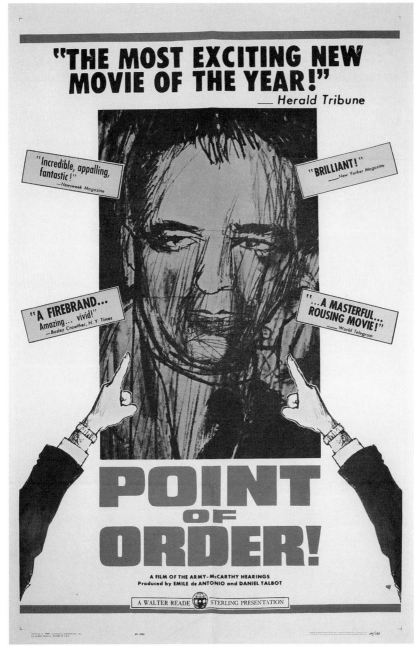

Point of Order (Emile de Antonio and Dan Talbot, 1964)

My Dinner with André (Louis Malle, 1984)

Dona Flor and Her Two Husbands (Bruno Barreto, 1976)

New Yorker Films catalogue cover:
Rainer Werner Fassbinder in
Wizard of Babylon (Dieter Schidor,
1982)

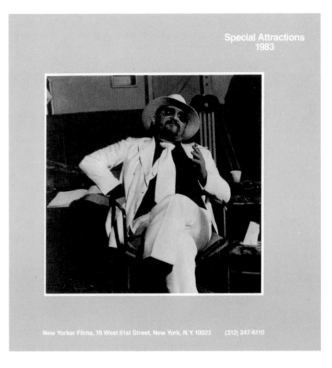

New Yorker Films catalogue cover:
Yaaba (Idrissa Ouedraogo, 1989)

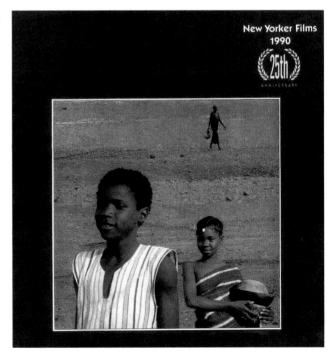

New Yorker Films catalogue cover:
Tampopo (Juzo Itami, 1985)

New Yorker Films catalogue cover:
Satyajit Ray

New Yorker Films catalogue cover:
Shoah (Claude Lanzmann, 1985)

New Yorker Films catalogue cover:
Ousmane Sembène

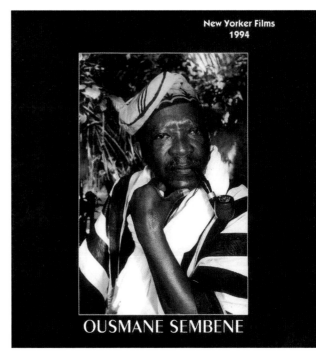

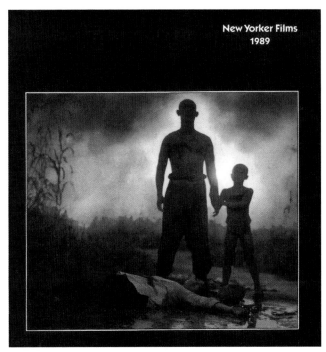

New Yorker Films catalogue cover:
Red Sorghum (Zhang Yimou, 1987)

New Yorker Films catalogue cover:
Phantom India (Louis Malle, 1969)

New Yorker Films catalogue
cover: *Orchestra Rehearsal*
(Federico Fellini, 1978)

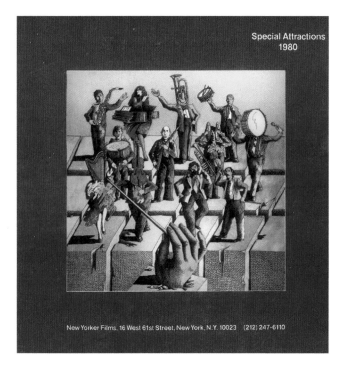

New Yorker Films catalogue cover:
Moolaadé (Ousmane Sembène,
2004)

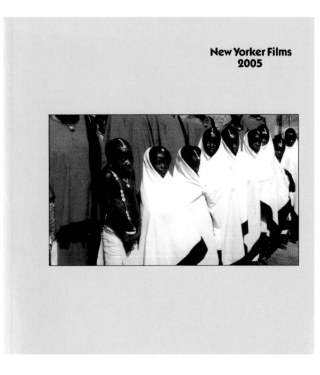

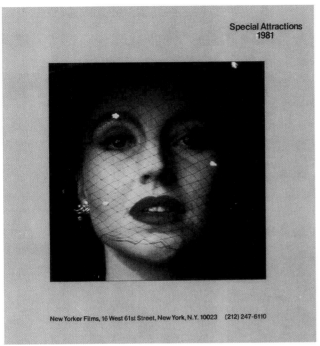

New Yorker Films catalogue cover:
The Marriage of Maria Braun
(Rainer Werner Fassbinder, 1978)

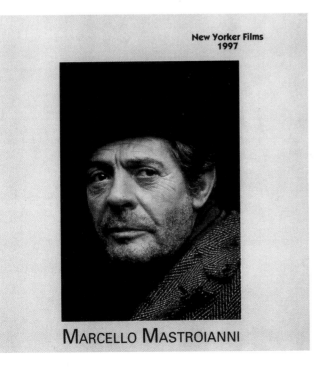

New Yorker Films catalogue cover:
Marcello Mastroianni

New Yorker Films catalogue
cover: *L'Atalante* (Jean Vigo, 1934)

New Yorker Films catalogue
cover: *Landscape in the Mist* (Theo
Angelopoulos, 1988)

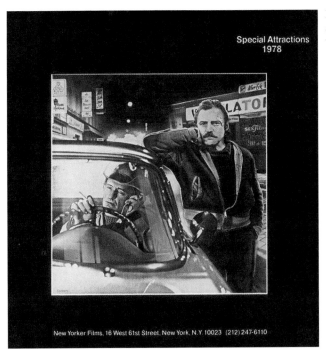

New Yorker Films catalogue cover: *The American Friend* (Wim Wenders, 1978)

New Yorker Films catalogue cover: *Ivan and Abraham* (Yolande Zauberman, 1993)

Postcard announcing New Yorker Films moving from Sixty-First Street to Sixteenth Street

Handwritten offer for *Stalker* (Andrei Tarkovsky, 1979)

A page from Dan Talbot's journals mentioning *The Piano* (Jane Campion, 1993)

Dan Talbot's handwritten notes for Rossellini Award acceptance speech given at the 1991 Cannes Film Festival

Toby on the balcony of Hôtel Splendid in Cannes

Dan and Toby Talbot with Dieter Kosslick on the occasion of Lia van Leer receiving the Berlinale Camera in 2011
Photo: Richard Hübner

Dan and Toby Talbot with Bernardo Bertolucci

Dan Talbot in New Yorker Films office; photo signed by employees

Dan Talbot's study on the Upper West Side

FROM THE SAFETY OF MY LIVING ROOM

I wonder at times how my life might have been altered had I undergone severe deprivation, physical suffering, extended trauma. From the safety of my living room, I've read the same catastrophe stories as you have in the daily papers and seen them on television. I read these stories and, within ten minutes at the most afterward, go about my business. Thinking of how I will make enough money to support my large family; deciding which movie to see as a form of pleasure; reflecting on the quality of the previous evening with friends; wondering when I will die and in what manner, in the meantime feeling physically and mentally strong.

I do not at all feel guilty about my good fortune in life, yet something is nagging away at me. I think about Korean comfort women who gave their bodies to Japanese soldiers as often as fifty times a day, of naked terrified Jews pushed by Jewish *Sonderkommandos* into gas chambers, of massacres performed on the innocent in Yugoslavia. I think about these daily tortures and I say to myself, *I must be at the office soon to be in time for my appointment.* I remember Toby and I seeing Louis Malle's *Calcutta*, a documentary about such ghastly mass poverty that our stomachs turned inside the theater. Afterward, we went to a two-star fish restaurant and ate sea urchins and grilled scrod washed down with Chassagne Montrachet, then returned home and made love.

■ ■ ■

Everything goes in the name of information and culture. What shall I do? Go to one of the world's trouble spots and put my shoulder behind the wheel of relief to sufferers? Shall I give an emaciated Rwandan child a Hershey bar with almonds? On the same day that four hundred thousand hungry Rwandans march thirty miles to their homeland, the Dow Jones goes up one hundred points. Where and how will book knowledge, street smarts, the transforming powers of art, the wisdom of Talmudists and Oriental sages make a difference?

Perhaps we should believe Stefan Zweig, who once said that every time you tell the truth you increase the measure of truth in the universe. And what about all those wonderful memoirs that describe life triumphing after deep suffering? I'm haunted by Nadezhda Mandelstam's *Hope Abandoned*. In her head, she carried her husband's verses written in prison so that they would not be forgotten, so that the assassins of memory would be duped. So that *Zakhor* (remembrance) might live. And think about the near death suffered in adolescence by that great Austrian novelist Thomas Bernhard, so meticulously inscribed in his memoir, *Gathering Evidence*.

I don't recall ever missing a meal as I grew up (nor in my subsequent life), except when sick with an upset stomach, which was almost never. Alongside our daily candy intake, my pals and I ate kosher hot dogs with sauerkraut and mustard, sour pickles, potato knishes, salami sandwiches from Schwartz's delicatessen. In my lifetime, I don't think I've ever gone more than ten days without eating, and that was from being in a hospital for minor surgery. Or because I'd wanted to skip a day of food after having overeaten for a week, my stupid stomach bulging with foie gras, bagels, and Léoville Las Cases '86.

Would I have endured the hunger that Knut Hamsun described in his great novel of that title? I have thousands of books that have given me pleasure and hopefully a glimpse of enlightenment. I've seen thousands of movies, plays, and operas. I've listened to most of the great works of Mozart, Handel, Bach, and Stravinsky. I've traveled to all of France and Spain, to Portugal, Italy, Brazil, Czechoslovakia, Morocco, Egypt, Greece, Yugoslavia, Turkey, England, Israel, Hungary, Germany, most of America, Poland, and over the years have seen how most of these societies were transformed by blue jeans, Coca-Cola, Mickey Mouse, Big Macs, dope, and violence—our chief exports.

In other words, in my travels I've experienced some semblance of a life lived, on the whole, expansively if stupidly amid extreme suffering on the planet. Are you interested in visiting Vietnam and Cambodia, countries that American

bombers almost sent back into the Stone Age? Or will your travel agent someday suggest Grozny or Kabul or Dubrovnik?

We attend a dinner party, and the after-dinner conversation tilts to retirement funds, vitamins, doctors, trips to France, Zabar's, a new supermarket on
Columbus Avenue. Will somebody, some major sage, please enlighten me? I
would like to understand all this madness. Am I hallucinating because I've lived
a life of more pleasure than suffering? Though I'm knowledgeable about literature, wine, money, movies, psychiatry, elegant manners, lovemaking, ethics, and
morality, I am ignorant about extreme deprivation. Will somebody run after
me with a machete so that I may know what it means to be informed about
near death?

There are times when I can't tolerate my well-being and yet know that I'm
not a masochist and would be unable to write these lines without being well.
I've struggled with quasi-nightmare thoughts but would like to truly appreciate what terrible things are happening on this planet. I think about super-rich
people who buy land and buildings like properties on the Monopoly board.
(One of John Jacob Astor's financial fellows said to him: "We have just taken
a position on lower Fifth Avenue," meaning that Astor had just bought ten
blocks of real estate.)

If you see the Earth from a jet plane 35,000 feet away, it looks eerily beauti-
ful but at the same time meaningless, proportionately foolish. I think about
Charles Wilson's comment: "What's good for General Motors is good for
America."

At our monthly lunches at the Four Seasons my dear friend and lawyer Bob
Montgomery and I are seated in the power room. Below are the regulars:
billionaire Ronald Lauder, real-estate magnate Jack Rudin, architect Philip
Johnson, Wall Street scion John Loeb, and publisher Dick Snyder. Bob and I
speculate as to why these super-richies need so much money. Why do they still
have the hots to earn more?

Thomas Merton embraced silence in a monastery after having lived the high
life. I think of all those complacent faces you see on the society page, and then
of past photos of the two ten-year-old Jewish boys with the Star of David on
their jackets, their hands raised as a Nazi soldier points his rifle at them, and
another showing an elderly Orthodox rabbi forced to clean the street with a
toothbrush, German jackboots a few feet away. There are the haunted faces of
poor hillbillies seen in the photographs by Walker Evans in *Let Us Now Praise*

Famous Men, and of dead Black bodies lying in pools of blood in American ghettos.

I just want to make sense of these things because my living room is getting crowded, and I am beginning to feel jittery.

ROZHINKEL

I f you run into someone who has the *rozhinkel*, it means that this person has *savor*. The Yiddish word—literally "little raisin"—denotes someone with a certain endearing manner, someone who expresses themself in an unexpected, original style, someone with an air of folk wisdom, someone with whom you simply want to spend a lot of time—in short, someone beguilingly charming. That person is endowed with Miguel de Unamuno's "tragic sense of life" and, in plain language, will steer you straight and good. That person sends off nifty vibrations.

We're talking about someone past fifty, for most young people are nervous or blindingly ambitious or hooked on strong sexual ways; and if you're busy all the time with an eye cocked on the main chance, be it running after a pile of money or a good fuck, you don't have the capacity to lie back and give off *rozhinkel* emanations.

There are no universities or lycées for learning the *rozhinkel* effect. Either you got it or you don't. It's not genetic. It more or less happens, a leftover piece of the bolt out of the blue. When in the presence of someone with the *rozhinkel*, you'll know it. In our lifetime, each of us meets at least one such individual. You walk away from that person with a cleansed soul. You feel like whistling or walking on the balls of your feet.

Toby and I have incorporated this word into our movie lexicon. It's our secret language, our private real estate of a word. Movies don't involve a single individual—there's director, actor, music, sound, editing. So, for a film to have the *rozhinkel*, it needs a felicitous blend of multiples.

An outstanding example of a movie with the *rozhinkel* is Idrissa Ouedraogo's *Yaaba*. When we first saw this film from Burkina Faso at Cannes, I turned to Toby toward the end and whispered in her ear, "This is a masterpiece." When it was over, we were ready to spring out of our seats. It's a simple story: about a friendship between a young boy and a little girl, his cousin, and an elderly woman, shunned by the community as a witch. Through that friendship he learns about tradition, prejudice, loyalty—in short, humanness. At one point his cousin falls ill, and the old woman's medicine saves her. Beautifully photographed, with long shots that give time to reflect, it's a film with soul.

One wouldn't characterize Andrei Tarkovsky's *The Sacrifice* as having the *rozhinkel*. We regard this philosophical film as a masterpiece, but it operates on superexalted levels—grandiose, millenarian, a film that diminishes you in the worldly scheme of things. *8½* has the *rozhinkel*. Nelson Pereira dos Santos's *Vidas Secas* has the *rozhinkel*. Werner Herzog's *Aguirre, the Wrath of God* doesn't have it, but his *Land of Silence and Darkness* definitely does. As do De Sica's *Umberto D.* and Ozu's *Late Spring* and *Tokyo Story*. I could go on . . .

I imagine a film geared around Toby's mother, Bella. She stands behind the candy counter of the New Yorker Theater, dispensing folk wisdom in her caring manner—someone with the *rozhinkel*. One can begin to understand why *Yaaba* has the *rozhinkel*, as do Leo McCarey's *Make Way for Tomorrow*, François Truffaut's *Jules and Jim*, Kenji Mizoguchi's *Sansho the Bailiff*, Carlos Diegues's *Quilombo*, Yolande Zauberman's *Ivan and Abraham*, and François Girard's *Thirty-Two Short Films About Glenn Gould*. In this cinema game of ours, we revere those who confront the blows of life yet retain an ineffable spirit.

MIURA

*M*iura is a Portuguese word that describes unfulfilled sexual activity between a bull and a cow and that Gianni Amico, the Italian filmmaker, applied to describe films of quality that are appreciated by cinephiles but—and this is the determining factor—are certain to be doomed at the box office.

Gustavo Dahl's *O Bravo Guerreiro*, if not most of Brazil's Cinema Novo, was a *miura*. As to the films of Straub–Huillet or Marcel Hanoun, or the early works of Philippe Garrel, *miura* would be inadequate. A new word, unless you wanted to be cute and say *miura-isimo*, would have to be invented. For those films that fell in between *miura* and *miura-isimo*, we sometimes said *miureen*, with the emphasis on the *-een*. It was a private game. The underlying note was affection.

In those days, we loved cinema so much that there was little room left over for discussions of national politics, let alone the global disorder during the seventies. The 360-degree pan in Godard's *A Woman Is a Woman* is a moral statement worthy of Rossellini. Do not forget Roberto Rossellini.

An excellent example of *miura* would be an obscure film by Dominique Benicheti called *Cousin Jules*. Let us now praise this exquisite gem, a masterpiece of humanity. A documentary about a couple in their eighties, peasants who live on their small farm in an undesignated part of France. The husband is a blacksmith of medium height, erect, comfortable in his sturdy plain cotton pants and shirt. He has an inquisitive look. The wife tends the vegetable garden and cooks. An uncommonly handsome woman, she looks optimistic. They have lived with each other for over sixty years. We do not know if they have children. The filmmaker is related to Jules, hence the title, though this is left somewhat ambiguous, for Benicheti was in his early thirties when he made the film. I'd be curious to learn how a thirty-year-old and this eighty-year-old can be cousins. No matter.

The film follows in minute detail the cycle of this couple's day over a period of three seasons. Both are up at the crack of dawn. Roosters crow. Cows moo. There's a slight breeze. The leaves of the magnolia tree near the house flutter. The ancient woman makes a wood fire in the stove. Coffee is cooking. They sit at a distressed wooden table looking out the window toward their fields strewn with red poppies while drinking coffee and eating huge chunks of peasant bread smeared with thick layers of butter. They look at each other but say nothing. He rises and puts his cup in the sink. He walks out of the room in his clunky wooden clogs and goes to the nearby shed to make a coal fire. He puts on a leather apron. He is working on a farm implement I've never seen before, which is undoubtedly a basic tool. He gives this piece of iron his undivided attention, a gaze fixed and intense.

He pauses, studies the contour of the tool, and then puts it back in the lathe to refine it further. At midmorning, his wife (no given name in the film) appears with a pot of coffee and two cups. She warms it up on a brazier. He stops work. She sits down on a small wooden stool, pours the coffee, hands it to Jules. They drink together, looking at each other, saying nothing, and you now understand the deeper meaning of ritual. After coffee, she goes to the garden and we see her harvesting leeks and potatoes. They will have leek soup tonight. The sun is so bright you imagine that you're in southern France. So far we are one hour into the film. Nothing and everything has happened. If Pudovkin had been alive at the time of this film, he would have embraced Benicheti. As the sun descends, we witness this harmonious couple eating dinner. Leek soup rests in a large wooden bowl. They eat with handmade wooden spoons. You hear the sound of clogs on the wooden floor as she goes to the stove for more soup. Throughout the film you hear the crunch of clogs on gravel paths. The film runs only ninety minutes, with not one word spoken by these two magnificent people.

Now, if your mind has been wandering, trying to figure out which stock to buy, please pay attention. Benicheti shot this film in color, CinemaScope, and stereophonic sound, in 1973, twenty years before the introduction of digital sound. No other way would do. A sort of predecessor of this film— *Farrebique*—was made in black and white, mono sound, in a 1:33 aspect ratio, the way most films were made in the thirties and forties, before color, scope lenses, and overly refined sound changed the look of films. Benicheti's aim was to give the film the sense of a lived life, without the fakery of artifice. You hear the buzz of bees, the crackle of fire, the crunch of gravel as if you were experiencing the workings of nature for the first time. Hollywood films since then, with their leviathan industrial insults to the brain, use soundtracks that deserve to be outlawed. If Sylvester Stallone, God forbid, were to sneeze in Dolby sound, it would sound like a herd of elephants farting; I could easily see those elephant farts rending mountains asunder, uprooting two-hundred-foot palm trees.

Benicheti organized a screening for me and Toby to learn if I would distribute the film. After seeing it, I said of course. But then reality intervened. The print I screened was the only one in existence. It cost $20,000 to make. The negative elements—in separate tracks—were at Technicolor in London. To order additional prints, the separate elements would have to be married. This, with an answer print, would run to $75,000. Benicheti wouldn't allow the print he showed me, a pristine print from the original negative, to be shown again unless I wanted to make additional prints to the tune of $20,000 a pop, and then only a maximum of six to seven prints could be made. Striking additional prints would invite destruction to the negative. If one were to entertain global distribution, with the remote possibility that the film would gain a halfway decent-sized audience, several hundred thousand dollars would have to be invested. Go show a film like this to a run-of-the-mill airhead audience. I consider myself among the privileged few for having screened it. I was unable to speak for two days afterward. I will never forget it. The film occupies a special crypt in my memory warehouse. It is actually incomplete. Benicheti managed to shoot the elderly couple over a period of three seasons. Jules's wife, Felicie Guiteaux, died before the onset of winter. It matters not. I am in Benicheti's debt for showing me such a great work of art. I still feel transformed by it.

"IGNATZ, DON'T GO SO DEEP."

At times when feeling good about myself, I talk too much. Or maybe it's not just a question of talking too much but a somewhat obsessive *digging* for the truth. As a youth, when dealing with an ambiguous event, I'd want to analyze it, circle it, probe for a new outrageous or unheard-of angle.

At which point, my mother would stop me and say, "Ignatz, don't go so deep."

My mother, apparently, had a relative in Lemberg, Poland, named Ignatz who drove everyone crazy with his questions and complicated answers. He was without trade or profession. Hung around the house most of the time. And with all that time on his hands, went about trying to get at the root of things. He was a nice fellow, according to my mother: likeable, talkative, attentive to his parents, brothers, and sisters. Given to reading professional medical books.

His mother—her name was Zipporah—was afflicted with a panoply of disorders, none debilitating, but of sufficient quantity that her day was occupied with doctors, medicines, bromides, hot-water bags, and half-empty glasses of water and tea. To compliment Zipporah on how well she looked was an affront—unacceptable, if not unprovable.

Ignatz was at her side much of the day and, as at a press conference, fielded questions about his mother from friends and relatives. "Her heart is strong, but she feels faint today," he'd say, "so I get her to lie in bed, but when in bed, she becomes anxious because she's afraid she won't be able to rise and walk around, which of course is what she should be doing, even if it means that she would trip and fall on her face." Ignatz!

It seems that I've inherited Ignatz's ruminative trait. My mother started calling me Ignatz when I was ten years old. I was the apple of her eye. When Chicago relatives would visit us in the Bronx and stay for a month, I was often put on display. And I'd want to know why Uncle Joe was wearing a green polka-dot bow tie, why Tanta Rosie was so fat, why my uncle Zachariah kept his teeth in a glass of water before going to bed, and why my cousins were twins. When I tried to make connections between the tie and the teeth and the twins, I'd hear my mother yell at me: "Ignatz! Enough!"

After my mother died, Toby kept the tradition alive of calling me Ignatz whenever my tongue went off track. But in her case, there was an additional element: imputing contrariness in my wisecracks.

These days it seems that everyone is a contrarian. It's a kind of *panacherie*, a scoundrel's attempt to be different, to appear original. This is especially so on Wall Street. Everyone there is a contrarian. It's how these brilliant money managers seduce unwitting investors. "I'm neither value nor growth-oriented," I heard one of these geniuses say. "I am a contrarian." In other words, an imbecile. My feeling is that since all those guys and gals are contrarians, they cancel each other out and study each other's styles to such a degree that they remain conformists.

I spent an hour trying to analyze *The Crying Game*. For example, the key scene in which the Black girl turns out to be a fellow—that is, an *alleged* fellow—with unresolved overtones to his/her sexual identity; I developed a case for him/her as a reincarnation of Virginia Woolf, since Ms. Woolf, in my estimate, could be construed as male.

"Ignatz!" Toby thundered. "Enough is enough."

MINYAN

I have to make a confession. The films I traffic in are chosen in collaboration with a phantom minyan. The people in my shifting minyan live in different parts of the city. We've often met—and continue to meet—at the various theaters I've operated on the Upper West Side: the New Yorker, Cinema Studio, Metro, and Lincoln Plaza Cinemas. They come from all walks of life. At various times, the minyan has consisted of a psychiatrist, a lawyer, a painter, a bookie, a sidewalk philosopher, a doorman, a writer, an opera singer, an editor, a rabbi. They're a fierce lot. Range in age from twenty to ninety. Opinionated, sometimes more than I can bear. Mostly A types. Lucky for me, they don't know that they're members of the floating minyan. Knowing that, they might ask for a share of the profits. For sure, they would try to take editorial control.

I think of these phantoms whenever I'm about to choose a film. If I turn down Film B and it turns out to be a great success, it might get out later, and I'd be accused of being left back. And if I choose Film C, what would Stan or another person in my minyan say? Once I opened a film that Stan didn't like, and he chased after me in front of the Ansonia, at which point his wife intervened.

At one point in our Monday Night series, as I described, we showed *Triumph of the Will*, Leni Riefenstahl's monumental documentary, commissioned by Hitler. It shows the Führer ranting before thousands of spectators at a Nazi party rally in Nuremberg. The film hadn't been shown publicly for over twenty years, and large crowds gathered for the screening. Isaac Bashevis Singer happened to be passing by, and unaware of the film's subject, he beamed: "How wonderful to see people lined up for culture, not for bread."

Who knows what invisible minyans exist in our audiences?

On another occasion, I was booed in my hostess's dining room for defending the art of a filmmaker deemed reactionary. A roomful of people clutched their heads.

From the moment I saw *Not Reconciled*, I committed myself to Jean-Marie Straub and Danièle Huillet. In that film, one generation of a family explains to the other the losses suffered and mistakes made over a seventy-year span, straight through the Nazi era. Straub is fascinated by the insistence upon utter cleanliness, regularity, and niceness in that German bourgeois household—both its genius and its undoing. Turmoil, never shown on screen, but always spoken of and compulsively explained, gives a unique understanding of the permanent scars left by Nazism on this fragmented family. Straub–Huillet's films are uncompromising. Challenging clichéd and "dull and boring naturalism," their goal is to bring the viewer into an active and thinking relationship to the film and, above all, to be analytical. Their films are admittedly "difficult," aggressive, and quite beautiful. Through new forms of sound and image, the viewer experiences film as film, and reality as reality rather than as realism.

After five years, I finally managed to turn a corner on *Chronicle of Anna Magdalena Bach*, the Straubs' second feature, perhaps their most accessible and often considered a monument of structural cinema. The serene visuals of the film, suggestive of Dutch painting, juxtaposed with a spoken text drawn from the letters and manuscripts of Johann Sebastian Bach, reveal a life of poverty and frustration. Bach, a Protestant, wrote most of his music for Catholic patrons, and he and his second wife, Anna Magdalena, performed on the harpsichord to support their thirteen children. The film, in its attention to Bach's compositions, is a music lover's dream: choral and instrumental selections, including the Brandenburg Concerto no. 5 and *The Art of Fugue*, are magnificently performed on screen by Gustav Leonhardt in his role as Bach.

As you see, there are no free lunches in my trade. I'm haunted by these minyan spooks; their voices lecture and nag me. This Gang of Ten has been put on earth as a whispering conscience—they've turned me into a slave.

Only once did I not obey and consult with the minyan. Quietly I ran off to Paris with Toby, and with Claude Lanzmann sitting behind us, we screened *Shoah*. In short order, without consulting the minyan, we brought this masterpiece into New York and presented it. This was the only time in our lengthy partnership that not one member of the minyan dissented. Let us appreciate the fact that there's at least one tradition among our people that has survived over the centuries. Long live the minyan!

PART 9

REFLECTIONS

CLUSTERS OF FRAGMENTED MOMENTS

I have railed against Hollywood films that wallow in gloom and float through an amniotic nightmare of severe mental crises, teary eye sockets, drab interiors, and mass family breakdown. Such films work toward a common denominator: preoccupation with the morbid. Whereas the common run of Hollywood films was previously concerned with simple-seeming affairs, such as how to get married, a graceful way to make love, how to make a success of one's job or project, and how to keep a community free of assorted freaks—all achieved by a kiss, a show of ritz, and some adroit muscular blitzing—it has become fashionable to begin with the complete disintegration of a personality. This is entertainment?

One goes to the movies, I thought, to see the more pleasurable aspects of our lives or greater insights unfold before us. In terms of entertainment, Hollywood has been spectacularly successful in the past. It's true that there exists an unbridgeable gap between it and life as really led in kitchens and streets; certainly only a fool or a serious politician would expect accurate representation. Yet there's so much in the way of small detail off screen that can be transmuted into exciting imagery on screen that a filmmaker has their work all cut out, even before getting too deeply involved in the lines or message they may want to sneak in. It is precisely the detail work that marks a film— how a cigarette is smoked, how a chair topples, a facial gesture; the intricate relationship between people and objects jammed together in isolated moments of tenderness, spleen, melancholy, clumsiness, and so forth.

Art emerges in the tradition of medieval cathedral building: just as one is moved by the collective efforts put into a cathedral, so one is struck by the detail and intricacies that go into a film. By dint of evocative eye billiards—ferocious fighting, gag making, or intensive lovemaking—we perceive the whole. I believe it was André Breton who, when asked why he went to the movies, said in effect: "I go to get all worked up. I want to see people hitting each other, making love for hours at a stretch, all of them having a big time on the screen."

I recall memorable gems of details that evoke *genuine* emotion, such as Erich von Stroheim in *Grand Illusion* putting on his white cotton gloves, tamping them elegantly, just before he shoots the French prisoner (a fellow officer) attempting to make a getaway; or the bit in *The Ox-Bow Incident* of Henry Fonda and his sidekick, standing at the bar and drinking whiskey and licking their chops at the painting of a nude; or the scene in *The Quiet Man* when Victor McLaglen and John Wayne are staging a fistfight to end all fistfights, going at each other with animal ferocity, the huge crowd following them in a loop-the-loop of all those marvelous Irish hills and dales. The catalogue is endless. Watching those films, you had the feeling that no one was trying to "make life," but that attention centered on the way people handled objects and related to one another.

We live our lives in clusters of fragmented moments, and for the most part direct our movements toward some vague, unspecified territory that goes under the heading of Goal. One thing we know is that what we're doing at the moment will simply not suffice. We all operate on the nirvana principle, and herein lies the essence of "a problem." One works forever toward the solution of "the problem," and if perchance—*heaven forbid!*—that problem is solved, then there is no purpose in life and it's time to roll over.

At some point we must face the fact that what we're doing in "making life" is perhaps "making book," betting as it were against losing one's job, family, or friends; the onset of illness; old age; and now, of course, radioactive fallout or nuclear disaster. But what makes us all so marvelously human is that we find it bad manners to scowl in public, and when we emerge into the company of others, we leave our gloom harness at home.

But it's precisely this aspect of real life—the uncharted realm of everyday psychic disturbance, depression, and gloom—that has crept into such disconsolate films in a shallow manner and unwittingly dramatized the New Hero: the Gloomster. Such films are so laden with false psychology, simplemindedness, and gloom making that there's no room for anything as casual as the enjoyment of a drink of water or some lighthearted repartee between a man and a woman.

So strangling is this that I start wondering where in our crowded and complicated city I could knock off for a few hours from life making and not be reminded of how difficult life itself can get.

Besides gloomy movies, my avoidance list includes doctors, lawyers, agents, memorials, funerals, and real estate brokers.

THE NEW FRANKNESS

Recent magazine articles describing "the new frankness" in films argue that movie content is suddenly being liberated, that deeper feelings—regarding incest, homosexuality, flagellation, adultery, etc.—are being given the opportunities they deserve on the screen.

Nobody says anything, however, about the fact that Stroheim, Griffith, and Pabst, among other greats of the past, dealt with this stuff with infinitely better judgment, taste, insight, and cinematic interest. No, the new frankness in movies is quite simply another way of legitimizing psychosexual melodrama at the box office. Psychosexuality has moved in on kitsch and taken over the mass psyche beautifully.

I don't know that *Sunrise at Campobello* gives me any more pleasure or information than a political convention or TV speech (neither of which gives me much pleasure or information) or that *Crossfire*, a well-made film, tells me something about anti-Semitism that wasn't already quite obvious—namely, that psychosis has a lot to do with it. American movies with serious themes are usually unbelievable—*Pinky, Gentlemen's Agreement, Lost Boundaries*—simply because our talent does not lie here.

Erwin Panofsky, a great art historian, once wrote: "To pre-stylize reality prior to tackling it amounts to dodging the problem. The problem is to manipulate and shoot un-stylized reality in such a way that the result has style." This proposition relates to the opening remarks of his magnificent essay "Style and Medium in the Motion Pictures," from which I quote:

Film art is the only art the development of which men now living have witnessed from the very beginnings; and this development is all the more interesting as it took place under the conditions contrary to precedent. It was not an artistic urge that gave rise to the discovery and gradual perfection of a new technique; it was a technical invention that gave rise to the discovery and gradual perfection of a new art.

These reflections invest in movies the serious aesthetic properties held by all the other arts, which sprang from a purely artistic urge and not a technical discovery. This, of course, doesn't make movies any less an art form. Now once the mammoth studios with their elephantine sets were built, and once the camera used by Billy Bitzer developed into a grotesque Martian eye that could zoom in and out of bodies and homes like a new secret inner life, and as filmmaking became an industry even more complicated than car manufacturing, we entered a new era of film realities. Almost anything could be done, re-created in the studios, and to paraphrase a saying about Marx, you may not be interested in movies, but movies are *surely* interested in *you*.

Initially, there was an almost exclusive interest in the moving image—how strange it must have been at the turn of the twentieth century to watch figures *move* about on a screen for the sheer sake of movement and nothing else, figures no different than us the audience. Then, having become at once an industry with technical and financial facilities and a form of expression that perforce had to explore its limits, movies focused on almost anything handy: novels, operas, newspaper incidents, poems, short stories, aphorisms. No doubt you've heard the aphorism "You can make a movie out of anything, including the phone book." Well, this maxim certainly came true with films like *Pillow Talk*.

But it didn't end there. With every place to go and an unlimited aesthetic vocabulary to choose from, moviemakers began exploring genres *within* genres: westerns with Freudian psychology (*Shane*), westerns satirizing westerns (*Along Came Jones*), comic parodies of old gangster films (*Some Like It Hot* satirizing *Scarface*), and elegant crime films imitating not-so-elegant crime films (*Rififi* taking up where *The Asphalt Jungle* left off).

Sophisticated moviegoers have gotten into the habit of sometimes going to movies simply to seek out isolated fragments of films, somewhat like a charade, with the express pleasure of identifying their previous source—what amounts to a copy of a copy. Movies no longer simply grow straight out of an identifiable event or dramatic fact in our culture but come out of a series of imitations. If this process, in line with Siegfried Kracauer's ideas, represents some of the authentically hidden fantasies of our national life, then all we're left to say is that nothing much real is taking place out there in the cities and plains; rather, life has gotten more and more abstract. This notion is easily documented. The mass intake of art is now so great that advertising trade magazines refer to huge groups of the population as the "art audience."

A digression: "Who *is* the art audience?" Basically, someone who gobbles up Picasso, Stravinsky, and Eisenstein like a slew of shrimp balls, who admires the works of these artists for any number of reasons, including guilt, being in the know, boredom, and, to this audience's credit, responding to an unfulfilled aesthetic urge. Generally these works are admired in a superficial way and barely understood.

On one hand, there's something good about a culture that has become visually oriented, in that we learn a great deal about the everyday details of dress and gesture and discover new forms and patterns. But if what the camera photographs turns out to be a cliché of a cliché, a copy of a copy, then what's the point? Indeed, a complicated paradox, and were I asked to pinpoint its source, I think it can be attributed to that American maxim: "Nothing succeeds like success itself."

Story editors and studio heads have a little box in their brain with this motto etched into it. How else to account for this positively weird phenomenon of movies imitating themselves so methodically? The next question: What is the source of the first success, that is, what makes a story editor or studio boss decide on what will make a movie with a "fresh angle" succeed? The answer would provide illuminating insights into the success mechanism of American culture. After all, these studio execs are not exactly earning monumental salaries for their good looks. Their jobs demand that they consistently turn up some new, "fresh" angle of a movie. This large subject demands a study in itself. To say it boils down to sex and violence and let it go at that is insufficient—particularly since sex and violence have taken on some pretty strange twists in our time.

I will look for tragedy on its highest level in Shakespeare, for an explanation of the schizophrenic personality in Harry Stack Sullivan, for sexual torment in the Broadway productions of some of Tennessee Williams's plays, and for a novelist's way of telling me about the failures of the material life, but I don't care for movie treatments of the above topics.

Then there's that nasty word, "packaging"—a new way of making movies by monolithic show-business agencies, in which almost totally anonymous packagers decide on the ingredients and stars of a movie as an exercise in market research. The implications of this coproduction mobility can only result in a certain sameness of picture making. For example, at one point the beatnik theme was hot, and it was astonishing how many films about beatniks were made in Poland, Italy, France, England, America.

One day I screened an Argentine film called *El Jefe* and to my dismay, there it was, a whole collection of miniature Brandos and Deans driving everybody in correct society out of their minds. The Argentine producer who brought the print to New York selected this film out of about ten others as the one most likely to gain distribution in the United States. Also worth noting is that many American films have scenes in them that are shot differently: one version for the American market, one for foreign markets. In the past, breast exposure was unacceptable in films here while it was all right abroad. This is probably the only instance I can think of where sameness would be quite admired.

■ ■ ■

Not enough attention has been paid in books and symposiums to the exterior conditions of the industry. I'm not talking now about *Variety* or *Film Daily*. In the thirties and early forties, everybody went to the movies. Anything on celluloid simply could not miss at the box office. This was a time of 2,000 and 3,000 percent returns on a studio investment. It stood to reason that, despite the vulgar tastes of such studio heads as L. B. Mayer, Harry Cohn, and Jack Warner, there had to be—among the large number of films produced each year—a substantial number of very good films made by sophisticated people who were close in time and spirit to such titans as Griffith, Pabst, Eisenstein, Murnau, Dovzhenko, etc. At their best in that era in America were Chaplin and Garbo, Lubitsch, the Marx Brothers, W. C. Fields, Mae West, Morrie Ryskind, S. J. Perelman, Donald Ogden Stewart, Val Lewton, Preston Sturges, Carole Lombard, James Cagney, Clark Gable, and Cary Grant—all of whom participated in a vast run of celluloid so inspired, so fantastic and entertaining that by comparison today's output seems dreary.

In those days, there were authentic struggles between businessmen and artists, and sometimes the artist won, even if it meant smuggling in one's talents. This was because the division between artist and businessman was clear-cut—each had clearer definitions of what they were and wanted to be.

Today a so-called film artist is likely to be producer, investor, and writer of their own film. Directors, writers, and stars have become big businessmen at the behest of their agents, which has tended toward a clearly conformist, safe product. I can't imagine, for example, a film comedian today, supposing they had the talents of a W. C. Fields, making a movie without a script, without a notion of where the story was heading, improvising in the splendidly wacky way that resulted in Fields's masterpieces. Instead, we get carefully planned, multimillion-dollar, nonsensical comedies.

Now, producer Jerry Wald extended this mania for making movies out of books and plays with *Ulysses* and *Remembrance of Things Past*. Kitsch swings full cycle. I can't imagine anything more distasteful or wrong-minded. Though it's true that *Ulysses* reads like a scenario, one of the glories of that book is its linguistic magic, while Proust structures a world of timelessness—precisely what movies do not do.

Wald is exploiting the superficial raising of the mass level of taste. This itch for identifying with high culture has become so strong that movies must now offer more than simply soap opera or "B" content. The trouble is that American movies never did have a literary tradition and are now bound to become even more unidentifiable than ever before.

Conceivably, this new trend has been influenced by foreign movies—particularly the French New Wave. Befitting the French and their culture, their literary movies are quite authentic. *Hiroshima Mon Amour* is a work of art, scripted by an extremely literary person, Marguerite Duras, and directed by Alain Resnais, a man heavily influenced by classical French literature (and I might add, by American westerns and gangster films). French movie critics have written extensively in the past few years about the *caméra-stylo*, namely, that literature is written with the pen, and movies therefore must be written with the camera. Happily, this has resulted in quite a few extraordinary French films.

Movie influences have become topsy-turvy. The French adore Howard Hawks's westerns and suspense films, almost anything by John Ford (a decidedly nonliterary director), and a spate of lesser-known directors, whose movies break on the RKO and Loew's circuits, like Nicholas Ray, Samuel Fuller, Joseph Losey, etc. As I understand it, the Cinémathèque Française in Paris owns more copies of American westerns and gangster films than the Museum of Modern Art, and for the equivalent of a quarter you might see three of these films a night at the Cinémathèque.

While we Americans admire international literary films—Bergman, Dreyer, Bresson, and Kurosawa—Dreyer admires *Suddenly, Last Summer*, and Bergman would like to try some Faulkner. The Japanese also like Faulkner but are adept at the supercolossal western. The English, good at dry comedy, are positively gone on the Marx Brothers. In fact, there was a movie house in the suburbs of London devoted exclusively to the films of the Marx Brothers.

What are some of the problems in making movies today? First and foremost, like it or not, it's money. In 1958, Orson Welles, embarking on *Touch of Evil*, remarked that unlike a typewriter, which needs only paper, a film requires much equipment and many technicians, and a filmmaker can never afford to foot that bill on their own. Money at one time was centralized in a few hands—the large studios—and in order to make a film, one simply had to accept the relationship between employer and employee, sponsor and creator. One went to work at a large studio and zeroed in on one's talents. Most directors weren't pleased by this, but at least it had the virtue of extreme definition. Beyond it being an era of good moviemaking, we wound up with lots of funny studio jokes about all the gauche money men and phony artists. Today, movie money is decentralized.

The illusion has been created that all one must do these days is find (a) a script, (b) a star, and (c) a name director, and somebody will put up the money. So many films were made this way in the past, one would think that we have here, as newspaper fictions would have it, a healthy independent production era. Wrong. The fallacy of this illusion is that the independents are infinitely more commercial than the old studio setup, simply because they have only one or at best two chances to succeed at the box office and are forced to play their aesthetic shots much cozier.

A second problem is again an old one: the studios in the thirties and forties were run like authoritarian states, whereby the head posed as a benevolent dictator. Those who accepted corruption profited, and those who bucked the system were either crushed or compromised. The talents who thrived were paid handsomely for their work—their values and commitments were essentially elsewhere—like Faulkner, Ben Hecht, Donald Ogden Stewart, etc., men who worked in Hollywood strictly for money in the way that a serious actor or director today will do freelance chores for an advertising agency or radio soap opera to gain their keep.

With the breakup of this authoritarian state of Hollywood into clusters of independent units all over the world, power has shifted, and nobody seems to know quite where it is. Almost anybody with access to large sums of money or talent can now make a movie. Many films are made anonymously and then sold to large distributors who tack on their studio colophons in the opening frames. The end result: movies as anonymous as their makers. Once, in three seconds you could identify an old Warner Brothers musical of the thirties (Busby Berkeley) or a Paramount comedy (Lubitsch, the Marx Brothers) or a Columbia comedy (Capra, screenwriter Sidney Buchman), but I defy anyone to identify anything that makes today's movie special, unique, or even marvelously vulgar (such as *Gold Diggers of 1933*).

What has happened is that the new filmmakers, by and large, are terribly young, serious, and aggressive and hope to make big names for themselves in the pantheon of movie art. They may know a lot about cameras and deep-focus photography and wide-angle lenses and handheld shooting, yet lack a sense of humor and perspective. They can't afford such things because their risk is too big.

■ ■ ■

At the New Yorker, I played *Sunset Boulevard*, one of the really good serious movies to come out of Hollywood with tragic themes and symbolic notations on America. Gloria Swanson came to see it, and we chatted a while. Having been awed by her performance in the picture, I began asking her serious questions about how Wilder directed her and playing with Stroheim. She laughed at my seriousness, thought there was even something grotesque about it, since all she could remember were the gags and pranks Wilder pulled off while shooting the film—even that last scene, one of the great moments in filmmaking, when she descends the stairway with indescribable magic and lunacy, with Stroheim crying (and she too seemed to be truly crying from within).

With regard to this scene, Miss Swanson said: "Oh yes, we had lots of fun doing that one. Someday I'll tell you what Wilder actually did." She began laughing; of course there was some vast private joke behind that great scene.

■ ■ ■

There is less humor and wit in today's movies and less cooperation on the set. This is visible in today's product: crazy tensions, intentionally sick subjects, tortured faces. The next time you go to a movie, take note of this. Just as our age has produced a spirit of pettiness and crankiness and mindlessness, this is reflected in our films. Much of it, I believe, stems from the collective movie apparatus gone dead. This brings us to the subject of commitment. I've heard young filmmakers in New York say: "Put something on film—anything. Make a film for $15,000. It doesn't matter how bad it is. A major studio is bound to buy it. They need product. Let's shoot something, boys. We'll make our *good* film afterward with *studio* money."

This is a shallow way to go about making a career in moviemaking. There's no substitute for the hard way, just as there's no substitute in literature for hard thinking. Time was when a director or writer really did start from the bottom, learned every facet of moviemaking through long years of osmosis, study, patience, picking up all the know-how of an artisan. Making movies nowadays seems to have become a kind of game—there's nothing better to do vocationally, so why not a movie? We live in a period of superficial talent, of the man in the street turned movie critic, of shortcuts, of psychopathic impatience, of businessmen playing with the arts.

I don't mean to say that nothing extraordinary can emerge in today's climate and that the past is always better. But before succumbing to the fake uplift in *Variety*, or even the *New York Times*, we must recognize what's happening around us, in both our filmmaking and our pretensions. In addition to some of the physical and industrial problems involved in making films today, there are those of distribution and exhibition.

Once a film is completed, it must go to a distributor, who attempts to place it in an appropriate house—an art house, Broadway, or a circuit break. New York remains the key play town. The opening of a first-run picture is watched like a hawk, and by the time the first week's grosses are reported in *Variety*, decisions have been made throughout the country's exhibition houses as to *whether* the film is to be played, how much money and playing time are to be guaranteed, and roughly when it will circulate.

Once distributors bring over a film, they plan their strategy. First it will be screened for some "key" people simply to get an opinion: a film critic, an old-time movie trade reporter, a big midtown exhibitor, a film enthusiast who occasionally writes a piece for a quarterly. After the first reaction, if a distributor is now convinced that he has a "property," they send out a publicity release stating that they've just acquired such and such a film and then drop a line or two of "copy" value that will gain a newspaper squib.

Time to wait. An exhibitor will call and ask to screen the film. The distributor then "baits" the exhibitor, telling them how everybody else in town is terribly interested in this film, but "since we're such close friends, I'll send a print over so that you can look at it. I'd like to get your opinion, at least." Meanwhile, several exhibitors have had a chance to look at this film. After about a month of playing one off against the other, the distributor tries for the best price and the best house, and a play date is set.

Then follow six weeks of intensive publicity. All those signed stories you see in the Arts section of the *New York Times* are the result of elegant high-pressure publicity and are very valuable, at least the equivalent of about a five-hundred-line ad. The film opens, reviews are published, and the course of the picture runs according to a peculiar combination of critical reviews and some unknown set of factors in the public's taste that make them want to see a film or not.

Exhibitors, to round out the picture, are essentially main-street merchants who try to exhibit "product" that sells. With rare exceptions, they're not in business to satisfy any deep aesthetic need, unless one wishes to apply this need to the ferocious pursuit of money. These facts are plain, even banal, but so pertinent that it's impossible not to mention them.

After artists have finished their work on a movie, it's taken over by a gang of the biggest crooks and dummies in the film system. Here we're in the realm of cutthroat business, and I could spend forty days telling you anecdotes about the forty thieves of this world. Distributors market films out of leather kits, and exhibitors book films on the basis of first-run grosses. If a film dies in its first run, it almost never gets a chance to be seen elsewhere in the country.

New York is, of course, the key spot. When there were roughly twelve first-run art houses in New York, a distributor picked from among hundreds, perhaps thousands, of films made throughout the world. Now, through the laws of chance, art houses do play some of the best films made these days, but within their own world they've created a pattern of what makes a movie commercial that would positively awe the RKO and Loew's circuits. In the fifties and sixties, you were literally as good or bad as the box office figures of your last Ingmar Bergman movie.

Occasionally, something risky was tried, like *Pather Panchali*, where we're blessed with the work of one of the leading filmmakers in the world. It took quite a while, however, before this movie could find a house. The same applied with Antonioni's *Il Grido*, which had been lying on a distributor's shelf in New York for roughly five years. Why? Because the movie was too risky commercially for a first-run exhibitor, and if someone should come along like myself who'd like to play it, the distributor had some money fantasy that could only be fulfilled by government subsidy or a tax-losing millionaire. Meanwhile, the movies of Antonioni—easily one of the most fascinating, important, and great filmmakers of our time—played all over Europe while we had yet to see one in America.

Strangely, all the power to see or not to see a particular movie is in New York art houses, and the rest of the country is in the hands of less than half a dozen individuals. The public, even trade people, don't know this, but it's a fact. A new director, who may very well be a genius, plans and plots his work for as much as ten years before it's put into the can, then has no guarantee whatsoever that it will even be seen by anybody. Now there's something wrong with a system that permits such prohibition and inhibition.

This aspect of moviemaking has much to do with the kinds of movies being made. For example, nobody in his right filmic mind would attempt a modest newspaper satire like *Blessed Event* or a Dadaistic anything-goes comedy like *A Night at the Opera*. The closer a director gets to knowing the ins and outs of the movie world today—and they must, if only to be up on practical matters—the more difficult it becomes to want to make the kind of movie that has always been the glory of moviemaking. At my New Yorker Theater, when I played films of the thirties and forties, I wish you could have seen the response of sheer delight from the audience. I know of few contemporary films with the power to do this.

To Have and Have Not, The Maltese Falcon, Gold Diggers of 1933, The Treasure of the Sierra Madre, the original *A Star Is Born*, and *Never Give a Sucker an Even Break* are movies working the authentic American idiom of wiseguyism, hallucination, the bad-good girl casting her slinky charms on the good-good guy. Rarely will you find their equal today for sheer filmic pleasure and insight into our mores. Perhaps the last movie made in a comparable genre was *Beat the Devil,* but many years have passed since.

What has happened is that the old masters have dried up and the avant-garde—which has every loyal and true feeling about the sense of revolt—has little to work with. Or having much to work with, has nothing that gains response. (In passing, we note that the avant-garde of today is acceptable in Larchmont and Brookline.) Movies are quite different from literature or painting in the sense of avant-garde acceptance. It takes about twenty to thirty years to catch on to an important writer, whereas in movies, the foundation of which is publicity, it may take three to five years to promote an avant-garde work, real or fake. Painting may take even less time; witness the title of the idea behind Harold Rosenberg's book on painting and the arts, *The Tradition of the New.*

■ ■ ■

One point about movies is so obviously before our noses, we almost always overlook it when introducing aesthetics. Not only is film an extraordinarily expensive form of expression, but so many livelihoods depend on it: from those of the grandiose producers and distributors to the less grandiose high-paid union men and directors to the exhibitors. We must go back to Egypt, the Middle Ages, and the Renaissance to realize the comparable energy expended and cost of producing pyramids, cloisters, and vast cathedral murals. How vulgar a movie must seem next to these revered objects—but in centuries to come I'm sure movies will be compared in the ever-shifting context of history to these past achievements. A movie says as much about our period as those other artifacts say about theirs. Imagine, Clark Gable and Marilyn Monroe will be our representative historical figures!

■ ■ ■

There's something extremely unhealthy about adopting an overly serious aesthetic about moviegoing; we watch for elementary pleasures. Yet there's something equally unhealthy about encouraging filmmakers to go on with their imitations of imitations, their preoccupations with morbidity and popular psychologizing.

I've no notion what can be done about changing these patterns. Perhaps the best we can do is to recognize the forces behind contemporary film and react accordingly at the box office. This cannot be forced: we either go or don't go to a theater; there's tremendous capriciousness in that.

I have no fear that good movies will die or no longer be made. There's obviously a huge audience for them. But our culture must change. We must somehow crash through the infinite boredom that plagues our society and hope that perhaps one or two or more astonishing young artists will break through this complex world of moviemaking to inspire the witty and meaningful works we genuinely desire.

Just as our culture inspires our movies, so our movies reflect our culture. It usually takes a long period of deprivation and suffering of one kind or another before significant work emerges. Just as we were great during and shortly after the Depression, and just as the Poles in the sixties were turning out one tremendous movie after another after all those horrible years, so we may very well be on our way to beating this boredom around us—if we have the spirit, energy, and brains do something about it.

If only we could utilize that marvelous human faculty for being terribly funny, very warm, and nothing short of very bright, and finally have enough courage and anarchy to wreck Hollywood and all the pretenders who talk art out of one side of the mouth and money out of the other. This may very well lead to making movies on the cheap and exhibiting them in little communities and cultural enclaves operated on shoestrings throughout the country.

When Bernardo Bertolucci was asked in 1966 whether artists always put themselves in their work, he responded by quoting an author he didn't identify: "We work in the dark—we do what we can—we give what we have. Our doubt is our passion, and our passion is our task. The rest is the madness of art." These words were spoken by a novelist to a young admirer in Henry James's short story "The Middle Years." What makes Bertolucci's memory of them more touching is his having omitted what the novelist had said right before: "A second chance—that's the delusion. There never was to be one."

Saint Augustine, when asked where time came from, said, "It came out of the future which didn't exist yet, into the present that had no duration, and went into the past which had ceased to exist. I don't know that we can understand time any more than a child."

DEATH EQUALS FREEDOM

What is it like to learn that we have cancer? That we'll die within a year? Does this awful knowledge provoke acts of terror, beauty, courage? Do we discover the unalterable truth that we've taken too much for granted in our lives? Do we find ourselves, in these petty, narrowing times, paying more attention to boring, meaningless work and enslaving compulsions than to the endless El Dorados of creative energy within ourselves that beg to be discovered and tapped for the good of self and society?

What does it really mean *to live*? Is life, roughly speaking, more natural (in the brute, animal sense) than spiritual? And if we *know* that the life of man is inherently more spiritual than natural, why *don't* we spring our traps and exploit the infinite freedoms of an unfettered spirit?

When these philosophic considerations show up in a movie we must, as a rule, exercise caution, if not downright suspicion, in our appraisal, inasmuch as they require the tool of closely reasoned words. Yet, upon rare occasions there are films—like *Umberto D., Bicycle Thief, Grand Illusion,* and *Citizen Kane*—that transcend visual imagery and tell us something about life that, to paraphrase Stefan Zweig, increases the measure of truth in the universe.

From Japan came a film that has to do with these very things: *Ikiru* (literally, in Japanese, "to live") by Akira Kurosawa (creator of *Rashomon, Drunken Angel,* and *The Men Who Tread on the Tiger's Tail,* among others). This great Japanese film was made in 1952 but is just as vital today.

The story concerns an old man who, though told by a doctor that he has an ulcer, knows intuitively that he has stomach cancer. The knowledge shatters him. He hides it from his son and daughter-in-law and his associates at the Citizens Section of City Hall, of which he is the chief. He feigns going to work every morning and wanders around the city in a state of shock. One night he meets a "writer of trashy novels" and tells him about the cancer, and at the writer's suggestion, they decide to paint the town red. They wander from bar to bar, dance hall to dance hall, watch a strip act, pick up two prostitutes. At the end of this pleasure binge, the usual letdown occurs.

A few weeks later, a young girl who works in his office comes to his home to get him to sign her resignation. He induces her to spend her free time with him. They go out for dinner every night, listen to music, and walk around. It is not a romance: he simply wishes to *be* in the company of a youthful girl. The gossip at his home and office is that he is having a shameful affair. By now he has come to terms with his situation and, desiring to spend his remaining months in the creation of something meaningful, he returns to his office. Through patience, perseverance, and a sustained hacking away at the dense bureaucratic jungle of City Hall, he fathers a playground for children. We see him swinging back and forth in that very place he has created, his expression luminous.

It's at his wake that the glory of this man and the smallness and meanness of those around him are revealed, through a series of arresting flashbacks. The son and daughter-in-law were concerned only with getting the old man's money and considered him selfish for spending it on the young girl. Of course, not only does he leave sufficient money for them to buy a new house, but it comes out that he had worked for thirty years in a stifling job *only* because he wanted to provide a better life for his son, whom he adored. As for the playground, the unctuous City Hall officials at the wake each try to claim credit in the eyes of the press and among themselves. The truth, abetted by alcohol and an official who knows the inside story, finally emerges.

The film is constructed on two major pinwheels of flashbacks, with frenzied cutting in each one. They build swiftly and consecutively into one image: the haunting, wracked, life-thirsting face of Watanabe-san (played superbly by Takashi Shimura, who will be remembered for his role as the woodcutter in *Rashomon*). This man's face is saying: I know I am going to die and therefore I feel life—pulsating life—in everything, every second, everywhere!

The magnificence of this film is in its totally unvarnished image of the physical sensation of being. Given a cancer victim as the core of a story, how easily it could have lapsed into the sheerest soap opera. But as you follow Watanabe-san's nightmare voyage, you feel you are in the presence of an indestructible human being. He refuses to submit to death; he makes a worship of his remaining days on earth—indeed, it is the notion of death on his doorstep that brings him the first full bucket of freedom he has ever dipped into.

Everything the hero does is inspired by the urgencies of life: when told by a cancer patient what the painful symptoms are, Watanabe-san groans maniacally in protest; the clang of an alarm clock, which reminds him of the passage of time, sends him diving under the bedcovers in retreat; the loss of his hat makes him fly after it in a thick crowd; and after being mired in a red-taped City Hall, whose sole function, it appears, is to keep anything from happening anywhere, he pursues city officials like a man possessed to bring about the playground project. His life is so enhanced by senses of purpose that the irony of his situation is tripled.

The imagery is as vivid as the idea of this film, particularly in the final flashback sequence. As the hero's last days at City Hall are reconstructed by the officials at the wake, the scene shifts frantically between Watanabe-san scurrying about the halls and the officials laughing and then crying out of guilt. The drunker they become, the more avid the hero (in flashback) appears. The camera—restless as a wild stallion—seems to have been taken over by Watanabe-san himself. But within this restlessness, there is restraint, contrast, and a sense of the divinely delicate.

Beyond this are sharp glimpses of postwar disillusion and despair in Japan. Some of the young people are portrayed as cynical, interested only in money and a plodding security; others go in for kicks of various kinds—booze, girls, crowd milling—in a state of utter confusion and stupor; the petty bureaucrats sit at long tables buried under tons of documents, sunk forever in the apathy of the clerk's world; and what could be more pathetic than a bunch of mediocre officials clamoring for a little attention and credit?

The U.S. Customs authorities delayed the importation of this picture on the ground that one sequence is obscene.

TAKE TO THE STREETS

1968: Outside our movie theater was Reality and interminable wars. Student uprisings were just a few subway stops away at Columbia University, as at the Sorbonne; there were antiwar demonstrations in Central Park, candlelight marches on the Upper West Side, brutal police intervention, and assassinations.

Inside, we were showing *Nixon's Checkers Speech*, Joseph Strick's *Interviews with My Lai Veterans*, Haskell Wexler and Saul Landau's *An Interview with Salvador Allende* and *Brazil: A Report on Torture*, Chris Marker's *Cuba: Battle of the 10,000,000*, Saul Landau's *Fidel*, and *Far from Vietnam* (by six revolutionary filmmakers, including Jean-Luc Godard and Agnès Varda, who demonstrate their contempt for the Vietnam War)—all distributed by New Yorker Films.

■ ■ ■

May is the month of hormone changes. These past few years, April has not been quite as cruel as the poet said it would be. Weather patterns changed, perhaps due to the radiation in the air, or the interest among the young in astrology and Jesus. Or conceivably a new psychic imbalance brought on by the numbness of deodorant commercials spliced onto air raids over foreign land. The new twists of time have altered the classic month of April, a month hitherto belonging to ritual human change. We make do with May. But the hormones are more nervous than ever. Paranoia has become calcified, if not pleasurable. Spengler has replaced *Reader's Digest*. Nova Scotia, Bahia beckon.

It feels apparent that we are on two roads: extermination within a month, or the end of what is commonly known as the social order. We hear this talk endlessly, daily, in those split human moments of the day when the soul goes oceanic and the pencils of compulsion can no longer write the stuff of our daily bread. Years ago, when many of us were more active in antiwar efforts, it was suggested by some smart one that the way to stop the bloody game was to "hit in the money," a massive economic boycott. There were no takers. Perhaps we should look into it now. Nothing else is working. Our imaginations are on death row.

May is a month of promise. Economic suffering is nothing compared to the mawlike onset of Zombielife. So why not start with a day off? Wouldn't it be nice to be out in the streets, all of us, talking to one another, *homo ludens*, the way they did in Paris in 1968?

Maybe one day will slide into a second day. And if the conversation is interesting, we'll have a week's vacation that our boss didn't count on. Can you imagine a second week with almost every shop in the land shut down? Okay! We may lose our jobs if we ever return, but we will still have our lives. Language, sequence, logic—to say nothing of the tatters of our humanity—drip down the face of our being every time the president speaks. To Moloch, we say: Strike! Strike! Strike!

PART 10

PORTRAITS

PETE MARTIN AND THE
NEW YORKER BOOKSHOP

I met Pete Martin back in 1954 when I was an editor at Avon Books. Pete was doing freelance editing for a publisher of sex magazines, which were beginning to flourish at New York newsstands. Prior to coming to New York, he'd been partners with Lawrence Ferlinghetti at San Francisco's internationally famous City Lights bookstore. He was also editing a magazine called *City Lights*. The story goes—possibly apocryphal— that one day he got into a tumultuous argument with Ferlinghetti and said: "I can't work with you anymore! I want out! Buy my 50 percent interest in the store! I can't stand it anymore. Give me a dollar, and I'm off like a bat out of hell!" And for one buck, he sold his interest. Who knows? It's possible that the store was deep in debt and that Pete was on the hook for a large bundle of money. Getting relieved of his 50 percent share of the debt for one dollar was, at the time, seemingly a bargain. He continued to edit *City Lights* for a brief while, until it folded. The magazine published articles by Manny Farber, Willie Poster, Barbara Deming, Parker Tyler, and others on the popular arts in America: movies, comic strips, cabaret comedy, theater, and lowbrow journalism.

Pete had recently married Madeleine Doubleday, a scion of the illustrious publishing family. She was not rich but was left a trust fund that threw off enough income for the two of them to live comfortably. They came to New York shortly after Pete's fight with Ferlinghetti.

They took an apartment on Gramercy Park in the same building where Nell Blaine lived. Nell was on the verge of becoming a famous painter—this was years before she was stricken with polio. By then Pete and Madeleine were heavy drinkers, not full-blown alcoholics but close to it. To assure that their money due the landlord was sent and not pissed away in drink, they paid their rent quarterly in advance.

It was in this period when I met Pete that I developed a fondness for alcohol. I first got caught up in drinking when I was an eighteen-year-old soldier during infantry training at Fort Wheeler in Macon, Georgia. The drinking then was mainly beer. Not to drink with your buddies on a night on the town was a show of weakness, an invitation to be known as a sissy. When I got out of the army, I had no interest in alcohol. I went back to school and had a normal regimen. It was when I got into book publishing, enjoying the martini-lunch brigade, that I entered a new period of drinking, this one considerably heavier than when I was in the army. Yet I was by no means a heavy drinker. It was all peer drinking, and I never drank alone. So, in the beginning of our friendship, Pete and I used to go to bars at night, where we drank and talked. I could never keep up with the vast amounts of alcohol he put away. Drinking one-fifth of what he had was enough to make me drunk.

Toby and I became good friends with Pete and Madeleine and would see them on and off over the years. Pete was the son of Carlo Tresca, a socialist anarchist leader of the 1930s. Pete had in his apartment a large photo of a few hundred workers on strike gathered around his father while he was playing cards on a wooden crate. Apparently Pete was raised by a series of women who were living with Tresca over the years. He grew up in the lap of left-wing militancy. His aunt was Elizabeth Gurley Flynn, a prominent member of the Communist Party. While Pete was always a little left of center, he was leery and suspicious of all the different radical left movements, including the New Left of the 1960s, which drew his sarcasm, as if it were a fake knockoff of the more serious left movement of the thirties and forties.

Pete inherited $10,000 from his aunt Elizabeth. He called to say that he was ready to open a bookstore with me—a project we'd often talked about. A few weeks later, I received a postcard from him from Moscow. He'd decided to go there at the urging of some of his aunt's friends, dedicated communists, who'd assured him that he would get the red-carpet treatment. He hung out there for a few months, on the drink with his new joyous-drinking Russian friends. Then he blew all of his inheritance, with just enough to make it back to New York.

Sometime later, in 1965, my friend Austin Laber—a lawyer who ran for Congress on a Democratic liberal ticket on the Upper West Side of Manhattan, and a very entrepreneurial fellow (a career that included real estate developing, hotels, variety stores)—and I formed a group of investors and we bought a taxpayer building on Broadway and Eighty-Ninth Street. It included the New Yorker Theater, a beauty parlor, a butcher (Joe Rosen), a luggage store (Sam Finkelstein, cigar perched in his mouth at all times), a dress shop, Benny's corner luncheonette, and a small tailor shop (Sol). On the second floor was Lynn Olivia's jazz studio, where the greats practiced: Dizzy Gillespie, Bob Brookmeyer, Zoot Sims. Next door to the studio was the office of New Yorker Films—two small rooms in which five people worked, including Toby and me. The building shook all day long from the jumping jazz studio.

Shortly after buying the real estate, I got in touch with Pete, whom I hadn't seen for a while, and proposed that we open that bookstore on our property. Austin Laber, ever ready to invest in whatever, agreed to help finance the store.

Pete immediately liked the idea. He was at loose ends, not engaged in editing or anything other than guzzling away. Sol the tailor's lease was up, and he decided to retire, so his shop was available.

It was a hole in the wall next to Benny's and became the entrance to a vacant space on the second floor. In the storefront, we installed popular magazine and newspaper racks and a cashier. We broke through the ceiling and built a staircase, which led to the bookstore: a generous space with large windows overlooking Broadway and Eighty-Ninth Street.

Our deal with Pete was simple. Austin and I put up 100 percent of the money. We gave Pete a decent salary for operating the bookstore and split profits and equity on a one-third basis. Effectively, we put Pete into business without him having to invest a dime. His investment was his body, his brains, his expertise, and an incredible imagination.

We hired Manny Farber to build the bookshelves. For many years Manny had earned his livelihood as a carpenter since he was unable to support his family on his film writing. He wrote only for serious magazines, which paid contributors a pittance. To pay the rent, he had to hustle. At the time he was building these shelves, bookstalls, and tables, both his wife and John Law were after him for money—alimony and parking tickets. For several months, to escape them, he slept at night in the store in a sleeping bag. Nobody except us knew of his whereabouts, sworn to secrecy.

Eventually Manny got a divorce and settled with his wife. As for the hundreds of parking tickets, he dealt with this by skipping town. He found love with a young woman, Patricia Patterson, and ultimately they headed west, from where he originated, settling down at the University of California in San Diego, where he gave courses on film aesthetics, occasionally writing pieces and painting. Over the years, Manny booked many of the films for his classes from the New Yorker Films library; the ones most requested were by Danièle Huillet and Jean-Marie Straub!

■ ■ ■

We had a party at the bookstore the night before opening. With glasses in hand, we roamed the store, stocking books in the peculiarly angled bookshelves built by Manny, proven incapable of doing anything straight on. He saw things and led his life in angled ways.

Pete instructed us as to where to put books on the shelves. He had his own system of sections, unlike those ever known in any other bookstore. Only he knew where every book was shelved.

"Pete, where do you want the book on JFK's assassination?" I asked.

"Put it in science fiction," he riposted in his drunken, raspy voice. He laid out all the magazines on a rickety bookstand, already on the verge of collapse, as Manny had neglected to attach angle irons as reinforcements. Pete's originality in stacking magazines was symbolized by putting *Commentary* next to *Mad* magazine, suggesting that *Mad*'s loony Alfred E. Neuman reminded him of Norman Podhoretz, editor-in-chief of *Commentary*. Pete had a large section on Black history, fiction, and sociology, possibly the first bookstore run by a white man that did so—in line with the period's emerging civil rights revolution. Aside from the normal inventory of classical and modern fiction, and topical works on current affairs, philosophy, sociology, and Marxist literature, Pete also stocked a large section of detective and espionage books. And on the magazine stand were the *Nation*, the *New Republic*, *Partisan Review*, *Granta*, *Kenyon Review*, and the *Sewanee Review*.

The store had a distinguished clientele. Isaac Bashevis Singer, who lived in the Belnord on Broadway and Eighty-Sixth Street, came by every morning for his *Daily Forward*. Alfred Kazin, Irving Howe, Richard Elman, and Jules Feiffer, as well as various book and magazine editors, were among the store's regular customers. The shop's unique spin and cachet spread around town, attracting writers from all over.

The New Yorker Bookshop was a financial disaster. Pete ran it intuitively, breaking all the financial rules needed in order to run a successful independent bookstore. He ordered books whimsically; they remained on the shelves for years.

Pete was in the store six days a week. Madeleine came in the afternoons and helped out. Pete's staff consisted of young hippies with sandals, torn clothing, and long hair rubber-banded in ponytails. After the first year, he spent more time at Wilby's Bar (a steakhouse on Broadway between Ninetieth and Ninety-First streets, a few doors down from Murray's Appetizing Store), dropping over for a few snorts while his hippie help—enlarged to compensate for Pete's absence—moved busy fingers in the cash drawers.

Pete disliked Austin Laber from the start. Austin, a control freak, went bananas over the way Pete operated the store. In turn, Pete regarded Austin as an establishment square. They had considerable difficulty communicating with each other. Pete, who always wore a navy-blue suit, a solid tie, and a dark checkered shirt, put an index card in his jacket pocket that read: GET AUSTIN OUT. Clearly, I had to intercede.

A few weeks after the store opened, I proposed that Austin and I give Pete as much time as he needed to pay us back, interest free, the money we'd invested. Pete thereby would own the store. It was a sort of utopian solution. And—incredibly—it worked. Pete managed to pay us back in one year. Although he was falling behind in his payments to book wholesalers, he nevertheless kept his nose to the grindstone during that first year. Once rid of Austin and me as partners, secure in his relationship with me as his landlord (I being the resident manager of the property), he also started falling behind in his rent. I never reported this to my partners; I was ready to make good if Pete defaulted.

We were friends. We socialized. We had wonderful conversations. Pete was a fabulous conversationalist. Charming, funny, well read, smart—his basic strategy was to knock down pretentiousness wherever he could. He was in the tradition of Dwight Macdonald, the great deflater of baloney.

It was huge fun just being with Pete. As he talked, his fingers, his hands moved around like those of an orchestra conductor. I'm sure this wonderful tic was inherited from his Italian father. As he drank more, his voice got raspier.

Hands flying, and with that fabulous voice—a basso profundo—he invariably gave his friends a one-man show.

After opening the bookstore, he and Madeleine had moved into a two-bedroom apartment in The Normandy, an art deco apartment building on Eighty-Sixth Street and Riverside Drive. Since they lived on an upper floor, Pete installed a high-wire fence around the small terrace's skimpy gate to assure that he and Madeleine wouldn't topple over after polishing off a bottle of hootch.

In less than seven years, Pete was in dire straits. Book publishers and wholesalers withheld book shipments to him until he paid some of the money owed them. It was difficult for him to fulfill individual requests from his customers. He was behind in his payments to Con Ed and New York Telephone. He had trouble scraping up enough cash to pay his thieving help. He was nine months in arrears in his rent.

While this doomsday scenario was unfolding, Pete spent more time at Wilby's. He would return to the store sloshed, holler at the help, and get into fights with customers, accusing them of not knowing anything about literature.

Upset that he couldn't pay the rent, he turned to me for help. I advised him to go into Chapter 11 bankruptcy. I told him to sell some books, marked down, to the public and to other booksellers.

In 1973, I decided to sell the New Yorker Theater, a sale I talked myself into doing because I was beginning to repeat myself, a prospect simply too boring for me to accept. Toby was opposed to the sale. She felt that too much creative energy had gone into this theater to let it go so casually. Years later, I regretted this impulsive decision.

The demise of the theater produced many nostalgic conversations across the Upper West Side and beyond, and again in 1982 when the New Yorker Bookshop closed. It was a sad day for the store's devoted patrons. They had become fans of this idiosyncratic place run by a genuine crank, an eccentric who loved books, ideas, smart talk, laughter.

Fortunately, Pete and Madeleine could survive on her trust income. With the little cash they had left, they put a down payment on a house on Long Island, where they lived for several years. We would see one another whenever they came to the city on a visit. About a year after they moved, I received a check in the mail for the bookstore's rent in arrears. Pete was not legally obliged to do this. For him it was a matter of honor. Had he not paid up, it wouldn't have jeopardized our relationship. I'd already covered the default.

Pete belonged to that rapidly declining race of people with "character." As I write these words, the entire world is infected with savage capitalism. Economic survival is more than ever a function of jungle existence. This statement may sound pompous and self-righteous, but (unhappily) I believe it is true.

PAULINE KAEL

Fueled by Fire

As 1996 drew to a close, Pauline Kael, in her mid-seventies, was living in Stockbridge, Massachusetts, suffering from Parkinson's disease and a weak heart. I called from time to time to check on her health.

She sounded her usual feisty self, with a hint of mellow. "Whoever said that getting older is fun is full of shit. It's no fun at all!" she replied, having recently published her sixth collection of writings.

My first contact with her had been in 1957. When putting together my anthology of writings on film, she was one of the first contributors I contacted. She'd published "Movies, the Desperate Art" in *Partisan Review*. At that time she was living in Berkeley, California, where she programmed and managed the Cinema Guild and Studio, the first twin cinema in America to play serious films from around the world on a fifty-two-week basis. She also wrote the program notes: short brilliant texts on all featured films. These notes, as well as her radio reviews for Pacifica, made it clear that one day she'd pursue a full-time writing career.

Pauline was pleased that I'd contacted her and made a few revisions for my anthology. In her piece, she expressed justifiable despair over the inadequacy of much of film criticism, as well as the downright staleness of Hollywood and many avant-garde filmmakers. In suggesting that today's audience had been conditioned by suave-looking films that would probably have been passed up by the more adult and more discriminating audiences of the twenties and thirties, she hit upon a useful approach for judging movies. She wrote:

The best films of recent years have not been spectacles and they have not been geared to a large audience; they have made more and more demands on concentrated attention. The trained eye of an adult may find magic in the sustained epiphanies of *Day of Wrath*, the intricate cutting and accumulating frenzy of *La Règle du jeu*, the visual chamber drama of *Les Parents Terribles*. American attempts in these directions have met with resistance not only from the public but from American critics as well. The critics' admiration for "action" and the "chase" leads them to praise sleazy suspense films and to fret over whether *A Streetcar Named Desire* or *The Member of the Wedding* is really "cinematic." . . .

Suspense films may reflect modern anxieties but they don't deal with them; the genre offers the spring of tension, the audience recoils. For critics, the suspense film has been a safety valve: they could praise it and know themselves to be in accord both with high "technical" standards and a good-size audience.

But critics have been quick to object to a film with a difficult theme, a small camera range, or a markedly verbal content (they object even when the words are worth listening to). . . .

The integration of meaning and style is almost always the result of the director's imaginative grasp of the story material and control over the production. A great film is one in which the range of meaning is so imaginatively new, compelling, or exciting that we experience a new vision of human experience (*Grand Illusion*).

In 1960, when I began the New Yorker Theater, Pauline was still running her twin cinema in Berkeley. We spoke to each other once a week. I was new at the repertory game, so I studied her bookings and program notes and asked how well certain films were doing and where she was getting her prints. Prints were often hard to unearth. Such was the subject matter of our phone conversations. When showing films of the twenties, thirties, and forties, I was working closely with William K. Everson (who had a library of more than five thousand films, many of which would have been irretrievably lost if he hadn't begged, borrowed, or stolen in order to save them). In due time, as I learned the tricks of the trade, I passed them on to Pauline. Sent her my theater flyers and occasional program notes. Whenever she caught an error—historical or grammatical—I heard from her.

Pauline was born and raised on a farm in California. She drifted to San Francisco, where she hung around painters, filmmakers, writers. Had a brief liaison with James Broughton, the avant-garde filmmaker, from which her daughter, Gina, was born.

Pauline and Gina lived on the margin for many years while Pauline was reading, going to the movies, writing. She was part of a group of San Francisco cinephiles who went to movie houses as if going to church or graduate school. I remember her radio reviews describing the emotional impact of films she and her friends saw. This manner of responding *personally, emotionally,* to a movie was unique, and it became her trademark during her days at the *New Yorker*. She was the first film critic I had come across who responded to movies in this way.

Raising Gina alone, Pauline had serious financial problems. She scraped some money together and for a while opened and ran a laundromat. Then she met and married a well-to-do exhibitor, Edward Landberg, who founded the Cinema Guild and Studio.

Pauline had a house in Berkeley stuffed, I was told, with Tiffany lamps. She was not romantically involved with Landberg; it was a marriage of convenience. He turned over his theaters to Pauline to program and manage. She was not a partner but a salaried employee.

This marriage lasted a few years, until one day they had a dispute over who would run the theater: he or she. As reported in *Variety*, Pauline resigned, and Landberg posted signs in front of the theater saying: "It was not Darryl Zanuck or Louis B. Mayer who started the Cinema Guild. It was Edward Landberg."

Pauline had already been flirting with the notion of coming to New York and writing full time. She'd submitted a few pieces to *McCall's*, which she asked me to read in manuscript to suggest changes. (She was given to randy language.) *McCall's* hired her as a film critic, and Pauline and Gina moved to New York.

She continued to show me her *McCall's* pieces in manuscript. As the months went by, we spent a good deal of time together. We shared a passion for movies and would stay up late drinking and discussing them. In those days, we were both heavy smokers.

Within a year or so, William Shawn offered her a regular slot as film critic at the *New Yorker*, sharing the movie beat with Penelope Gilliatt. From the beginning to the end of her days at the magazine, Pauline wrote as if her life depended upon it, passionate reviews that were fueled by fire.

At first I agreed with her taste, but as the years went by, she became more and more obsessed with the sexual dynamics in films. Her review of Bernardo Bertolucci's *Last Tango in Paris* made Toby and me uncomfortable, as did the film—she compared its showing to the scandalous premiere of Stravinsky's *The Rite of Spring*.

We saw it again a week later to confirm our initial displeasure, and try as we did, found little to recommend it. Pauline's review was grandiose, if not grotesque, almost like a front-page headline. I don't recall how other critics responded to her outrageous review. I saw the film again twenty years later, and it crumbled before my eyes: an indulgent, adolescent male fantasy about outré sexuality.

Years later she moved to the house in Massachusetts. Since Pauline didn't drive, her daughter would ferry her every Tuesday to Pittsfield, where she took a train to New York. There she organized film screenings back to back, then went home and wrote her reviews in the country.

She had many quarrels with *New Yorker* editor William Shawn over the use of what he regarded as dirty language. He'd never allow her to use the word "shit," certainly not "fuck." Shawn was old-fashioned; a prim, correct man, a great editor who loved the English language and doted on his writers. Pauline made him nervous, but he respected her.

There was one serious controversy between Pauline and myself: she came out flat against Claude Lanzmann's *Shoah*. In a blistering attack on the film in the *New Yorker*, she criticized the way it was made and what she perceived to be bias and distortion by Lanzmann. It was the only negative review of the film that I can remember, shocking and totally nonsensical. Her negative review had less to do with the film as a work of "artistic" documentary filmmaking than with Pauline's reservations about her own Jewishness, with which she obviously felt uncomfortable.

The review made me angry, and I wrote a response to her piece that I sent to Shawn, with a copy to Pauline. Shawn phoned me and said that while he was in total disagreement with Pauline's piece, he never published letters in response to articles in the magazine. I subsequently learned that this was the only time during his tenure as editor-in-chief of the magazine that he had been seriously considering *not* publishing an article by one of his weekly contributors. I also sent my letter to Irving Howe at *Dissent* and to a few other magazines, and for whatever reason, everybody turned it down. I didn't speak to Pauline for a year. Not long after, we made our peace.

LETTER IN RESPONSE TO PAULINE KAEL'S REVIEW IN THE *NEW YORKER* ON *SHOAH*

January 3, 1986

Pauline Kael
THE NEW YORKER
25 West 43rd Street
New York, NY 10036

Dear Pauline:

What is so troublesome about your piece on *Shoah* is its wrongheadedness. Yes, it is criticism in your usually crisp style, with all the personal touches and closely reasoned arguments. But you're using your considerable equipment on an extraordinary movie that will not go away so easily, that in fact will in my opinion surely go down large in the history books. There are not many precedents for *Shoah*'s kind of moviemaking. Marcel Ophuls is indeed correct when he writes in *American Film* that the film is "the greatest documentary about contemporary history ever made, bar none, and by far the greatest film I've ever seen about the Holocaust."

I'm upset about how *unmoved* you represent yourself in the face of such emotionally disturbing testimony in the movie. You write: "I found 'Shoah' logy and exhausting *right from the start*, and when it had been going on for an hour or longer, I was *squirming* restlessly, my attention slackening" (my italics). It would be arrogant of me to suggest how you should react to a movie. Still and all, I simply cannot understand how you were unable to respond *in some way* and even failed to write about survivor Simon Srebnik's visit, for the first time in over thirty years to Chelmno, where 400,000 Jews were murdered. His account of what happened at Chelmno in the 1940s is truly one of the most moving episodes ever put on film. This scene occurs at the beginning of the film. Minutes later, Mordechai Podchlebnik, the second survivor of Chelmno (out of 400,000 only these two people survived, a fact in itself which is overwhelming in its emotional dimension) recounts in very poetic Yiddish how he placed his wife and children in the grave at Chelmno and then asked to be killed. The Germans kept him alive; they said he was strong enough to work. He is crying as he tells this tragic epic.

How is it possible not to respond deeply—Jew or Gentile—to all this? And indeed, these two episodes are only a handful out of so many stirring accounts in the film.

Those coming to see this film are not film buffs or general audiences who go weekly to see the latest Hollywood fluff or the new "art" movie. It is the peculiar irony of your article that you are addressing your remarks to *your reader* who, to a certain extent, would not be interested in seeing *Shoah*. It's as if you are exhorting some potential buyers to be wary of the merchandise, when in fact *this* merchandise will not interest all your buyers. The audience, then, is atypical. It has been consisting of middle-aged and older Jews, many of whom haven't been to the movies for as long as twenty years. There are also younger, intellectually curious people. And, finally, a sprinkling of survivors, their children and relatives, as well as very religious Jews. Younger people and more Gentiles are beginning to come as word of the power of this movie spreads. For the first month of the run I monitored audience reaction daily. It was extraordinary to witness how visibly moved these people seemed to be. On opening day, a Rabbi and his wife travel fifty miles from a small town in New Jersey to see the film. At the end of the film, after the audience emptied out, the Rabbi wandered back into the auditorium and, alone, he prayed and made blessings.

I find it so irreverent for you to write: " . . . sitting in a theatre seat for a film as full of dead spaces as this one seems to me a form of self-punishment. A large proportion of the audience may agree: Part I plays in a crowded theatre; only a handful of people attend Part II." As the film's distributor and exhibitor, I have the figures and I can verify that at least 40 percent of those who saw Part I are seeing Part II, certainly not a "handful." As the weeks go on, the audience for Part II keeps growing. People do have busy schedules, and many are coming from great distances. I fully expect, in time, that a majority of those attending Part I will catch up with Part II.

Those who come are eager to learn a *history lesson*. You have to watch and listen carefully to what's being shown and said—not with the film aesthetician's bag of tricks but with the humanist's sense of curiosity and humility. Kitsch, like *Genocide* or the TV series *Holocaust*, uses music, stentorian voiceover (Orson Welles), and *acting* (disgrace! disgrace!), while *Shoah* is concrete, honest, simple, a Niagara of information, not one frame of manipulation.

Did you learn something? Did you know before seeing the film that children under four rode the death trains free of charge while those under ten went half-fare? And that these trains were booked by German travel agents? And paid for by the proceeds of confiscated Jewish property? That the Jewish workers in the gas chambers were not allowed to use the words "corpse" or "dead bodies" but instead "puppets" and "rags"? Can you imagine a great fiction writer improving upon all this? Don't you at least think that Lanzmann's *selection* of material out of 350 hours of footage he shot is done with the mind and heart of a great artisan, if not an artist? And not, as you reveal, a Doctor of Philosophy? If the *New Criterion* critic erroneously refers to Lanzmann as a "medical doctor," then why do you have to perpetuate the myth that he is a tourist in filmmaking and not "a great movie-maker"? You criticize Lanzmann for wanting to be taken seriously as an artist. What's the point of all this? Why bring someone down to the lower rungs of the artistic ladder? Don't you think at the least that he is entitled to *think* and *feel* that he's an artist? One way or the other, what's so sacrosanct about being an "artist" or a "great movie-maker"? Isn't it the work that matters? Are we going to subject ourselves to all those boring platitudes about Great Art and Great Movies? And why do you speak of "moral blackmail" in his approach? Don't you think that eleven years in the sewer of Holocaust-work is by any stretch of the imagination the deed of a saintly person? Is it more urgent that he be a great moviemaker rather than a humanist teaching us something important without resort to all the guileful tricks of moviemaking?

You write: "Lanzmann is not a stirring interviewer. You don't feel the play of a wide-ranging intelligence in his questioning . . . *Shoah* has nothing resembling the moral questions raised in Marcel Ophuls's *The Sorrow and the Pity* . . . *Shoah* is certainly a vivid presentation of the nuts and bolts— and the hideousness—of genocide." There are indeed no moral issues explored by Lanzmann in the film since this was not his intention. We may have to leave these questions to the philosophers. However, you are on to something else here, but you drop it too quickly. It is precisely these "nuts and bolts" that represent the true meaning and intentions of the film. Lanzmann spins a circular web of information, the totality of which is so powerful that when you piece it together in your mind weeks after seeing the film, it is not possible to remain exactly the same person you were before having seen the film. *This is finally what great art is about.* These are "nuts" and "bolts" engineered by alleged human beings. Contrary to what Hannah Arendt argued in her banality-of-evil thesis, the viewer's imagination inside *Shoah* is constantly inflamed by all the reported incredible acts and happenings. There was nothing banal in the evil that occurred, and for Hannah Arendt to have promoted this false idea is a historical conspiracy against the dignity and heroism of those who survived. When you study the *faces* and *expressions* of the Nazis who are interviewed by Lanzmann, you enter a new realm of drama. These men (except for Franz Suchomel, the former SS Unterscharführer at Treblinka) are lying through their teeth. They have escaped extreme punishment and they are still capable, forty years later, of making fiction out of old reality. At one point, Suchomel contests Lanzmann's statement that 18,000 Jews were "processed" daily on peak days at Treblinka. "No, Mr. Lanzmann," he says, "that's an exaggeration. Believe me. The figure is too high. No more than twelve to fifteen thousand per day. *But we had to spend half the night at it.*" Forty years later these words are spoken. I kept wondering what occurred in Suchomel's daily life in those intervening years. At every turn in the film, my imagination was set ablaze as no other spectacle has ever done before to me. The genius of this film is that it keeps your mind going on all the unanswered questions for months on end. You, in effect, become an accomplice to Lanzmann in his making of the film.

I'm absolutely puzzled when you write: "the whole film can be seen as a Jew's pointing a finger at the Gentile world and crying, 'You lowlifes—you want to kill us!' This is not necessarily an aberrant or irrational notion." On the contrary, it is indeed an irrational notion if you include among "the Gentile world" the hundreds of millions of Catholics, Protestants, Irish, Italians, Brazilians, etc., etc. who were neither Nazi killers nor Ukrainian or Latvian death camp colleagues of the Nazis. Lanzmann did not make a film about "the Gentile world," nor is he "moaning," as you put it. Nor does he mean to be "morally complex," which you accuse him of failing to be. Why are you making such a to-do about Lanzmann's seeming unfairness to Gentiles when in fact he is not at all so. (This is, by the way, not a film about Gentiles vs. Jews.) Did you also want him to interview a gently disposed Gentile manicurist in Warsaw? A Gentile medievalist at the University of Cracow—at the risk of making the film even longer than it is? The Poles interviewed are not all members of "Woody Allen's convention of village idiots." There are at least a half dozen Poles interviewed who are quite sympathetic, including one Polish peasant who spontaneously breaks into tears when recounting how he saw a Nazi shoot a Jewish mother through the heart. The strategy here was simple: to interview only those who had a ringside seat at the death camps. Is there anything inappropriate about this? Furthermore, *Lanzmann didn't tell these Poles what to say*. In fact, I'm told there is at this moment another of those raging anti-Semitic campaigns in Poland as a result of the Government-sponsored television showing of the Polish sections of *Shoah*. Lanzmann has been accused of *bribing* these Poles in the movie to say what they said. Indeed, the village idiots, I'm afraid, may very well constitute a significant slice of Polish life.

Your attack on the film seems to *start off* with a chip on your shoulder. I suspect that you're leery of all the movie reviewers throughout the country who were moved by the movie. You seem to be playing the role of Don Quixote in righting all these wrongs in the cause of defending Great Moviemaking. There is not one false detail in the film, not one false note. The critics around the country are right. I think that you are wrong. You're often on target but some forces outside of film criticism prevented you from experiencing this work in a whole way.

Cordially,
Daniel Talbot
cc: Mr. William Shawn

VINCENT CANBY

With Brains and Heart

Vincent Canby was writing stories and reviews for *Variety* while I was running the New Yorker Theater. One day he phoned and invited me to lunch at the Algonquin Hotel, which was around the corner from *Variety*.

He was wearing a buff-colored tweed jacket with hints of orange and violet, a white button-down Oxford shirt, and a rep tie—a costume I got accustomed to seeing him in over the years. Of medium height, with thin, warm, inquisitive eyes, sandy-haired, he struck me as someone who could have taught Latin at an Ivy League university.

His purpose of the luncheon was to find out what I was up to in my strange new theater. It never occurred to me that I was being interviewed for a story. He took no notes. We chatted about movies, personalities, the state of the industry, the importance of the Upper West Side Thalia theater in our movie lives.

I filled his ears with stories of the people who hung out around our theater: drug addicts, hookers, rough lowlifes rubbing elbows with writers, artists, elderly European refugees, some of them Holocaust survivors, some so elegantly described by Saul Bellow in *Herzog* and *Mr. Sammler's Planet*.

The next issue of *Variety* had a story by Vincent about the New Yorker Theater. It included many quotes of things I'd said, and they were pinpoint accurate. It reminds me of a description by Ben Hecht of Lee Garmes, the great cinematographer. Garmes was able to tell the color of someone's cufflinks in a passing car going ninety miles an hour. Vincent had a prodigious memory. He was a master of summarizing a movie.

As the years passed, Vincent reviewed films and wrote thoughtfully about Rohmer, Truffaut, Fellini, Woody Allen, Robert Altman, Bergman, James Ivory, Fassbinder, Juzo Itami, and others. Each film, each review, was like a snapshot in his family album. He wrote from the heart and brain about their work. With generosity, wit, sincerity, wisdom. Vincent's writing presented a wonderful way to follow a director's career.

I remember telling him about my weekly lunches with Irvin Shapiro at the Russian Tea Room. Shapiro had begun his career in movies as manager of the Little Carnegie Theatre on West Fifty-Seventh Street. He was there in 1928 when Carl Theodor Dreyer's *The Passion of Joan of Arc* was a big hit: a ten-week run. Irvin had also imported *Breathless*. Toward the end of his career he operated as a representative for foreign producers, selling their wares to the new high rollers on the block. It was Irvin's job to know whose pockets were flush. His table at the Russian Tea Room was at the entrance, a position that allowed him to jot down in his leather Mark Cross notebook who was coming in. Many of them were marks with fresh bundles of cash, and as Irvin and I dined on sliced salmon, capers, black bread, and vodka, he told me who could expect a phone call from him the next day, and how much of this cash he was going to relieve them of in exchange for the French and Italian movies he represented.

Vincent's response to all this *meshuga* activity was his usual resounding laugh. It was a great treat to hear Vincent laugh.

I kept him up on Ed Harrison's activities. Ed was Satyajit Ray's distributor, and of course Ray was another favorite of Vincent's. I spoke to him of my visits with Jacques Tati in Paris in my attempt to deal with this mercurial fellow to distribute his works here. Also of my adventures with Don Rugoff, the volatile, contentious, but always brilliant head of Rugoff Theatres and Cinema 5, whose reign marked a golden age of movie viewing in New York. And of some of the wise guys in our business who were into tangolike accounting, and of some of the new directors I was excited by: Eustache, Tanner, Fassbinder, Sembène, Kieslowski. Vincent couldn't get enough of this stuff. His curiosity was endless.

■ ■ ■

One day Vincent asked me if I'd heard of any apartments in my neighborhood. Since I knew many building superintendents through the theater, I was able to find him an apartment in short order. So, we became neighbors, and would refer to our quarter as our little Polish village. Surely it was a figment of our celluloid imagination, springing from Polish villages we saw in movies. We frequently bumped into each other at Barzini's, a neighborhood grocery store run by two Iranians.

Vincent and Toby, both good cooks, often discussed recipes and store prices. He knew where to get the best fish, the best artichokes, as well as the best prices on limes and lemons. Quality food and prices were as important to us as the stylishness of a good movie.

We did much of our socializing on these streets. From time to time, we had dinner at each other's apartment. I invited Vincent one evening to our place, along with Andrew Sarris and Molly Haskell. Before dinner we screened a documentary on Billy Wilder by Volker Schlöndorff. Commissioned by German television to make the film, Schlöndorff needed clearance from Wilder to show it in the United States, which Wilder refused to give. It seems that Wilder's wife didn't like one of the scenes, in which her husband was scratching his back with a long ivory backscratcher while yakking away. Schlöndorff asked me to help unblock the film. We were all big fans of Wilder and liked the film enormously. I wrote to Wilder, pleading with him to give the clearance, mentioning that I'd shown the film to Canby, Sarris, and Haskell, all of whom were taken by it and promised to support the film vigorously.

No sale. Never heard from Wilder.

Vincent and I seldom spoke about his reviews, except when I disagreed with him. Always aware of the immense power he wielded as the *New York Times* chief movie critic, I felt constrained by his complicated position. An incredibly modest man, a gentle soul, he never spoke disparagingly about directors, producers, stars. He seemed content—although God knows he was not a simple man—to be a recording angel of movies that touched him deeply, that were simply thrilling, as well as of controversial events in our industry that made headlines.

Vincent reviewed films for the *New York Times* for twenty-seven years. His love of films persisted until the end of his life.

TOSCAN

Gaumont's Wit

In late 1977, I was contacted by Swiss producer Yves Gasser. He told me that I'd be hearing shortly from Daniel Toscan du Plantier, Gaumont's *gérand*, or managing director. It seemed that Gaumont wanted to have a presence in the United States and wanted to work with me as their ally in film distribution. Gasser told Gaumont it was unlikely that I'd want to do this, since I had the reputation of being very independent and insular in my activities.

A film distributor since 1965, I had amassed a library of close to four hundred films—among them the works of Chabrol, Rivette, Resnais, de Antonio, Korty, Marker, Skolimowski, Wajda, and many other auteurs of this period. It was an exciting moment in film history: an explosion of great modern cinema, independently made artistic works not seen since that time. I worked closely with some of the filmmakers, especially Godard, Bertolucci, Sembène, and Tanner. And along came Gaumont, a company with a great history going back to its founder, Léon Gaumont.

Toscan, as he was always known, contacted me in New York. I was instantly charmed by him. Whatever reservations I had about teaming up with a great film company vanished. Subsequently, I met Nicolas Seydoux, the company president, and was impressed by his intelligent grasp of our complex, knotty business. As alluded to earlier, I never regarded "film" as a "business" but rather as a casino.

In short order, we drew up a contract that gave me a sufficient amount of "independence" to satisfy me. The first film that we worked on together was

Claude Goretta's *The Lacemaker*, starring Isabelle Huppert, which we opened at the Cinema Studio. It was Isabelle's first major film.

The film opened softly. So much so that the panic was on. Toscan, Isabelle, and I went the next day to the advertising agency, where we changed the ad campaign. At the same time, we spent more money on ads. It paid off—the film became a hit and launched Isabelle's amazing career.

Gaumont stepped up quality film production under Toscan's guidance. Numerous wonderful films emerged: Maurice Pialat's *Loulou* and *À Nos Amours*, Andrzej Wajda's *Danton*, Robert Bresson's *Lancelot du Lac*, Joseph Losey's *Don Giovanni*, and others.

Gaumont invested in twinning the Cinema Studio, which I had owned for a couple of years, and we became partners in this venture. We now had two screens, and Nicolas came up with the idea of assembling the stores on Broadway between Sixty-Sixth and Sixty-Seventh streets, hoping to find a developer who would put up a tall building with a large cinema complex at the base. I would have an interest in exchange for letting the Cinema Studio give up its lease. I worked with Joe Browdy (a real estate lawyer with Paul, Weiss, Rifkind) in assembling the other parcels on the block. I enlisted my friend Daniel Rose in negotiating to construct a tower building on the block, along with a cinema complex at the base belonging to Gaumont, with some as yet undetermined part of this for myself. Nothing came of it. Rose Associates was asking too much. In the end, Nicolas sold most of the block to ABC Television for a significant sum of money. I received a 10 percent commission for my work.

The next venture was the Lincoln Plaza Cinemas, under a thirty-story building on Broadway and Sixty-Second Street. I got to know the Milstein family, who owned this building. It fell to Howard Milstein to negotiate with me the construction of a triplex in the basement. Initially, I was alone with Howard in financing this proposition. Since I had no experience in the world of New York City construction, with little or no knowledge of cost overruns, I allowed Nicolas, who was eager to be a partner in this venture, to join us. The theater complex was built and opened in April 1981 with Federico Fellini's *City of Women*, Michel Deville's *Le Voyage en Douce*, and Jacques Doillon's *La Drôlesse*. The cinemas became so successful that we built three additional rooms in this complex some years later.

Over the years of our partnership, Toby and I became close friends with Toscan. Several times we stayed with him in his lovely manor home in Ambax, a tiny village in Gascony, not too far from a small village that had a weekly goose auction, setting the worldwide price of goose liver pâté. Irrepressible, charming, witty, passionate; a lover of cinema, life, women; and a stand-up conversationalist, Toscan died of a massive heart attack—far too early at the age of sixty-one—in front of our hotel in Berlin during the film festival. In Paris, a service was held at a grand cathedral, where Nicolas Seydoux was moved to tears.

THE INDOMITABLE LIA VAN LEER

Founder of the Jerusalem Cinematheque

Toby and I met Lia van Leer and her husband Wim in 1974. They were both cinephiles and had cranked up small cinematheques in Haifa and Tel Aviv before building and opening the Jerusalem Cinematheque in 1973. Besides having large vaults where they stored 35mm prints, videos, and tapes, the Jerusalem Cinematheque had theaters showing films 365 days a year with audacious programming. For years, members of the Jerusalem *haredim* leaned on Lia to stop showing films on Friday night and Saturday, for them a religious taboo. Lia did not give one inch.

Born in Romania, Lia came to Israel in 1940 to visit her sister, and when World War II broke out, she remained. Her parents died in a concentration camp. She met and fell in love with Wim van Leer, the scion of a prominent wealthy Dutch family and an astonishing person, given to witty sayings and jokes. Wim had participated in World War II as a British Royal Air Force pilot and spy for the Allies. After the war, he flew a single-engine plane for crop dusting in the United States and engaged in drug rehabilitation work in Israel—often visiting police stations abroad to observe how they handled this problem. He became a prominent journalist and film connoisseur and produced a film by French director Chris Marker. I remember the many conversations about films that both of us championed.

Toby and I were invited to the Jerusalem Cinematheque in 1984. This film palace was a modern sleek white stone building overlooking the walls of the Old City. Lia greeted us at the Mishkenot, a beautiful residence for visiting scholars, appearing with a vast smile and a bag of provisions: milk, eggs, bread, and fruit. In addition to screening halls, the cinematheque houses the Israel

Film Archive, an archive of films from the 1920s to today. The cinematheque programs were—and still are—of the highest standard. They represent a way of studying our film legacy in a world that deems art secondary to moneymaking and technological emptiness.

As an admirer of the Van Leers, I donated over one hundred 35mm prints to their cinematheque, representing the basis of New Yorker Films: Godard, Herzog, Bertolucci, Rocha, Tanner, Sembène, Varda, and many others. The rooms storing their prints had the latest in controlled temperature storage.

We recall those early days of excitement with deep nostalgia. In ongoing years, the four of us went to East Berlin, then under Soviet occupation. On one occasion, the border guards examined every inch of our car for contraband and other hot goods. All was kosher. Our driver, however, apparently didn't have the perfect credentials and was sent back! That left us in the snow to make our way on foot into East Berlin. In those days, the city was sad, grim, with bad food and suspicious "soldiers." We quickly realized how privileged we were in our lofty Western standard of living.

Lia, an engine of energy, was 24/7 with her film activities—raising money to expand the cinematheque, looking for prints, establishing deep relationships with festival directors, film directors, producers, editors, actors, and actresses the world over. On top of this, she organized and ran the Jerusalem Film Festival, an international festival gem. It was a life's work of preserving and showing the best of cinema without borders.

In 2015, while in Berlin, Lia was hospitalized for a kidney ailment. Toby and I were staying at the Hyatt, the same hotel as she, and we'd met for breakfast virtually every morning in the elegant spacious dining room. Although she had already been ailing in Jerusalem, she'd insisted on coming to Berlin. Fortunately, she had a wonderful Argentine attendant. Lia went to screenings every day and then on to parties where she met filmmakers, distributors, actors, and actresses, ever alert to meeting somebody who might make a contribution to the cinematheque or come to Israel with their film for the annual July festival. She wound up in the hospital in Berlin, stayed a week, then returned to Jerusalem, where she died three weeks later.

Lia van Leer was truly one of the outstanding figures in the world of cinema: a memorable woman who yearned for a peaceful solution between Israelis and Palestinians.

KIESLOWSKI, MALLE, AND MASTROIANNI

Three Lives and Three Deaths

When Krzysztof Kieslowski and Louis Malle died just months apart, their deaths created a void. Great artists of their caliber do not grow on trees. Their absence makes our lives emptier. Then, when Marcello (as everyone called him) died in December 1996, less than a year after Kieslowski, it was even more painful. Imagine, never a new Mastroianni film!

I met Kieslowski in 1980 when I invited him to New York from his native Poland to do publicity on *Camera Buff*, his second film. It's about a young man who buys an 8mm camera to film his new baby daughter but gets sidetracked into making a film about his factory's twenty-fifth anniversary. Kieslowski, at the time, spoke no English. I asked Annette Insdorf, who speaks more foreign languages than you can count on your fingers, to interpret. My sense of Kieslowski was that he was a lonely man, cautious in his expectations. It couldn't have been much fun living in Gomulka's and Jaruzelski's Poland, with all those horrible, dreary Stalinist apparatchiks dictating cultural life. You had to work miracles to say what you really wanted to say. Perhaps this accounts for much of the art and craftiness of so many postwar Polish directors.

Kieslowski swooned over classic American movies. It reminded me of de Kooning's remark about why he came to America. "While I was growing up," he said, "I saw a lot of Paramount pictures. I liked the color of the sun in those movies. I knew I had to come eventually to the U.S."

Kieslowski went on to make some of the most remarkable movies of our time. I remember seeing *Dekalog*—two episodes a week—in a Paris movie theater. I'd planned to stay in Paris for only two weeks, but because of him I couldn't leave. Hypnotized by his art, I stayed for another three weeks to see the rest of this majestic work inspired by the Ten Commandments. *Dekalog,* at the time, had only a few showings in the United States. It had become the victim of an absurd plot hatched by a bumbling speculator who'd been trying to peddle the U.S. market for a million dollars. From time to time, this happens in our trade. Once again, the money-art stew. What a drag.

Kieslowski then made his *Red, White,* and *Blue* trilogy. Such beautiful movies! Transcendent, mystical films that will, I'm sure, have a long life—not unlike some of the great Ingmar Bergman films. Worn out, having had heart surgery, Kieslowski eventually announced that he would stop making movies. All he wanted to do was smoke cigarettes and play with his dog in his backyard.

Over the years, since 1981, I often ran into Kieslowski at festivals in Cannes, Berlin, elsewhere. He'd learned English and we spoke about our health, our ageing, the films of other directors. He was chattier yet still cautious. Rarely would he talk of his own films. Turned off journalists who asked him questions about such and such symbols and mysterious scenes in his recent work. Kieslowski knew that powerful art does not lend itself so readily to explanations.

In *Mr. Sammler's Planet* Saul Bellow wrote: "Intellectual man had become an explaining creature. Fathers to children, wives to husbands, lecturers to listeners, experts to laymen, colleagues to colleagues, doctors to patients, man to his own soul, unexplained."

■ ■ ■

Sadly, Louis Malle died too young, like Kieslowski. I had become his intimate. Upon his death in 1995, a rush of memories overwhelmed me. I remember being introduced to Louis in Paris in 1970 by Claude Nedjar, the manager of Les Nouvelles Éditions des Films, Louis's production company. We became friends.

Over the years New Yorker Films handled many of his early works and a few later ones. I went to Munich with Louis to visit a twin theater that he owned there, managed by François Duplat, later to become a producer. So many memories. I visited Louis in his chic Paris apartment, where he was casting for *Lacombe, Lucien.* We once shared a sumptuous dinner at Darbar (Louis loved Indian cuisine) in celebration of the opening of a new Satyajit Ray film. And, of course, after he asked me to read the script of *My Dinner with André,* I encouraged him.

Toby and I were traveling through France with our friends Mike and Gloria Levitas when we visited Louis in his seventeenth-century country home near Cahors. In this house, *Black Moon* was shot. Vincent, Louis's younger brother, prepared a tasty truffle omelet. We drank a robust local red wine. We chatted with Louis's older brother, Bernard, a book collector. I remember visiting Louis in Los Angeles to tie up the distribution rights for *Phantom India*. There I met Terrence Malick, a first-rate filmmaker.

Louis was a terrific filmmaker. He loved movies. He was up on everything, making it a point to see all the new films of his fellow directors. And he revisited, time and again, the films of some of his favorite directors—Robert Bresson (for whom he once worked), Carl Theodor Dreyer, Nikita Mikhailkov, Satyajit Ray. He also knew about the business. He was an exhibitor. He built a twin theater out of an old Chinese pagoda. La Pagode still stands as one of the more enchanting movie houses of Paris. He also knew everything about film distribution. He founded Pyramide Films, which continues to distribute films in Paris. He was an elegant dresser. He had a good eye for the ladies.

His choice of what film to make next was always unpredictable and eclectic, so that you couldn't find a common thread in his work. What made Louis so interesting was his doubting nature, ever in doubt about the validity of his new undertaking. When he finished a fiction feature, his next film would be a documentary.

If you don't have doubts about yourself, you are not an artist. Doubt makes you strive for perfection, for a spot in art heaven. And that's where Louis is now, in his snappy clothes, reading an offbeat novel that will result in an offbeat movie. Hey, Louis, you hear me?

■ ■ ■

Marcello Mastroianni was my man. In his seventy-two years, he acted in nearly two hundred movies. Plus, theater work. True to his nature, he continued to work for unfashionable directors if the script was honorable. He made a lot of bread in his lifetime. Didn't have to squander his protean talents on crap. He was the opposite of those Hollywood bums who, in cahoots with their manicky, bug-eyed agents, work the system for zillions of dollars while appearing in one turd after another—in the process mugging the American brain, or what little there is left of it.

Marcello was a real person. I've been told that on a shoot, he'd say, "Let's get this shot done and then we can all have cutlets." There wasn't a synthetic fiber in his body. I first met him in 1981 when I invited Fellini, Giulietta Masina, and Mastroianni to come to New York for the launching of *City of Women*. Unpretentious to a fault, Marcello engaged me in a quasi-comic riff on American station wagons. For one reason or another, he was hung up on American station wagons. Would I inquire if a Buick was superior to a Pontiac? And how about the Chrysler? I wasn't sure if he was putting me on. In any case, we all spent a few pleasant days together.

Our Italian visitors were shepherded around town by Suzanne Fedak and Mary Lugo, our bright in-house publicity team. One night we went—there were ten of us—to Il Nido for a wonderful Northern Italian meal. The maître d' was beside himself with excitement when Il Maestro arrived; Fellini ordered various Piedmont reds. He knew the owners of these Italian vineyards. We ate and drank heartily. Marcello did a few mimetic turns, impersonating a drunk, then a waiter. The bill came to two thousand bucks. It was worth every penny.

GIANNI AMICO AND JACQUES DEMY

Journal Excerpts

*O*ctober 22, 1990: Bernardo Bertolucci phoned from London. He needed advice regarding the 57th Street Playhouse, where Warner Brothers was planning to open *The Sheltering Sky*. An excellent choice, I said. The theater was "hot," had premiered Kurosawa's *Dreams* a few months ago. Good notices. Huge business. Now playing Barbet Schroeder's *Reversal of Fortune*, as are two other theaters, also good notices and business.

"Now the bad news. Gianni is very sick," said Bernardo, and I quickly realized *that* was the real reason for his call. Gianni Amico had a serious liver cancer, which I'd already learned of a month before from our friend Fabiano Canosa. I'd tried to phone Gianni in Rome but got no answer. Bernardo said he spoke to Gianni daily. We then discussed Alberto Moravia, who'd died a few weeks before of a heart attack in his sleep. Eighty-three years old. I thought of our visits with Moravia, his wife Dacia, Bernardo, and Pasolini at Moravia's house in Fregene and at his apartment in Rome. So many splendid times together.

■ ■ ■

October 28, 1990: I called Rome and reached Gianni's wife, Fiorella. She recalled our visit, some twenty years before, at a house she and Gianni had rented in Cinque Terre, near La Spezia. She passed the phone to him. He sounded extremely weak: voice barely audible. For me it was a conversation of emotions since the words between us didn't register. Gianni, co-scriptwriter and assistant director of Bertolucci's *Before the Revolution* and *Partner*, had played a small role as a cinephile in *Before the Revolution* where he said, "Cinema cannot live without Rossellini."

A great aficionado of jazz and Brazilian music, Gianni was instrumental in introducing Cinema Novo directors to Europe: Glauber Rocha, Nelson Pereira dos Santos, Ruy Guerra, Walter Lima, and Joaquim Pedro de Andrade—all distributed by New Yorker Films.

In 1967 Gianni made *Tropici*, a 16mm black-and-white film about a poor family from the northeast who trek to São Paulo, where the father becomes a construction worker building the Hilton hotel. A tragic and familiar tale in Latin America: desperate rural families migrating to big cities in search of livelihood.

■ ■ ■

October 30, 1990: Jacques Demy is dead, age fifty-nine. He'd been ill for over a year. Fond memories of his early films quickly surface: *Lola, Bay of Angels, The Umbrellas of Cherbourg*—especially *Lola*, one of my favorites. I recall an argument I once had with Agnès Varda over dinner at our apartment, when I accused her of being silly and cowardly for not marrying Jacques, loving each other and having two kids together. Marriage was a boring, stifling institution, she thought. Shortly thereafter they *did* get married.

■ ■ ■

November 3, 1990: Fabiano called this morning. Gianni Amico died yesterday, having endured much suffering those past months. He was one of the gentlest creatures I knew. But no simpleton—well read, a music maven, versed in classical, jazz, and Brazilian music. A later work was based on Goethe's *Elective Affinities*, while his first, *Tropici*, was an elegant tribute to Nelson Pereira dos Santos's great *Vidas Secas*. Toby reminded me of an absolutely splendid evening at Bernardo's house when we ate well, drank a lot, smoked pot. Gianni spun endless surrealistic narratives, stories that could have made a dozen films.

He also explicated at length on the Portuguese word *miura* (bull), a code word in our circle for beautiful artistic films with no chance of making a dime at the box office. Years later, Luiz Carlos Barreto, producer of *Dona Flor and Her Two Husbands*, dubbed me "King of the *Miuras*." I adore these films.

Although we hadn't seen Gianni in recent years, I shall miss his magnificent presence on earth. "I live with my dead," as Truffaut once said. He himself died of a brain tumor at the age of fifty-two. Soon after, Toby says to me, "As we grow older . . . " And I interrupt: "I'm moving sideways until one day when I fall over."

PART 11

UPPER WEST SIDE CINEMAS

UPPER WEST SIDE

Very often, I bump into friends on the Upper West Side—Linda and Aaron Asher, Carol and Jack Gelber, Judy and Jules Feiffer, Nelson Aldrich, so many. I run into Stanley Engelstein at least once a week. He lives in the Seventies, and since I walk back and forth every day from my apartment in the Nineties to the office, it's not unusual for us to meet each other in that thirty-block stretch. Stanley and his brother invented the elbow that binds the microfiche, and Stanley, now retired, is ever present in our neighborhood. Once a powerful handball player and a big-time walker, but with knees hobbled from years of handball, he now finds it troublesome to walk long distances. Yet he does walk and works the treadmill in the Sixty-Third Street YMCA. Stanley and his wife, Feema, both born in Russia, are close friends of ours. We see each other often, if not in Manhattan, then in the Hamptons, parts of which can be considered an extension of the Upper West Side.

All of us relish the hectic activity on Broadway, a carnival of whirling souls and endless food stores. We know what to buy at Zabar's, Fairway, and Citarella. We know where to get the best bagels and which supermarkets are overpriced. And with the profusion of Chinese, Vietnamese, Turkish, Italian, Thai, Japanese, Indian, Spanish, French, Southwestern American, Lebanese, and Portuguese restaurants on the UWS, Stanley can, with the rest of us, assuage the haunted appetites of our pogrom mentality.

Recently, on one of those autumnal days when New York gives off whiffs of youthful romance, I was sitting on a bench near Lincoln Center enjoying a pretzel with dabs of mustard on it. It was four-ish in the afternoon, the time of day when hypoglycemic individuals such as Stanley and I experience an energy dip this side of dizziness and require a snack. I love soft pretzels, ate many as a kid growing up in the Bronx, and now eat them in Manhattan and in Berlin when Toby and I are there for a film festival. Stanley came by and sat next to me on the bench. He was on his way to the YMCA, carrying a plastic bag with his gym togs.

Stanley enjoyed going to our Lincoln Plaza Cinemas. When younger, he'd sometimes fight with me over a booking. Once, when we were close to blows, his wife had to intercede in front of the Ansonia building on Seventy-Ninth Street. Now, with his finely developed *schmecker* beak, he knows what to avoid and what to see, and is also a fan of the Walter Reade Theater.

He promptly runs through his takes on the movies showing at the Lincoln Plaza: he liked *Secrets and Lies* but thought that *Big Night* was thin ("easily forgettable"); found *Three Lives and Only One Death* too dense; was knocked out by *Looking for Richard*. On leaving, he thanked me for "the pleasure you've given me with your theater."

I like these encounters. They allow me to reflect on my friends and on my work. It substantiates my enterprise, since I've a tendency to be very doubtful about how I spend my time as well as the validity of it all. But I also think that Stanley, who had a low threshold for the brusqueness of business life, retired too early.

In his mid-fifties when the chips came in, he said *basta*. Since then, he reads even more voraciously than ever; and in his sixties he went to law school, became a lawyer, and wound up doing pro bono casework for the Human Rights Watch. He's an expert on Russian and Polish history—I've seen him hold his own with learned history professors from Columbia University. His daughter is a renowned scholar of Russian history; his sons are successful lawyers; his wife is a brilliant psychologist who teaches at Einstein Hospital; they travel a lot. At age seventy-two, Stanley studied Hebrew, which he then spoke and wrote fluently, though like so many secular Jews, he had abandoned this tongue after his bar mitzvah. Indeed, I'm awed when I encounter someone with such brainpower.

An accomplished debater, Stanley can get noisy and obtrusive at times. Like myself, he's a devoted follower of Yosef Hayim Yerushalmi, the great Columbia University professor of Jewish history and disciple of Salo Baron. If stuck on an important issue relating to Jewish history, we may consider consulting Yosef.

At one point in one of our marathon discussions of a film, while I was eating my pretzel, Stanley echoed Saul Steinberg's *New Yorker* cover cartoon, "If only the rest of the world could be like the Upper West Side." We agreed.

■　■　■

Toby and I have lived in the same apartment on Riverside Drive for over fifty years. Here our three daughters were raised. Hundreds of friends and acquaintances have crossed our threshold over the years, and we discuss aspects of our neighborhood as if it were a continent. Rarely do I go below Fifty-Ninth Street or east of Central Park West. My new hangout has become Barnes & Noble on Broadway and Eighty-Second Street.

It became a study house. Try to find an empty chair in the store! Every day, young and old—black, white, and yellow—have their heads buried in books, exploring the endless mysteries of life, awaiting some bulb in their head to light up. I've walked almost every street on the UWS—know the brownstones, the churches, the art deco apartment buildings. When not stuck in daydreams or problem solving, I discover something new on each walk. I learned that the two Zabar brothers own that particular Barnes & Noble block. To their credit, it has been kept as a two-story building. They could have easily developed it into another hideous apartment building, the kind that crushes our spirits in New York. I know most of the stores in my area. For one, there's the Town Shop on Broadway and Eighty-Second Street, founded by Mr. and Mrs. Henry Koch, who were our neighbors back in the 1940s. It's now run by their son and grandson. They sell ladies' undergarments and have survived the Filene's of this world by carrying exclusive brassiere and panty lines. Customers come to them from all over the city. These brassiere and panty retailers are in the tradition of proud merchants throughout the world who feel they have something special to offer. My wife claims that one of the saleswomen can at a glance know what size you are! When Victoria's Secret appeared, I asked Toby: "How many bras does a woman need?"

Recently, I walked past a supermarket on Broadway and 105th Street, a few blocks from the Metro, my old theater with the elegant art deco medallions on its facade. That spot was once a Horn & Hardart automat but is now landmarked. Next to it is a sliver of an empty store slicing through the middle of a property. This sliver, I learned, is also owned by the Zabars.

ALL SEATS $1.00 AT ALL TIMES

On January 12, 1969, I took out a full-page ad in the *New York Times* to promote a new series of exciting works by international filmmakers that would premiere at our New Yorker Theater. The films were to open on a Sunday; critics were not invited to advance screenings—and had to buy a ticket, same as everyone else. Moviegoers could form their *own* opinions. This is how it read:

There must be one hundred problems in trying to introduce unknown works by new directors to a "serious" audience, let alone a mass audience. The cost of launching such films is prohibitive. This advertisement, for example, costs over $5,000. It appears only today; tomorrow it joins the scrap heap of thousands of other advertisements.

Worse, the traditional system of launching films is senseless and archaic. It involves a series of pre-opening screenings for critics, tastemakers, and trade people. Overnight, an aggressive publicity machinery goes into competition with other aggressive publicity machineries, whose aims are to get a still from the movie in the papers on opening day, or to extract some advance quote from an "influential" or even the foolish attempt to "prime" critics to write favorably. In this auction market atmosphere, very few films get good reviews. The day after reviews appear, they are raked over for good quotes. Then, in proportion to the Machinery's pocketbook and ego, all those noisy advertisements you see every day fight each other for audience attention. Out of this confusion, the ultimate metamorphosis takes place: movie-goers become passive, subject to easy manipulation.

The problem is to find a thrifty and commonsensical way of joining interesting work with audiences who are tired of being seduced day in and day out. Films are expensive to make, and in many instances a film-maker has only one opportunity. It is possible, for example, that several of the film-makers whose work is presented in this series will never get to make another film. The only people who stand to profit from the films of these film-makers are producers, distributors, and exhibitors. The losers are the film-makers and the audiences.

The fact is, most of the films that are recognized as truly important movies—as influential, suggestive works that set people thinking along new lines—are not greeted with raves in their first showing. They may even irritate. Indeed, the films that irritate people and the press are often the most interesting and the most influential ones—the ones people talk about years later. Some of the movies we've launched in the past nine years—films by Bertolucci, Buñuel, Antonioni, Wajda, Bresson, Renoir, Ichikawa, Ozu, Dreyer, Godard, Kurosawa—are now recognized as among the key works of the past decade. Influential movies are not always movies that *can* be greeted with raves; often they are only interesting in part or interesting upon reflection.

We think that the films in this series represent some of the novel directions taking place in movies today, even though we cannot offer unqualified raves ourselves. It is with some of these thoughts in mind that we are presenting this series of new (and, in a few cases, older) work. We have not held any screenings for critics or trade people in advance; today's projection is the first to take place in this country. These films come from Africa, Brazil, France, Germany, Italy, Poland, and the U.S.A. They are films that are made with thought and, for the most part, reveal fresh, youthful tendencies in film-making today. We invite *everybody*, for $1.00, to see these films on an equal footing. Our aim is popular theatre.

The films in the series were: *Black Girl* and *Borom Sarret* (Ousmane Sembène), *Pickpocket* (Robert Bresson), *Bad Company* (Jean Eustache), *Me and My Brother* (Robert Frank), *Identification Marks: None* (Jerzy Skolimowski), *Les Créatures* (Agnès Varda), *Not Reconciled, Machorka-Muff,* and *The Bridegroom, the Comedienne and the Pimp* by Jean-Marie Straub (Straub and Danièle Huillet),

Six in Paris (Claude Chabrol, Jean Douchet, Jean-Luc Godard, Jean-Daniel Pollet, Éric Rohmer, Jean Rouch), *Le Socrate* (Robert Lapoujade), *Tropici* (Gianni Amico), *The Fire Within* (Louis Malle), *Morire Gratis* (Sandro Franchina), *Chronicle of Anna Magdalena Bach* (Jean-Marie Straub and Danièle Huillet), *Walkover* (Jerzy Skolimowski), and *The Smugglers* (Luc Moullet) with short film *The Accompaniment* (Jean-André Fieschi).

This program was a total disaster at the box office. But since I had the distribution rights for most of the films, launching them collectively was cheaper than doing it picture by picture.

CINEMA STUDIO

I sold our New Yorker Theater to the Walter Reade Organization in 1973 to devote myself fully to distribution. For the following three years, I was without a theater and dependent on other exhibitors to open my distribution company's films. Don Rugoff was the ideal choice, a tyrant with excellent taste, but impossible to do business with.

In 1976, on a leisurely walk along Broadway, I noticed an empty movie house between Sixty-Sixth and Sixty-Seventh streets. The Studio, its marquee, announced it was for lease.

In those days, nobody was building or leasing theaters. The movie exhibition business was in the doldrums. But I missed it and was eager to get back into it. Moreover, I needed a living room for my own films. This theater had six hundred seats and had originally been showing Spanish-language films without English subtitles before switching to move-overs of Hollywood junk. It was owned by Dave Sanders, booked by the Brandt Organization, and managed by Carlos Canossa. The area around Lincoln Center, at that time, was a virtual ghost town. Next door to the Studio was Vorsts, a family fish restaurant; a small coffee shop; and a funeral parlor.

I took over the theater, cleaned it up, installed new seats, and renamed it the Cinema Studio. We eventually split it into two theaters, one with 300 seats and the other with 185. Now as both distributor and exhibitor, I could show our own New Yorker films.

In the first six months, there were countless difficulties: the theater couldn't run with just my films, and I did not have enough money to advertise and promote them. Moreover, distributors—notoriously gun-shy and never liking new kids on the block—would only give me second-tier stuff to show on onerous terms. I was getting angrier and angrier.

But then I opened *Aguirre, the Wrath of God* to strong reviews and strong box-office numbers. Followed by another Herzog film, *Stroszek*: again, good reviews and good numbers. But with Fassbinder's *The Marriage of Maria Braun*, I hit the jackpot. It went through the roof, playing fifty-three weeks. After that, distributors began lining up, begging me to play their films.

At the Cinema Studio, we launched Andrzej Wajda's *Man of Marble*, Jean-Luc Godard's *Every Man for Himself*, Werner Herzog's *Woyzeck*, Wim Wenders's *The American Friend*, Satyajit Ray's *The Home and the World*, Andrei Tarkovsky's *The Sacrifice*, Fred Schepisi's *The Chant of Jimmie Blacksmith*, Pedro Almodóvar's *Women on the Verge of a Nervous Breakdown*, Gabriel Axel's *Babette's Feast*, and Steven Soderbergh's *Sex, Lies, and Videotape*. Claude Lanzmann's *Shoah* opened on October 23, 1985, ran for twenty-six weeks, and grossed $729,290, an unprecedented figure for a film more than nine hours in length.

■ ■ ■

The Cinema Studio became a springboard for many films that we'd seen in Cannes and Berlin. At festivals, Toby and I would split up at times so as to cover more films. In 1986, she was the first who saw Juzo Itami's *Tampopo*, and before I went, she issued strict orders: *Do not laugh!* This would signal to the other distributors in the room that I'd be going after that film and then playing it— thus bringing more attention to the film and more competition for us.

I contained myself, but it wasn't easy. Here's the story: Goro, a tall, dark, cowboy-hatted stranger, rides into town on a milk truck and swaggers into the nearest noodle shop, owned and operated by the beguiling Tampopo, whose name means "dandelion" in Japanese, but whose noodles are terrible. Immediately, Goro resolves to elevate her to the top of that noble profession and produce the Perfect Noodle. The film is a lark, totally delicious. And it had a long run with us. What joy to hear our audience noodling with laughter.

In 1978 in Cannes, emerging from a screening of Ermanno Olmi's *The Tree of Wooden Clogs*, Toby and I agreed: this three-plus-hour film was a masterpiece. It won that year's Palme d'Or. Written and directed by Olmi, it takes place in

Lombardy, his native region, at the end of the nineteenth century. It has no single narrative line, but authentically captures peasant lives (a grandfather showing his grandchild how to secretly grow tomato seedlings in winter; a peasant attempting to cure an ailing cow; a young man courting a woman). All of this is magnificently done with quiet pacing and beautiful cinematography. When it premiered at the Cinema Studio, moviegoers in the audience vowed to return and see this humanistic work again.

THE METRO

Our first glance at the Midtown movie house on Broadway and Ninety-Ninth Street, which ultimately became our Metro, was in the late sixties, passing it as we accompanied our young daughter to the Montessori school on 102nd Street off Broadway. It was showing "adult" movies—the stuff you found in Times Square joints. Pornography and nursery school, an amusing juxtaposition!

The theater was not in a desirable neighborhood for an art house—Verdi Square, just a few blocks away, a favorite haunt for drug pushers. Yet Columbia University, fifteen blocks or so uptown, might attract students who'd previously attended our old New Yorker.

In August 1982, I signed a five-year lease and hired two talented young architects to spiff up the place, with a brand-new candy stand and art deco motifs. The renovation cost $300,000. With 535 seats, it was the largest revival house in the city. In 1989, the beautiful facade was landmarked. Neither I nor any subsequent tenant could alter it. Three years later, we split the interior in two, with separate screens offering moviegoers even more choices.

Though our Cinema Studio on Sixty-Sixth Street was running full speed with first runs, the Metro, almost like riding on a wave of nostalgia for the New Yorker Theater, would show repertory programs. Sample marquees: *Metropolis* with *Alphaville*, *The Deer Hunter* with *The Best Years of Our Lives*, *The Tin Drum* with *Young Törless*, *Tokyo Story* with *A Geisha*, *Sunset Boulevard* with *The Last Tycoon*, and so on.

Programming it was thrilling. Toby, on her way home from teaching at Columbia University, often couldn't resist popping in. But changing that marquee daily was daunting, even for our nimble young usher atop a ladder. In 1987, with the Lincoln Plaza Cinemas in full swing, I terminated our Metro lease.

THE LINCOLN PLAZA CINEMAS

The Lincoln Plaza Cinemas is a complex with six auditoriums. The first three were built in April 1981. When they were finished, I rewarded myself with a Buster Keaton Festival. There I was, in my new place, amid a matinee audience, watching our poker-faced hero in *The General*, rubber-band body dangling from a train. There I was, watching him in *Sherlock Jr.*: a projectionist (my alter ego) dreaming himself into the film. How many times had I, too, dozed off at an early morning screening? We owed those beautiful restored prints to Raymond Rohauer, collector and preserver.

So we now had even more room to launch our own films, along with those of other distributors. In came Fellini's *City of Women*, Rohmer's *The Aviator's Wife*, Krzysztof Zanussi's *The Contract*, and Malle's *My Dinner with André*.

In April 1992 we began construction of three more screens. On October 29 of that year, 98 percent done, I noted in my journal being exhausted, exhilarated, anxious. Two weeks of high anxiety followed. Would I need Xanax (first time) to calm down? In the new section we brought in Maurice Pialat's *Van Gogh*, Nikita Mikhalkov's *Close to Eden*, and Stephen Gyllenhaal's *Waterland*, and with the old section extended, Errol Morris's *A Brief History of Time* and María Novaro's *Danzón*. Business was disappointing until we opened Alain Corneau's *Tous les Matins du Monde* on November 13, but the theaters really exploded with Neil Jordan's *The Crying Game* and Régis Wargnier's *Indochine*. At which point—Christmas week—I spent seven days a week, twelve to thirteen hours a day at the theater, overseeing things, learning about the staff and the newly enlarged operation. When busy, it was a difficult theater to run.

We now had six theaters with over one thousand seats, and it was a smashing success. The year 1993 had ended well. I was continually screening—distributors all offering us films—and as usual, keeping notes. By January, we were holding over Jane Campion's *The Piano*, Kieslowski's *Blue*, Claude Miller's *The Accompanist*, Chen Kaige's *Farewell My Concubine*, Wenders's *Faraway, So Close!*, and Stephen Frears's *The Snapper*.

The refurbished theater has a spacious lobby with a vibrant mural of moviegoers gazing at a film. It was painted by our daughter Nina. A refreshment stand offers pastries selected by Toby, along with sandwiches of smoked salmon, Polish ham, and cheddar cheese; espressos; soft drinks; and, of course, popcorn. (Once, trying to ban popcorn at the New Yorker, I was bombarded by a deluge of protests in the guest book.) Atop the stand, the vase of flowers changes from week to week—Toby loves doing this. Beyond the ticket taker, an entire wall is lined with four giant movie posters: *The Passion of Joan of Arc*, *Zero for Conduct*, *L'Atalante*, and *Fantômas*. These are old Gaumont posters.

Access to the theaters is from an escalator enclosed by a twenty-five-foot-high glass hutch held together by metal beams. We installed the glass enclosure over the escalator so as to eliminate the fierce winds, rain, and snow that attack the area during winter. Once inside this cocoon, moviegoers are safe from those nasty elements.

On the other side of the escalator (which we've had since the construction of the first three halls in 1981) is an exit stairwell, built when the apartment building above was completed in the early seventies. It served originally as both entry and exit for that building. When it became a theater exit as well, we installed a ceiling-to-floor rolling gate at the bottom of the stairs to block stray individuals from entering the theater area between midnight and noon.

For a decade or so, the stairwell served its purpose well. It was clean, efficient, barely visible. Then, with the onset of a new wave of homelessness, the lower portion of the stairwell became a bedroom for a homeless person during the hours that the theater was closed.

Homelessness in New York City seems to be intractable. As most comfortable, liberal, well-educated New Yorkers torment themselves with the problem, nobody has the guts to speculate that their discomfort with homelessness, sad to say, might be an aesthetic issue. Mine was a different problem: as a theater operator, I have obligations to my audience. Once I get beyond programming, quality of projection, and an agreeable mise-en-scène of lobby and auditoriums, there's an obligation to deliver a few hours of protected pleasure and stimulation to very picky New Yorkers. I'm also concerned about the safety of the theater area, and of the exit stairwell in particular.

For several months, a surly guy slept there every night. At first he seemed harmless. At eleven each morning, one hour before showtime, an usher would roll up the gate at the bottom of the stairwell, ascend a few steps, and poke him—a wake-up call. I was told that he grumbled when awakened, and furthermore, pissed on the stairs during the night. For several hours this produced an overwhelming stench. I felt sorry for him, but something had to be done.

But what? He wasn't breaking any law. We didn't want to evict him forcefully, so we asked the building superintendent if he had any ideas. Without much thought, he dispatched one of the building porters, a short, mean-looking, barrel-chested fellow who resembled a Basque wrestler, to lean on the guy. This didn't sit too well with the *pischer*—he pulled a knife.

Things were getting out of hand. If Hannah Arendt were alive, in view of her thoughts about the necessity of legitimate authority in *The Origins of Totalitarianism*, I'd have sought her counsel. What would she have advised me to do? Then, *bang*, the obvious hit me.

Why not build a glass enclosure, like the one over the escalator, and install a rolling gate at the top of the stairwell? This would keep such guys out after the theater closed. I contacted the building's construction manager, Bob Gross, also built like a Basque wrestler. He called in the person who did the job over the escalator.

A week later, I was told that our homeless tenant had sadly died of a heart attack on the stairwell. I knew nothing about this man's life. He was in his thirties, white, always with a two-day growth on his face. Might have been a brilliant mathematics professor who one day dropped out of The Life. But dead he was, poor guy, and with it our stairwell problem was solved—we dropped our plan to build a hutch.

A week later we had a new tenant. Evidently, word had gotten out on the street-vine that there was a vacancy in the stairwell and the spot became home to a new kid on the block. This time we went ahead with that hutch. Once installed, it eliminated the vacancy problem. Life went on with the usual New York City craziness, unsullied by dried-up patches of acidic-smelling piss.

Then, several weeks later, another problem arose, this time with birds. I noticed a large patch of pigeon shit at the top of the stairwell. Apparently they had been hanging out there for a few weeks, since shortly after the glass enclosure was built. During this period, I'd been away on vacation in Spain. Upon my return to the city, I saw that the pigeon shit had encrusted itself all along the stairwell. This would be the final image moviegoers would take in on leaving our theater. Instead of walking out in a Satyajit Ray dream, that person's sensibility would be assaulted by this Jackson Pollock *geschrei*. So, as Lenin once said, "What's to be done?"

I brought this matter up with Jose Lopez, the former manager of the New Yorker Theater, and subsequently office manager of New Yorker Films. We'd worked together intimately for thirty years. You could describe our relationship as A and B. If I say B, he says A. We often argue, like a married couple, but in the end work it out. He was aware of the pigeon problem and had been in touch with Steve Rossi, the landlord's building manager. Jose came up with a unique idea.

Apparently there exists a battery-operated stuffed owl. This bizarre-looking creature is placed in the area where the pigeons hang out. Pigeons are scared shitless of owls. Upon seeing one, they flee. The Owl has real-looking glass eyes, shiny black and green, and a battery-operated device that makes the creature flap its feathery wings. If you imagined the *malekh ha-moves* reincarnated in an animal, that Angel of Death would look like this Owl.

"Where did you find out about the Owl?" I asked Jose after hearing about this ingenious solution.

"Well," he said, "I'm a country boy and know about these things."

"What do you mean?" I said. "You've lived in a two-bedroom apartment on the Upper West Side for over twenty-five years!"

"I was in the country while growing up in Cuba." I knew for a fact that he'd lived in Havana as a boy, and I couldn't imagine that pigeon shit would have been a problem in Castro's Cuba. I would have thought pigeons were part of the Mariel exodus. What self-respecting pigeon would take all that shit from Castro?

At the risk of deflating my colleague's ego, I dropped the country-boy fiction. Later that day, I went to the theater and ran into Marlon Hecht, our chief manager. Marlon had been one of the original managers when we'd first opened the theater in 1981. After a few years, he left New York to pursue an acting career in Hollywood. Got married, and nothing came of the acting career. He divorced his wife and took a job as an assistant manager at one of AMC's megaplex theaters. There were fourteen managers in this complex, and Marlon was not moving up the ladder. Sometime afterward, we contacted Marlon and offered him the job at a handsome salary, plus moving expenses. He remained with us for years. I raised the pigeon-shit problem. "Oh, yes," he said. "I told Jose that we dealt with this problem at AMC with the Owl."

I went to my country house that weekend, with scaffolds, owls, and pigeon shit on my brain. Jose was on the case. He assured me that an Owl was on the way, although I had no concrete evidence that it had been actually ordered or of where one could buy one of these odd creatures. Slipping into my country mode, I forgot about the Owl for all of thirty minutes. I went to our farmstand to buy a muskmelon, green beans, cucumbers, and corn. The farmer who runs the stand is a savvy talkative type. He has something to say about everything, including his forty-year-old son who has a huge black beard, is living in California where he plays the mandolin, and supports himself doing odd jobs. The kid visits his father every Christmas, and his father can't wait until he goes back to California. But the farmer knew nothing about those Owls.

When I inquired in another nursery, I was told to try a sports store. But then another knew all about the problem. He told us that Long Island University's Southampton campus, where he sold vegetables, had this pigeon-shit plague in several buildings. He gave me the name of John, the building foreman, whom I contacted as soon as I got home; I learned the following: pigeon shit was an ongoing problem at Long Island University.

John's predecessor at Long Island University had a dozen Owls at different locations on campus. When John came on the scene, he discovered that the Owl was only good for two to three months. Apparently the pigeons caught on that it was a fake and would sit next to this shitless imposter on the scaffolding and return to splattering the grounds.

John contacted Kevin of Eliminex, a Long Island exterminator who'd come up with a new solution: a bed of long plastic spikes on which it was impossible to sit.

So the pigeons, not to be one-upped, built straw mats on top of the spikes in order to evade this medieval device. John has a squadron of assistants climbing ladders every few days with broomsticks, clearing away the squatters' residence. But it seems that the pigeons have been heading west since then—"west" being, of course, west of Long Island: New York City.

I can tell you, my fellow Americans, that I'm waiting for these fuckers with broomsticks and spike beds.

THE NUTS AND BOLTS OF RUNNING
A MOVIE THEATER

R unning a movie house is inundated with detail. Toby applied her researching skills to seek out the best pastries and food—many sources were involved. She found a Jamaican woman who baked the gingerbread (Robert Caro, on his way to work, would come down daily for his beloved gingerbread), an Italian family eatery from the Village who made the ricotta cheesecake, brownies from Two Little Red Hens, and so on. Thus, a moviegoer who worked until 5:30 might have a tasty repast of sandwich, pastry, and an espresso before the show.

When we added three screens to the Lincoln Plaza Cinemas in 1992, there were basics to attend to. I examined the paper towels and toilet paper fixtures for our new bathrooms. Until then we'd used paper towels, which came rushing forth from their holder four to six at a time. A new roller fixture was installed, clearly more efficient. In the Bronx, where I grew up, toilet paper was rough, often causing skin infections. In France, twenty or thirty years ago, it was *very* rough—but has improved since. All in the interest of wiping one's ass!

A business acquaintance of ours, on being presented with any question in a transaction, would say, "That's just a detail." Whereupon that transaction inevitably collapsed, having overlooked each detail. I recalled having read that the space shuttle *Challenger* in the eighties disintegrated after one of its rings failed to connect properly with another. Apparently NASA scientists had overlooked the importance of that one small detail—and the result was catastrophic.

But, on with the details involved in the physical management of our now expanded theater. They were abundant.

1. We needed a larger lobby where ticket holders could line up before a show, and needed to construct a larger concession stand.
2. We needed to replace the escalators and seek competitive bids.
3. We had to add a twenty-ton water tower unit to our current one to cool off three screens and a twenty-ton water tower unit for the expanded lobby.
4. We added five 35mm projectors, and the latest sound system available at the time (Dolby SR).
5. We installed the most comfortable theater seats sold at the time of our expansion (in both new and existing theaters).
6. We computerized our ticketing system and made advance purchasing available.
7. We upgraded the box office showtime display to a modern LED display.
8. We expanded our staff from approximately twenty to thirty-five.
9. Toby redecorated the lobby.

An international staff—from Europe, the United States, Turkey, Haiti, Puerto Rico, Jamaica, Trinidad, and Ethiopia—had worked at the Lincoln Plaza Cinemas for a very long time. They shared their life stories freely, with the exception of Rena Shana, our full-time cashier, with us since the theaters opened in 1981. She answered the phone with Old World manners: "This is the Lincoln Plaza Cinemas. How can I help you?" Her devotion to me was total, even supplying fish oil capsules to strengthen my heart, with an injunction to take them daily.

In light of her deliberate silence regarding her background, Toby and I conjectured that she might have served as a guard in a concentration camp, or even in the dreaded *Sonderkommandos*—prisoners (usually Jews) forced, on threat of their own deaths, to aid with the disposal of gas chamber victims. Only at the end of her life, in the hospital, did she tell our manager Ewnetu Admassu that she'd been in the Lodz ghetto following the invasion of Poland by Germany and that her parents had been sent off to the Chelmno extermination camp. She, young and strong, was detained to work, manufacturing Nazi war supplies. Unmarried, without relatives, Rena worked with us until the end of her life. We were her family. How sad that she lived with that horrific secret, and we were unable to provide any consolation.

Ewnetu arrived in this country from Ethiopia when he was eighteen. He'd been part of a student revolt against a military regime in which three thousand youths were killed, mainly from his school. At one point they came to his house and threatened to shoot him blindfolded. Luckily he had hidden at a neighbor's. His father, a judge, urged him to emigrate to the United States, where he had sisters. He began working with us shortly after the theater opened. At his cubby of a manager's office, every wall is pinned with schedules and Post-its, every surface covered. Regulars would drop by to greet him, discuss the movie, or simply chat. Someone referred to him as "the mayor of the block."

Ron Thomas, another manager, was born in Trinidad and grew up in Guyana. At the age of seven, he and his brother were on their own; ate at other people's houses, stole mangoes, slept under trees, and were scared of night spirits. When he was eleven, he came to the States. Once again, home was the street. Years passed, with intermittent small jobs, until 1988 when he came for an interview at the Lincoln Plaza Cinemas. Starting as an usher, he became a manager, and met the young woman who worked in the ice cream parlor next door to the theater, who became his wife. They have three kids and bought a house in Queens. Never having had a paternal role model, Ron is determined to be a good father—takes them on outings, oversees their homework, keeps a schedule.

Iberto Plácido, born in the Dominican Republic, lives in Washington Heights. He is the slender, slight man in the lobby, taking tickets, directing you to Theater One, Theater Two, and so on, and providing showtimes and running times. He dresses for work as if going to church, always arrives ahead of time, even in blizzards. There's an air of alertness to him. He recognizes and greets many of our customers, particularly those on our guest list, consisting largely of friends. He keeps an eagle eye out for anyone trying to enter another theater after their own show is over—after all, that's his job! He and Toby speak to each other in Spanish; he has a soft melodious voice. He married a Jehovah's Witness and adheres to their convictions. After a heart attack, when advised by a doctor to have a stent inserted, he refused. Finally some mechanism was found that could be worn externally. And it worked. Trained in the guitar since childhood, Iberto has a vast repertory that includes classical music. He has played in our living room.

I could go on. Each employee, each with a different history and story. Customers have commented on the atmosphere of harmony.

■ ■ ■

One of the most pleasurable "tasks" is selecting the music we play during interludes. Toby and I spend hours delving into our CD collection, deliberating. Here is what we came up with:

Lincoln 1:   Habib Koité & Bamada
Lincoln 2:   Jean-Yves Thibaudet: *Satie: The Magic of Satie*
Lincoln 3:   Amália Rodrigues: *Com Que Voz*
Lincoln 4:   Maurice Ravel: *Piano Favorites*
Lincoln 5:   Frederica Von Stade: *Chants d'Auvergne*
Lincoln 6:   Béla Bartók: *Romanian Folk Dances*

■ ■ ■

Projection Booth Checklist:

1. Intermission music should be turned off before each show begins.
2. Ceiling lights should always be out.
3. Proper masking should be checked before the show begins.
4. Always observe the correct use of aperture plates and lenses vis-à-vis aspect ratios.
5. Check sound level at the beginning of the day.
6. Please stand by the machine whenever there is a changeover.
7. Keep prints clean.
8. Keep gates clean at all times.
9. Report any print damage immediately to the manager.
10. Check focus on all screens at all times.
11. Report any strange noises that come from the machines to the manager.
12. Keep machines oiled and greased at all times.
13. Relief projectionist cannot work on weekends.
14. There are to be no incoming calls unless urgent.

15. Any conversation in the booth must be kept at a low level.

16. Adhere to the showtime schedules unless the manager indicates otherwise. It's a good idea to check with the manager on Friday and Saturday nights since he may be too preoccupied to advise you in case he wants to start a little later.

17. Always keep a generous supply of parts on hand as much as possible in case there is something wrong with the print.

18. Do not hesitate to tell us anything that will result in the improvement of the booth. Whenever a new show begins, try to watch the first time around.

FESTIVALS

At the heart of operating a movie theater, as I've always said, is programming. We screen films all year round: at the theater, at home, and at festivals. Festivals are an important source for us as distributors and exhibitors, for they initiate the process of selection, premiering films we may want to distribute or play at our theater. Call it a head start. Toby and I follow auteurs and their work—the new Truffaut, Bertolucci, Herzog, Kiarostami, Von Trier, Soderbergh. But we may also stumble upon a new director. A discovery!

Nowadays, with over five hundred film festivals around the world, you can attend a different one each day of the year. Venice, London, Edinburgh, Rome, Tehran, Montreal, Los Angeles, San Francisco, Sundance, Palm Springs, South by Southwest, and the Hamptons for starters. In addition to New York, we regularly attend Cannes, Berlin, and Toronto. Industry folk from all over gather at these festivals. We meet up with friends seldom seen the rest of the year. In Berlin, for instance, we have breakfast daily with Lia van Leer, who runs the Jerusalem Cinematheque and its summer film festival; we exchange notes and schedules, and enjoy each other's company. Often joining us is Beki Probst, head of the European Film Market, an important festival component since it gives directors and producers of films, whether or not official selections of the Berlinale, the opportunity to show their work.

In 1967 we attended our first film festival overseas, Cannes, which takes place in May, and we've been going ever since. The city is on the glorious Côte d'Azur, facing the Mediterranean. We stay at the small Hôtel Splendid run by

Madame Cagnat and her very capable female staff, directly across from the Palais, where Main Competition films are shown. We generally reserve #504, a corner room, its balcony overlooking the sea and harbor, where boats and yachts are docked. Also at the hotel are eminent Chicago film critic Roger Ebert and his wife, Chaz; Larry Kardish, film curator at MoMA; Phillip Lopate, covering for the New York Film Festival; Tom Luddy, programmer of the Telluride Film Festival; and I could go on.

I barely sleep on the transatlantic flight, yet on arrival around noon, I hasten to obtain our accreditation, catalogues, tickets for the next day. Since more and more people attend the festival each year, registration at the office has long lines and several hours are needed to obtain our badges, catalogues, and letters to offices for top-of-the-line credentials.

All in a day's work.

With our convenient location, it's easy enough to tumble out of bed, grab an espresso, and land in front of the screen. With over a hundred or so films to choose from, at times Toby and I split up. How to cover the Main Competition, Films Out of Competition, Un Certain Regard, the Directors' Fortnight, Critics' Week, and Market Screenings? As my mother-in-law, Bella, would say in pungent Yiddish: "You can't be in two places with one bottom!"

The Promenade de la Croisette is jammed with hordes of pedestrians, not just festival goers but also vacationers and retirees. At the Hôtels Carlton, Ambassade, and Majestic, there's plenty going on. In lobbies and back rooms, deals are struck among sales agents, producers, distributors, and filmmakers seeking money for their next production. Toby and I are there, however, to *look at films*—as many as can be squeezed in. I usually see from four to six a day.

Each morning, invitations for parties slither beneath the door. But we're party poopers—party at night, and you're sunk for the next morning's films. Some evenings we enjoy a tranquil repast on our balcony from bounty Toby garners at the old Forville market: mesclun, strawberries, giant artichokes, an array of sausages and cheese, accompanied by a Provençal wine, say, a Pedro Domecq. And always, she brings lush bouquets of peonies and roses.

After dinner, I write up notes of that day's films: brief plot summaries culled from a welter of images. Spontaneous responses for reference back home; speculations as to what will get picked up; what high rollers will overbid on; and what we'll want to play. On our return to New York, friends invariably ask,

"What did you see? What did you like?" I began keeping notes in 1968 but in 2008 decided to send them to a small circle of friends and colleagues. [See "Festival Notes" in the appendix.]

In Cannes, we often run into the wonderful Pierre Rissient, an expert in world cinema and one of the most influential behind-the-scenes figures for discovering and guiding directors he believes in, among them Jane Campion, Hou Hsiao-hsien, and Lino Brocka, to name but a few. Many years ago, he ran an offbeat cinema in Paris, had his fingers in various film productions, and was a Cannes film scout in Asia. His tastes are on target, and I listen carefully when he speaks. Partly impaired in later years, he sits with his cane in a corner of the Splendid's small lobby. Professionals from all over the world come to greet him, to hear what he has to say about such and such film—even Gilles Jacob, then president of the festival, came by to pay homage, as did his successor as artistic director, Thierry Frémaux. In 2002, Pierre told us about a screening that evening of a film from Mauritania, and go we did. It was *Waiting for Happiness*, in the Main Competition, by Abderrahmane Sissako, which we wound up distributing. We recalled that back in 1997, Pierre was enthusiastic about Kiarostami's *Taste of Cherry*. Of course, we went and saw it. And agreed with his high opinion.

Tips from colleagues can be tremendously useful. You can't see everything. On the other hand, more than once I've been told by a distributor: "It won't play." And then it did!

Here's how the process of a film reaching audiences goes: it begins when a professional sees it and decides to bid. If a big distributor—say, Sony Pictures Classics or Miramax—knows that we'll play a particular film at our theater, it serves as strong encouragement for them to acquire it. The Lincoln Plaza Cinemas is often a launching pad for art houses throughout the country.

After seeing Michael Moore's *Fahrenheit 9/11*, we immediately went out on the Croisette, phoned the distributor, and told him we'd give it two screens. Among the films our New Yorker Films distribution company took on for distribution were *Belle Toujours*, *Distant*, and *The Wind Will Carry Us*. Many distributed by others also wound up at our theater: *In the Mood for Love*, *The Page Turner*, *The Diving Bell and the Butterfly*, *The White Ribbon*, *Habemus Papam*, and *La Vie d'Adèle*.

■ ■ ■

For a long time, we avoided the Berlin Film Festival. Members of our own family were among the six million Jews murdered by the Nazis. Yet, as distributors of so many excellent films by German directors such as Herzog, Wenders, and Schlöndorff, we were often invited to attend. In the early seventies we finally did. The trigger perhaps was Fassbinder's *Ali: Fear Eats the Soul*, which we'd seen in Cannes and immediately took on for distribution.

The Berlin Film Festival, which takes place in February, became our favorite, with excellent categories and politically engaged films. The pace is not as frantic as in Cannes, for it's less of a marketplace. Among the many films we saw there were *A Separation, Taxi, Lemon Tree*, and *A Film Unfinished*. All eventually appeared on our screens. Sometimes I'm keen on a particular film and decide to play it, and though it doesn't have "the numbers" (size of audience), I still try to hold it over. I want to give it a chance. Occasionally I'm resistant to holding onto one that has had a decent run and no longer warrants keeping it on two screens as a distributor wants. Through the grapevine, it's been reported to me that that particular distributor said: "Dan is so restless, itchy brain, always looking for new stuff."

Yes, new stuff! Exhilarating!

EPILOGUE

TOBY TALBOT

O ur Lincoln Plaza Cinemas are no more. Closed on January 28, 2018. After almost forty years, its lease not renewed.

Our last shows were *Darkest Hour*, *Happy End*, *The Insult*, *A Ciambra*, and *Wonder Wheel*. On December 22, 2017, Dan came to the theater and we watched Michael Haneke's *Happy End*. When it was over, he headed for the manager's office and asked Ewnetu, "How's business?" Then studied the ledger with the week's figures. On top of it, to the end.

He died one week later. On the morning of December 29, 2017, his heart gave out. It was my darkest hour. Gone, my dear husband of nearly seven decades.

On the very day of our closing, a joint memorial for Dan and the Lincoln Plaza Cinemas was held at the theater—five auditoriums filled. There were clips from among the nearly fifteen hundred films that he had played: *Aguirre, the Wrath of God*, *Shoah*, *Tampopo*, *My Dinner with André*, *City of Women*, *Tokyo Story*, *Secrets and Lies*, and *Cinema Paradiso*. Interspersed were tributes: Werner Herzog (remotely) thanked Dan for courage in taking on new directors, as he himself once was; Wally Shawn marveled at Dan's confidence in his choice of films, and how he *enjoyed* what he was doing; Michael Barker of Sony Pictures Classics reported that it was difficult to get Dan to play a movie he didn't like; Phillip Lopate recalled his days as a Columbia University student, hurrying to the New Yorker Theater for his film education; Molly Haskell praised the rich program notes of that theater and how Dan's programming transcended geographic and gender barriers; Jonathan Sehring of IFC Films told that countless members of the film community had started their careers at New Yorker

Films—and that the IFC Center at Sixth Avenue and Third Street (the old Waverly Theater) strove to be a downtown Lincoln Plaza Cinemas! Quite emotionally, he expressed his admiration of Dan as a *genuine* person. Michael Moore then railed against the power of one wealthy individual to destroy a cultural icon! Finally our managers, Ewnetu Admassu and Ron Thomas, spoke of Dan's warmth and closeness to his staff: "We were a family," said Ewnetu. "He helped me buy a house," said a tearful Ron.

Lastly, Dan himself appears on the screen, seated in front of our living room bookcases, in white shirt, sleeves rolled up, utterly modest. "All that I do is go out and look at films and choose the ones I want to play—films that stimulate, and give some insight into our lives. I hope that people will come, but if they don't, that's okay, too."

Here, I dissolve.

■ ■ ■

That very day, outside the theater, a woman was passing out flyers that announced the New Plaza Cinema, a coalition "committed to programming the kind of films shown at the Lincoln Plaza Cinemas." Its mission is to find a permanent space on the Upper West Side. This dedicated group has regularly been showing films ever since, in auditoriums and virtually during the pandemic. When the Lincoln Plaza Cinemas closed, twelve thousand signatures appeared on an internet petition, expressing love for the theater, with grief and outrage that it was gone. Dan created a cultural community of discerning moviegoers. Trusting his judgment, they came and saw everything he showed. "An audience is as intelligent as you want them to be," he said, and often stayed after the show to hear opinions. For months, I keep bumping into people in the neighborhood who ask, "How could you let this happen?"

■ ■ ■

The theater was Dan's labor of love. From the very day it opened, he kept notes on the films he or the two of us had screened early in the morning before the first show. Not simply "Will it play?" But the *look* of it. How original? How engrossing? What did it tell us about ourselves? About what it means to be human? Early on, he developed his own criteria for what made an artistic work.

Some random notes: "Strong narrative." "Meticulous mise-en-scène." "Didn't get to me." "Dippy." "TV look" (most damning). "Not commercial" (no deterrent). Once in a while, on the fence: "If there's an opening, I'll play it." He commented when we disagreed: "T. thinks it's silly and clichéd. I don't." Some of our best conversations would take place over dinner, or in a car, or on a walk. We'd recall images: a ferocious duel between two women in *Crouching Tiger, Hidden Dragon*; men joyfully slurping noodles in *Tampopo*; a ship being hauled over the mountain in *Fitzcarraldo*.

■　■　■

Three years after the theater closed, the landlord had still not removed our name from the marquee. There it was: LINCOLN PLAZA CINEMAS. The rest, blank. Whenever I passed that marquee, on foot or by bus, I was upset, then angry. Eventually I came to regard it as a kind of tombstone: IN MEMORIAM. In fact, Dan is buried in a seventeenth-century cemetery within walking distance of our house on Long Island.

Inside, the theater is empty. Screens empty. Seats empty. My own emptiness barely assuaged by memories unspooling in my mind: screenings at the theater, screenings at home, screenings at festivals. Choosing music for interludes. Dan in back of the theater, one eye on the screen, the other on the audience. "I love theaters and their atmosphere," he said. "They're magic."

He watched films with a lover's eye. Sometimes, while screening a new one early in the morning or rewatching, say, *The Rules of the Game*, *Sansho the Bailiff*, or *Pather Panchali*, I'd peer at his face in the dark. Illuminated by the light on the screen was an expression of rapture. Once again, he was my young companion, discovering films at the Beverly, the Paris, or the Thalia, and falling under the spell of movies.

■　■　■

I enter his study and sink into the tan leather reclining chair, molded to his form, which rests on the red and indigo kilim we bought in Marrakech.

Leaning against three walls are some thirty posters from among the hundreds of films Dan launched. A small museum. The posters stand alongside each other, overlapping, in no particular order. Robert Bresson's *A Man Escaped*, Chris Marker's *Sans Soleil,* Agnès Varda's *Lion's Love (. . . and Lies)*, Jacques Demy's *Lola*, Glauber Rocha's *Earth Entranced*, Jean-Luc Godard's *La Chinoise*. I could sit here forever, creating unlikely double features, the kind Dan delighted in coming up with at the New Yorker.

Sprawled against the opposite wall is a bank of black lacquered filing cabinets with Dan's reading stand on top. A kind of pulpit exacting total concentration. History, biography, or fiction—he was a voracious reader. It was a quality that first drew me to him. The book now on the stand is *Bloodlands* by Timothy Snyder. It describes the systematic murder of civilians by the Soviets and Nazis through starvation and shootings in the very villages where those victims lived. The book is open to page 352, a blue Post-it marking his place. This was the last book that Dan read there. I'm not surprised to see it. In the wake of *Shoah*, he read insatiably in Holocaust literature.

At some point, I shall go through those file cabinets: all fifteen. Legal documents—certificates of birth, marriage, and death; contracts, licenses, and such—along with correspondence and obituaries. Several of them contain journals with screening notes of every film played at the Lincoln Plaza Cinemas. Dan was superorganized and orderly. I, of a rather disorderly stripe, joked that he would've made a perfect bookkeeper! Interspersed with the screening notes are daily activities—visits to the gym, to doctors, what the kids were up to, meals we ate, wines we drank, music we listened to, books he was reading, birthdays and Thanksgiving, family matters—that sort of thing—also random reflections.

I can't resist scanning one of the journals, which it turns out has his Locarno notes of 1989, when he was on the jury. "A very primitively made film, crude in its narrative thrust, with strong feeling. The director doesn't, as yet, know how to compose his screen." Still another: "Disgusting, a film made for the sake of violence—pornographically so. Several murders, vouyeurism, ugly sex, chi-chi party, exhibitionism, etc."

Now I go to his desk. At its upper left is a wire mesh DVD holder. And inside, Vittorio De Sica's *Bicycle Thief,* Chaplin's *A Woman of Paris*, Giuseppe Tornatore's *Cinema Paradiso*, Herzog's *Land of Silence and Darkness*, Satyajit Ray's

The Apu Trilogy, Kieslowski's *A Short Film About Love*, Andrei Tarkovsky's *Ivan's Childhood*, *Mirror*, and *Nostalghia*—films that Dan loved and seemed to want ever at hand, like a kid needing a favorite toy at elbow's reach. At the center of the desk are two books: the oversized one with stills and precise production notes of Erich von Stroheim's *Greed*, compiled and annotated by film critic Herman G. Weinberg. On top of it is Kafka's *Complete Stories*. How many times had Dan read those?

At the upper right corner is a ledger listing films that played at the Lincoln Plaza Cinemas, their distributors, individual grosses, and how many entries each had drawn. Based on those figures, Dan would decide how to program the theaters. A movie on two screens for a few weeks or months might be moved to one, while a film in the large auditorium might get shifted to a smaller one. I marveled at his ability to predict how long a film might run and when to bring in a new one. It seemed like a juggling act. At the left of that ledger is a gray manuscript box containing *Fragments of the Dream World*—the basis of this book.

■ ■ ■

I swivel in his chair and envision him gazing out the window, at the trees on Ninetieth Street, at the American flag waving over the Soldiers' and Sailors' Monument in Riverside Park, and at the Hudson. On the river I can see one boat, two, a third in the distance—a trawler, a cargo ship, and some other. And *Tokyo Story* comes to mind. In its last scene, the widowed husband is sitting stoically on a tatami mat when a neighbor goes by. "You'll be lonely," she remarks. "Yes," he says.

■ ■ ■

I once asked Dan in his last months what he had to say. "I have nothing to say. I've said it all," he replied. Yet a few days later, there *was* something else that he said, to a nurse testing his pulse, heartbeat, and blood pressure for "vitals." Motioning with his head in my direction: *"She's* my vitals!"

What might I have said? "Dan, you have the *rozhinkel*."

■ ■ ■

On the last day of his life, at two a.m., Dan was watching W. C. Fields in *It's a Gift* and laughing at our triumphant hero sipping orange juice in his new grove while tippling a bottle of booze. It was Dan's last laugh. As he'd say, "Who could imagine a better life?"

EXCERPTS FROM DAN TALBOT'S FESTIVAL NOTES

CANNES

Taste of Cherry *(1997, Abbas Kiarostami, Iran)*

Mr. Badii, a middle-aged man, drives around Tehran, looking for an accomplice to perform a certain task for him. Planning to kill himself, and having already dug his grave, he needs someone to then throw earth over his body. His first recruit is a shy young Kurdish soldier, who refuses to do the job and flees. His second, an Afghan seminarist, also declines for religious objections to suicide. The third, an Azeri taxidermist, is willing, since he needs the money, but tries to talk Badii out of it. In the course of the drive, the taxidermist reveals that he too once wanted to commit suicide but chose to live upon tasting mulberries. Still, he promises to throw earth on Badii if he finds him dead next morning. That night Badii lies in his grave while a thunderstorm begins. After a long blackout, the film ends with camcorder footage of Kiarostami and his crew filming *Taste of Cherry*. Yes, audience, this is a film!

Toby and I loved it, but descending the steps after its screening, we ran into a prominent distributor who gave his pronouncement: "Won't play."

[A smaller distributor, Zeitgeist Films, picked it up and opened it at the Lincoln Plaza, where it got a great review from Stephen Holden in the *New York Times*. But that distributor on the stairs was (commercially) right. It did not have a long run. No matter, it's a great film. Won the Palme d'Or.]

Fahrenheit 9/11 *(2004, Michael Moore, USA)*

Often, if we liked a film at a festival and wanted to play it at the Lincoln Plaza Cinemas, this was strong encouragement to a distributor to take it on. Such was the case with Michael Moore's *Fahrenheit 9/11*. Both Toby and I knew immediately that this was a winner. Straight out of the screening, standing on the Croisette, I phoned Harvey Weinstein at Miramax and told him that I'd give it two screens to start with. In my midnight notes I wrote: "By far the most powerful film, so far, in Cannes this year. Moore recounts the events surrounding 9/11: Bush cozying up to Arab oil interests, the false premises of why we entered Iraq, the tragic consequences of Americans in Iraq, casualties, etc. Above all, it's an acid portrait of George W. Bush. His cynicism and dunce-like stupidity are at the core of the film, with the heartbreaking scene of a mother grieving over the death of her son in Iraq."

This is an urgent film everyone will want to see. Moore makes just a few appearances in this artfully constructed film. He received a rousing twenty-minute ovation. In the crowd I caught his attention, told him I'd give his film two screens. He shook hands for my support. "I'm in talks with Miramax over the opening date." [The film played initially on four screens, ran for six months, and was one of the top-grossing films of all time at the Lincoln Plaza.]

Moolaadé *(2004, Ousmane Sembène, Senegal)*

A devastating feature dealing with female circumcision in Africa by the great eighty-one-year-old Sembène, "father of African cinema," whose films I've distributed for forty years. It's about the revolt of women against that barbarous practice, its heroine a fiery woman who protects her daughter against the ceremony. Set in a tiny village, this battle pits elders and religious practitioners against young women who don't want to have their bodies be mutilated. The film ranks high in Sembène's canon. Roger Ebert called it a masterpiece and Richard Peña is inviting it to the New York Film Festival. Sembène and I did a deal over a cup of coffee—no agents involved—one on one. I'll open it immediately after the festival. Curiously, some of the critics in Cannes (e.g., Dan Fainaru, whom I usually respect) came down hard on it. Many at the festival were outraged that it wasn't presented in the Main Competition, including Todd McCarthy of *Variety*.

The Diving Bell and the Butterfly *(2007, Julian Schnabel, France/USA)*

At forty-three, Jean-Dominique Bauby, the rakishly successful and charismatic editor-in-chief of French *Elle*, suffered a massive stroke, brain stem rendered inactive. After lapsing into a coma, he awakes twenty days later to find himself the victim of a rare locked-in syndrome—mentally alert but permanently deprived of movement and speech. Refusing to accept his fate, Bauby is determined to escape the paralysis of his diving bell and free the butterflies of his dreams and imagination. The only way to express that frustration is by moving his left eye. These movements and a blinking code that represents letters of the alphabet became his sole means of communication. Slowly—painstakingly—words, sentences, paragraphs, and finally an affecting, life-affirming memoir emerged.

A very moving film. Schnabel's third in eleven years. I'm not a fan of his paintings, but his filmmaking is exhilarating. He won the Best Director award, and we'll play it.

The Band's Visit *(2007, Eran Kolirin, Israel)*

Possibly the most highly touted audience pleaser in Cannes this year. A small Egyptian band arrives in Israel. They come to play at an initiation ceremony but due to bureaucracy and bad luck are left stranded at the airport. They try to manage on their own, only to find themselves in a desolate, near-forgotten small Israeli town, somewhere in the heart of the desert. Several moving encounters with Israelis emerge.

A hilarious, almost Keatonesque work. The audience ate it up. All the moneybag distributors went after this *tchotchke*. Sony Pictures Classics snapped it up—two hundred clams. We'll play it at the LPC.

Persepolis *(2007, Marjane Satrapi and Vincent Paronnaud, France/USA)*

Based on a four-volume series of graphic novels, this autobiographical work deals with the growing up of Marjane, who co-made the film, from eight to young womanhood. It begins just as the shah falls, rides through the repressive mullah-controlled society, includes the eight-year Iraq-Iran war, then goes into Marjane's teenage rebellion while a student in Austria, then returns to Iran where she ridicules the mullah and listens to her liberal secular parents and especially her hip grandmother.

A wonderful inspired film, lovely black-and-white animation, and a powerful feeling of what it means to be a free spirit. This film got a bigger ovation than Michael Moore's *Fahrenheit 9/11*. Toby and I were wowed by it. Sadly, it won no prizes. Voice-overs were done by Catherine Deneuve, Chiara Mastroianni, Danielle Darrieux. Sony Pictures Classics co-financed it. We'll open it in December.

Waltz with Bashir *(2008, Ari Folman, Israel/France/Germany)*

An animated feature, dealing with the long-term effect on Israeli soldiers who participated in the first Lebanon War of the early eighties, culminating with the massacre of Palestinians at the Sabra and Shatila refugee camps, perpetrated by Lebanese Christian paramilitary fighters allied to Israel. Ariel Sharon, the minister of defense, looked away and actually helped the Lebanese with sky flares during the night when the massacre took place. But the film is about two soldiers who are troubled by their dim memories of what actually took place. As they probe their memories, we witness some of the carnage (all of it is grotesque animation, except for the final footage of dead bodies in the camp in the middle of the night). One of the most powerful antiwar films I've ever seen. A truly haunting work.

No One Knows About Persian Cats *(2009, Bahman Ghobadi, Iran)*

A documentary-fiction portrait of the underground music scene in contemporary Iran. Recently released from prison, two young musicians—a man and a woman—decide to form a band. Together they travel the underworld of contemporary Tehran searching for others to join them. Forbidden by the authorities in Iran, they plan to escape from their clandestine existence, and dream of performing in Europe.

A witty, moving film, probably inspired by *A Hard Day's Night*, superb dialogue, hip references, very political; it seems a miracle that this film was made in Iran. It may turn out to be one of the best films in Cannes this year. The film should have been in the Main Competition.

Wild Grass *(2009, Alain Resnais, France/Italy)*

With Sabine Azéma, André Dussollier, Anne Consigny, Emmanuelle Devos, and Mathieu Amalric. When middle-aged Georges Palet accidentally finds a wallet belonging to the similarly middle-aged and charming dentist Marguerite, who has a license to fly planes, Georges's imagination flies in all directions as he circuitously pursues Marguerite upon returning the wallet to her.

The end of the film is mysterious and complicated, but the story moves along with great charm and a Resnais-like complexity. Resnais rarely makes easy films, but this one has a pleasurable simplicity to it. T. and I really loved the film. The audience greeted it enthusiastically. I met with Resnais before the film began. He'll be eighty-seven shortly. We spoke about the time he came to New York forty years ago. I lent him money to go to Boston to do research on H. P. Lovecraft, which turned up in his later film *Providence*. Despite his frailty, he told me that he is starting his new film in January.

Another Year *(2010, Mike Leigh, UK/USA)*

A story of friendship, family, loneliness, companionship among a small gallery of folks over the four seasons. A truly lovely poetic film with deft character acting. A real genuine audience film. Some hard-nosed cinephiles could object to the film, but the audience in the Grand Palais was swept away by it (including us). High-roller bidders went after it, reputedly for seven-figure bread. Sony Pictures Classics won the bidding contest, and we will open the film at LPC on December 29.

A few days after seeing the film T. and I both thought that it was influenced by Victor Erice's *El Sol del Membrillo*, a masterwork. The film didn't cadge any prizes in Cannes. Ironically Victor Erice was a member of the jury, but my guess is that he would have thought the film too soft in the head. Isn't cinema wonderful? So many different responses to the elusive magic inside a film.

Hahaha *(2010, Hong Sang-soo, South Korea)*

A kind of shaggy-dog story of two close friends, one a filmmaker (Jo), the other a film critic (Bang). Before Jo leaves on a trip to Canada, the two friends meet and over drinks they recount what happened at a seaside resort recently, but only agreeing to talk about the pleasant memories. A very low-budget film ($100,000) that has the freewheeling ambiance of the early French New Wave films. Not much of a plot. Yet, involving and fresh. It won the Camera d'Or prize.

We Need to Talk About Kevin *(2011, Lynne Ramsay, UK/USA)*

With Tilda Swinton and John C. Reilly, the parents of fifteen-year-old Kevin, shown at different ages: toddler, ten-year-old, and finally, fifteen, a very troubled sociopath who winds up killing numerous people as an archer, a skill learned from his father. The film centers on Kevin's mother, played very powerfully by Tilda Swinton, who expresses her ambivalent feelings about being a mother. Toby and I were both very enthusiastic about the film. I left Michael Barker a note, telling him to go for it. (I'm a large fan of Lynne Ramsay's superb *Ratcatcher* as well, which wonderful Ismail Merchant bought for the United States.) I thought *Kevin* would win the Palme d'Or.

I was wrong. It didn't win a single prize. Yet I'm still strong on it. Picked up by Oscilloscope Films.

The Kid with a Bike *(2011, Jean-Pierre and Luc Dardenne, Belgium/France/Italy)*

Another gem from the great brother team the Dardennes. It's about Cyril, almost twelve, who has only one plan: to find the father who temporarily left him in a children's home. To achieve this, he tries to retrieve his stolen bike, which means everything to him. By chance, he meets Samantha, who runs a hairdressing salon and lets him stay with her. He gets mixed up with a petty thief who encourages him to assault and rob a newspaper vendor. The upshot is that he gets caught and almost remanded to a prison for young criminals. In the end he is freed and rides his bike to Samantha. Shades of De Sica's *Bicycle*

Thief, yet more complex as we try to figure out if Cyril's anger over abandonment and loss will ultimately imprint him.

Toby and I were deeply moved by the film. If this were a first film by the Dardennes, it would have won the Palme d'Or. They had twice received this top award, so the jury decided to give it the Grand Prix. IFC picked up the film. We will play it.

Melancholia *(2011, Lars von Trier, Denmark)*

A wedding at a sumptuous estate takes on a problematic air as the newly married wife (played by Kirsten Dunst, who won the Best Actress award) sinks into an unexplained depression, triggered possibly by the planet Melancholia as it heads toward Earth. The bride's sister (Charlotte Gainsbourg) takes charge as the wedding scene descends into hysteria and madness, owing partly to the bride's unsympathetic parents (Charlotte Rampling and John Hurt). As the frenetic scene turns feverish, birds in the sky die, and the planet of doom moves closer and closer to Earth, an apocalypse about to unfold. While the film at times seems a bit too precious and stagey, underneath there's a powerful feeling about Man's Fate. Not everyone's cup of tea; still, more accessible than some other Von Trier films.

I'm on the fence on this one. If push comes to shove, I'd play it. Unfortunately, Von Trier behaved boorishly at the press conference. Said he liked Hitler and made slanderous anti-Semitic remarks, taking a poke at Israel, and also put down Susanne Bier, the Jewish Danish film director. The festival immediately banned Von Trier—not allowed to be anywhere nearby. Postfilm events were canceled, including Magnolia's evening beach party for the film and its director. The question now is whether or not I can play the film.

Amour *(2012, Michael Haneke, France)*

About a devoted couple in their eighties, retired music teachers (played by Emmanuelle Riva and Jean-Louis Trintignant, both brought out of actual retirement by Haneke) and their needling daughter (Isabelle Huppert). When the wife suffers a stroke, her husband faces an ultimate, grueling decision. The film is a masterpiece: magnificent acting, filled with insight, powerful feeling.

Remarkable that the same Haneke who made *Funny Games* has made this truly compassionate work. We saw it immediately as a shoe-in for the Palme d'Or, which indeed it got. Will open at LPC on December 21. I predict a long run.

The Past *(2013, Asghar Farhadi, France/Italy)*

Stylistically in the vein of Farhadi's great film, *A Separation* (winner of the Golden Bear at the 2011 Berlinale), this new long film pivots around Marie (Bérénice Bejo, the star of *The Artist*) in the throes of formalizing a divorce with Ahmad (played by Ali Mosaffa, the star of *A Separation*). Marie's insistence that he stay with her and her troubled teenage daughter is just one of the several signs that she is unsure about a closure that she herself has requested. Her uncertainty is picked up by Marie's new partner, Samir (Tahar Rahim), who most of the time lives at Marie's with his son. The first hint there is something darker going on comes when it is revealed that Samir's wife is in a coma in a hospital following an attempted suicide.

The search for the truth keeps being derailed by fresh revelations (leaves of an onion peeling away) and by doubt until we begin to question whether there is one truth about what happened in "the past." Like in *A Separation*, Farhadi keeps pulling the rug from under the spectator's feet, always casting doubt on "the truth." An obsessive narrative of twists and turns that constantly challenges the viewer. This is not an easy film to follow, yet I found it rewarding in its examination of how the mind, full of "tricks," sometimes works. Bérénice Bejo walked away with Best Actress accolades. Sony Pictures Classics picked up the film. We will open it at LPC on December 20.

Henri *(2013, Yolande Moreau, Belgium/France)*

Henri, a man in his fifties of Italian origin, runs a little restaurant, "La Cantina," near the Belgian city of Charleroi with his wife, Rita. After the place closes Henri meets up with his rummy buddies; they kill time over a few beers, chatting about their shared passion: homing pigeons. Then Rita dies suddenly, leaving Henri bereft. Their daughter suggests that Henri get some help with the restaurant from a "white butterfly," as the residents in a nearby home for mentally handicapped are known. Rosette is one of them. She is upbeat and kindly.

She yearns for love, sexuality, normality. With Rosette's arrival, a new life takes shape, for Henri as well as Rosette.

A gentle, observant kind of fairy tale by Yolande Moreau, the director of *When the Sea Rises* (2004) and the star of *Seraphine* (2009), both of which played at LPC. Her first acting role was in Agnès Varda's *Vagabond* (1985). She has acted in a dozen other French films. She is a first-rate actress and director. For whatever reason she has never received the high accolades abroad such as François Truffaut et al. T. and I have a very high regard for her work and track whatever she does. We will play her new film if picked up.

A Touch of Sin *(2013, Jia Zhangke, China)*

An angry miner revolts against the corruption of his village leaders. A migrant worker at home for New Year discovers the infinite possibilities a firearm can offer. A pretty receptionist at a sauna is pushed to the limit when a rich client assaults her. A young factory worker goes from job to job, trying to improve his lot in life. Four individuals, four different provinces: a reflection on contemporary China, an economic giant slowly being eroded by violence. A major work by a major talent, arguably China's top filmmaker (forty-three years old), has made numerous feature films. China's Angry Young Man has not sold out as has Zhang Yimou, whose first film (*Red Sorghum*) we distributed years ago.

The newspapers report on China's explosive economic growth, its familiarity with such Western icons as Louis Vuitton, the Crillon in Paris, Swiss banks that hide tax money, etc., etc. On the other hand, our friend and former physician, the brilliant Jeremiah Barondess, whose brain is an archive of offbeat information, told us that 80 percent of the Chinese population have no shoes. We saw the film at a press screening at the Debussy, after which we ran into Michel Ciment (on the Cannes *Screen International* jury), Amy Taubin (critic on the selection committee of the New York Film Festival), Scott Foundas (chief film critic of *Variety*), Kenneth Turan (film critic at the *Los Angeles Times*)—all of whom were turned on by the film as much as Toby and I were. We all speculated that the Chinese government wouldn't allow it to play outside China, let alone inside China.

To our surprise, Jia Zhangke, who won Best Screenplay, revealed at the closing ceremony that the film *will* open in China. Kino Lorber picked it up, and we're destined to open it at LPC after it premieres at the New York Film Festival in October.

The Missing Picture *(2013, Rithy Panh, Cambodia/France)*

Rithy Panh, the director, had been looking for a certain photograph attesting to the mass murders committed by the Khmer Rouge in Cambodia from 1975 to 1979. Unable to find the photographic image, he re-creates it by using clay figurines to depict the story of the unspeakable horrors orchestrated by Pol Pot.

The director, a modest man, has made the most moving film I've seen on this subject. It brought tears to my eyes, and I was not alone. I saw Michel Ciment, editor-in-chief of *Positif* and member of the *Screen International* jury, teary-eyed as well at the end of the screening. Rithy Panh was on hand, having been introduced before the film by Thierry Frémaux, artistic director of the Main Competition and Un Certain Regard. The film won the Prix Un Certain Regard. I imagine it will be picked up for the States. If so, I'll stand in line to play it. Toby is eager to show it in her documentary class.

The Last of the Unjust *(2013, Claude Lanzmann, France/Austria)*

In 1975, Claude Lanzmann filmed a series of interviews in Rome with Benjamin Murmelstein, past president of the Jewish Council of Elders in the Theresienstadt ghetto in Czechoslovakia, the only "Jewish elder" (according to Nazi terminology) not to have been killed during the war. Murmelstein, a rabbi in Vienna following the annexation of Austria by Germany in 1938, fought bitterly with Adolf Eichmann, week after week for seven years, managing to help around 121,000 to leave the country and preventing the liquidation of the ghetto. The footage was shot during the making of *Shoah* and deposited by Lanzmann in the Holocaust Museum in Washington, DC. He retrieved some of it to make this film. He appears in the film discreetly, just the back of his head, questioning Murmelstein, a powerful figure with a strong articulate voice, describing his forceful arguments with Eichmann. Interspersed with this footage is a filming, some thirty years later, of Lanzmann reading aloud what actually occurred in Theresienstadt at that time. Murmelstein emerges as a heroic figure. Eichmann comes across as a monster who hated Jews, not the person described in Hannah Arendt's wrongheaded book, *Eichmann in*

Jerusalem, where he's depicted as a "banal man," an apparatchik who turned the wheels of evil like a fearless corporation executive.

A strong film, perhaps a bit too long. Before it went on, I greeted Lanzmann, wearing a tuxedo. He acted a little surprised to see me, his distributor in the United States, coming from Planet Nine!

La Vie d'Adèle *(2013, Abdellatif Kechiche, France)*

Subtitled *Blue Is the Warmest Color*, the film is largely about a love affair between two lesbians. Blue-haired Emma, the older woman in her twenties, is an artist who hangs out in lesbian bars. There she encounters fifteen-year-old Adèle, blonde, uncertain about herself, looking for some sort of action. Emma: "You don't often get girls like you in here." Adèle: "What's my type?" Emma: "Your type, well . . . don't know . . . underage kids cruising bars at night." Adèle: "How do you know I'm underage?" Emma: "Don't know, it's obvious. Or maybe, well, a straight who's a bit . . . curious." Adèle: "I told you, really, I just came in here by chance." Emma: "But you know there's no such thing as chance?" Adèle: "You think so?" Emma: "Yeah . . . what's your name?" "Adèle." In short order, we see these two women in bed with each other, passionate sex that goes on for twenty minutes.

Normally I'm revolted by explicit sex scenes in a movie. I find them unsexy, exploitative of women in that every part of a woman's body is revealed, whereas never does one see a man's hard-on. Usually these scenes are short, violent, a false "bridge" to the next action. In her Cannes report, Manohla Dargis, a *New York Times* critic whom I admire, took umbrage at the director's representation of the female body. She quotes John Berger: "Men look at women. Women watch themselves being looked at." Watching this twenty-minute sequence, I didn't for whatever reason feel like a voyeur. I regarded it as part of her story about a genuine love affair between a savvy, bright older woman whose first priority is not sexual adventure but who is focused on her burgeoning art career.

As for the younger girl, fifteen is a tricky age, though in this case, it led to a genuine relationship. Eventually, a few years later, when it had ended, Emma had become a successful artist, while Adèle was a teaching assistant. The controversial sex episode aside, the film is essentially about the feelings—raw as they are—moods, and aspirations of these two women, which I thought Kechiche handled artistically. Kechiche, born in Tunisia, is in his early fifties.

I distributed two of his earlier films—*Games of Love and Chance* (*L'Esquive*) and *The Secret of the Grain*. I don't regard him as a "major" director yet admire the risks he often takes. He makes solid craftsmanlike films about young people. No doubt this film will divide audiences.

Toby and Kenneth Turan (*Los Angeles Times* film critic) dislike the film, as does Manohla Dargis. I think it's a solid work and I hope to play it at LPC. My golden-oldie audience may take umbrage, but it's worth the challenge.

The Salt of the Earth *(2014, Wim Wenders and Juliano Ribeiro Salgado, France/Brazil/Italy)*

A film about and with the great, internationally famous Brazilian photographer Sebastião Salgado, who has made exquisite, sometimes shattering photographs of people and events throughout the globe, including the Rwanda holocaust, various catastrophes in Africa, starvations, exoduses, primitive tribes, discoveries of pristine territories of wild flora and fauna and grandiose landscapes. Sebastião's life and work are revealed to us by his son Juliano, who accompanied him during his last journeys, and by Wim Wenders, a photographer himself. The film often brought tears to our eyes. Both Toby and I thought it was far and away the most powerful film in Cannes this year. It received a ten-minute standing ovation from the packed house in the large Salle Debussy auditorium.

We greeted Wim after the film. Sony Pictures Classics has grabbed it. Indeed, SPC has made glorious pick-ups this year in Cannes. We'll open this superb film at LPC. It won the Special Jury Prize at Cannes but deserved a higher award.

Winter Sleep *(2014, Nuri Bilge Ceylan, Turkey/France/Germany)*

Shot in a small Cappadocia village (a region known for its mineral spring waters, which T. and I visited over twenty years ago) with a small hotel in the middle of it and a lot of poverty all around. This Chekhovian tale takes place mostly in the hotel that the lead character, Aydin, a former middle-aged actor, has inherited.

I thought the film could win the Palme d'Or, but there were still many films to see. New Yorker Films had distributed Ceylan's *Distant* (2002). I wrote in my midnight notes at the 2003 Cannes Film Festival: "A quiet movie, country/city mouse story of two cousins with little in common forced together by circumstances in Istanbul. Constructed from curmudgeonly silences and prickly exchanges, this rumination of male detachment is both humorous and heartbreaking." I made an offer, which he accepted. Then five minutes later, after we shook hands on the deal, he said to me: "Would you step aside if I got a higher offer?" I said I would. After all is said, new filmmakers have a tough time starting their careers. Ceylan didn't get a better offer, so we distributed *Distant*, which won the Grand Prix.

We became friends. He came to Cannes every year even if he didn't have a film. I always visited him in the Turkish Pavilion for a chat. Nuri is a lovable, modest man. I looked for him this year at his stand but missed him. I left him a note saying that I thought he would win the Palme d'Or. Isn't it nice that dreams sometimes come true?

Wild Tales *(2014, Damián Szifron, Argentina/Spain)*

The film was co-produced by Pedro Almodóvar. Six roughly twenty-minute tales, sort of thematically linked, dealing with road rage, corrupt municipal car park authorities, a rich man who does what he can do to cover up his son's involvement in a hit-and-run accident, and a final wonderful episode about a deceived bride who goes ballistic. A rich cinema fruitcake, the atmosphere high as a kite. Audiences will eat this one up. Sony Pictures Classics will distribute, and we'll play it at LPC. Don't miss it!

Fear *(1954, Roberto Rossellini, Italy)*

A new restoration in 4K from the Cineteca di Bologna, *Fear*, based on a Stefan Zweig novel, played in the 2014 Cannes Classics section. This highlight was the last film we saw in Cannes. Ingrid Bergman stars as Irene Wagner, the wife of a prominent scientist professor, Albert. Irene has been having an affair with Erich Baumann. She does not disclose this to her husband, or she'd ruin their "perfect marriage." This fills her with anxiety and guilt. Erich's jealous ex-girlfriend learns about the affair and begins to blackmail Irene, turning Irene's psychological torture into a harsh reality. When Irene finds out that the extortion plot is truly an experiment in fear, she is driven into a homicidal/suicidal rage. But she is saved from suicide by her husband at the last minute, both sorry for what they did.

This neat little package of a plot is used by Rossellini to examine the dynamic of "fear." A taut, masterful gem of a film with suave acting, as only Rossellini can elicit from his fine players. For me it was a fitting finale for this year's A plus festival.

Son of Saul *(2015, László Nemes, Hungary)*

One of the strongest films of the festival. Set in Auschwitz in 1944, the film follows the activities of Saul Ausländer, a Hungarian Jew. He is a member of the camp's *Sonderkommandos*, Jewish inmates delegated to send new arrivals to the gas chamber and crematorium. Saul is obsessed with finding the body of a boy who appears to be his son, and finding a rabbi to say the Kaddish with a proper burial. At the same time, he must choose whether to participate in a clandestine uprising being planned by the prisoners.

The narrative is disjointed, the environment quasi-surreal and dreamlike, the effect powerful. Another film on the Holocaust, each one part of a horrific mosaic—from Alain Resnais's *Night and Fog* to Claude Lanzmann's *Shoah*. The director was an assistant on Béla Tarr's *The Man from London*. *Son of Saul* gained the Grand Prix. Sony has it and we'll certainly open it in December.

BERLIN

Sophie Scholl: The Final Days *(2005, Marc Rothemund, Germany)*

Spring 1943. The Germans have lost the battle of Stalingrad, and in Munich, members of the White Rose infiltrate the city with wave upon wave of anti-Hitler activities. Sophie and her brother Hans distribute flyers in the main hall of Munich University, where they are arrested, interrogated, and put on trial, condemned, and executed. Sophie's last words are: "You're hanging us today, but tomorrow, it'll be your heads that will roll." This is the director's first feature film—he has made seven TV films before. This film looks like a TV film: studio-shot exteriors and back-and-forth dialogue. Julia Jentsch gives a superb performance as Sophie Scholl, but I found myself annoyed by the TV-ness of the film. I kept saying to myself: "Oh, where are you, Fassbinder?" I was premature in leaving after an hour. Word on the film was very good. Julia Jentsch won the Best Actress award, the director won Best Director, and the film won the "Ecumenical Jury Prize." I will see the whole film in New York. A big distributor will buy this film and I will want to play it at the LP.

Absolute Wilson *(2006, Katharina Otto-Bernstein, USA/Germany)*

A documentary on Robert Wilson—his background, his voyage into the higher spheres of his magical art as an avant-garde opera creator. Our first experience of his work was *Einstein on the Beach*, one of the greatest stage spectaculars I have ever seen. Since then we ran to whatever new work he presented. Although the film is somewhat conventionally made—with endless talking heads—it works, especially if you are a Wilson buff. Many famous artists and promoters are interviewed—among them Philip Glass, Susan Sontag, Harvey Lichtenstein, John Rockwell, etc. We talked with Wilson after the film ended. He comes across as a very sincere man. I told him I would play the film at the Lincoln Plaza Cinemas.

Beaufort *(2007, Joseph Cedar, Israel)*

A small band of Israeli soldiers hole up in an old seafarer's fortress, Beaufort, a former British military base. The film depicts the difficult military situation of these young Israeli soldiers as Hezbollah fighters shell the fort with mortars. The soldiers are brave, frightened, eager to complete their mission—the last group of soldiers pulling out of Lebanon. I was gripped and moved by this film. It is simultaneously an antiwar film and a patriotic portrait of Israeli soldiers. [Cedar] won the Best Director award. I thought the film deserved the Golden Bear. It was one of the best films I saw in Berlin.

Katyn *(2007, Andrzej Wajda, Poland)*

A powerful film about the murder of officers of the Polish army—including reservists, police officers, and intellectuals—in September 1939, the period when Germany invaded and crushed Poland in the West, and the Soviets, with a handshake from the Germans, occupied the Eastern Zone of the country. The story moves along when Andrzej, an officer, refuses to flee with his wife, Anna, because his allegiance to the army is more important to him than his marriage vows. The film swings back and forth between the Soviet prison camp and Cracow, where many professors were arrested. After the Nazi defeat in 1945, propagandist newsreels show the Soviets charging the Germans with the massacre at Katyn. There are also episodes of Polish compliance with their Soviet masters in order to keep their jobs. It was the Soviets who killed these Poles—in an effort to destabilize the country so that they could rule during the Occupation more effectively. In the last ten to fifteen minutes of the film Wajda shows how, one by one, each officer was murdered by a shot in the head from behind; then a bulldozer arrives and covers up the mass grave—as powerful a scene of brutality as I have ever seen. It turns out that Wajda, who was eighteen when the massacre occurred, was the son of one of the officers murdered (not shown or explained in the film, a biographical detail I knew about). Wajda wanted to make this film for twenty-six years but couldn't figure out how to do it. The result is a major film. The irony is that there are no American takers so far. If New Yorker Films had the money I would snap it up in a second. Screened Out of Competition in the 2008 Berlinale.

Shine a Light *(2008, Martin Scorsese, USA)*

Opening night. Performance film. The Rolling Stones at the 2,800-seat Beacon Theatre on Broadway at Seventy-Fourth Street in the fall of 2006. Some of Hollywood's top cinematographers shot the film (at least six cameras). The Rolling Stones perform (then in their early sixties) with the same kinetic energy that made them such a legend forty years ago. Their music is not my cup of tea, but their pulsating singing and guitar playing is a wonder to watch. The audience ate this one up.

Lake Tahoe *(2008, Fernando Eimbcke, Mexico)*

The director of *Duck Season*. Similar deadpan style but it takes place outdoors and is in color (shot by Alexis Zabe—*Duck Season; Silent Light*). A young man has crashed his car into a telephone pole. He goes in search of a mechanic and has run-ins with a series of goofy characters in an increasingly circuitous attempt to fix the problem. Somehow he can't find the right part, and we are in Kafka territory. He meets Lucia, a punk young woman who works behind the counter of a mechanical equipment store. Soon enough they sleep with each other. Finally, David, a teenager and kung fu fan, shows up and being somewhat of a mechanical wizard figures out how to fix the car. A strange, often hypnotic film that will probably be picked up. I'll play it—although *Duck Season* lasted one week at the Lincoln Plaza.

An Education *(2009, Lone Scherfig, UK/USA)*

A fairy tale that rubs up against harsh old reality. 1961. Jenny is a high school student whose ambition is to go to Oxford. She's sixteen, attractive, charming, bright, lives at home with her conservative parents in Twickenham. Her father is a wisecracking genial man whose targets are outside the insular world of correct behavior. Along comes David, a Jewish man in his thirties. He's handsome, charming, wordly, playful, a dreamboat. Jenny slowly falls for him, shakes off her conservative coils, and eventually acquiesces in bedroom sport. Meanwhile David manages to enchant her parents and at one point proposes to take them to Paris for a fun trip. One day Jenny comes across a document in David's glove compartment that reveals that he is a married man. Jenny's world collapses, as well as that of her parents. Ultimately she gets it together and winds up going to Oxford. What makes this simple tale fly is smart dialogue, charming acting, the bliss of romance while it lasts. The director, Lone Scherfig, is a Dane, some of whose previous films are *Wilbur Wants to Kill Himself* and *Italian for Beginners*. She and Susanne Bier are among the best directors from Denmark. I was smitten by *An Education*, which was picked up by Sony Pictures Classics at Sundance for 3 million bucks. It'll open on two screens this summer at LPC. For me this film was a festival highlight.

Budrus *(2009, Julia Bacha, USA)*

A powerful documentary about the effect on the Palestinians living in Budrus (population 1,500) when Israel decides to extend The Wall through a grove of olive trees. At the center of the film is Ayed Morrar, a Palestinian of this village. He is a nonviolent activist who organizes a peaceful protest movement that includes Hamas, Fatah, and Israelis, all of whom (after numerous violent reactions by the Israeli soldiers) stand their ground and in the end persuade the

Israeli government to move the wall to a Green Line, thereby preserving the olive groves so necessary for the town's economy. A very moving film. Ayer Morrar deserves a large Peace Prize.

The Kids Are All Right *(2010, Lisa Cholodenko, USA/France)*

With Annette Bening (Nic) and Julianne Moore (Jules) as a lesbian couple leading a bohemian life in the sun-drenched Los Angeles hilltops. When their teenage children seek out their biological father, the sperm donor who brought these kids into the world (played wonderfully by Mark Ruffalo), complications begins. Paul (Ruffalo), an organic crop farmer and restaurateur, starts coming to family dinners. He offers Jules, who is starting a landscape business, some work in his scruffy backyard. They wind up having sex. . . . Witty dialogue, unselfconscious acting—a delicious romp with serious implications since Nic and Jules's marriage is treated as normal, with none of the nasty undertones that some people attribute to gay couples. A very progressive film, fun to watch. It will play well at LPC.

Honey *(2010, Semih Kaplanoglu, Turkey/Germany)*

A moody, beautifully shot film in the heavily wooded mountains of Rize province, northeast Turkey. From the Berlinale catalogue:

> Six-year-old Yusuf has just begun attending primary school where he is learning how to read and write. His father, Yakup, is a beekeeper. He goes about his trade deep inside the woods where he hangs up his bee hives in the treetops of the highest trees. The mountain forest is a place of deep mystery to Yusuf and he derives great pleasure from accompanying his father there.
>
> One morning Yusuf tells his father about a dream he had the night before. Yakup turns on him curtly telling him never to share his dreams with others. The same day, Yusuf is asked to read out a text in front of the class. He suddenly begins to stutter and he is laughed at by the rest of the class.
>
> One day the bees suddenly disappear, throwing into question the family's means of earning a living. Yakup decides to set off for the remote mountains. But no sooner has he left, than Yusuf stops speaking. . . .

The days pass—and still Yakup does not return. . . .

Yusuf and his mother set off on a fruitless search for signs of his father's whereabouts after which Yusuf decides to continue the search for his father on his own. His is a journey into the unknown.

A gorgeously shot film with a host of exotic country scenes (e.g., dancing celebrations by archaically costumed men). Derek Elley panned the film in *Variety*. I'm sure Werner Herzog pussy-whipped the jury. The film is right up his alley.

The Turin Horse *(2011, Béla Tarr and Ágnes Hranitzky, Hungary/ France/Germany/Switzerland/USA)*

At the outset a voice-over explains the backstory: in Turin in 1889, the philosopher Nietzsche witnessed a horse being whipped, and subsequently retreated into silence and madness. "We do not know what happened to the horse," the voice tells us. The body of the film depicts what we can assume to be the horse's career. In chapters set over five days, the action, such as it is, takes place at a farmhouse in a brutally windblown landscape where an elderly man lives with his daughter. The film follows the two human characters' daily routine in great precision and with deliberate repetition. The man has a lame arm and so his daughter helps him get dressed every morning, then they eat a boiled potato with their fingers. At one point a band of gypsies show up—the man chases them away. On another day a townsman shows up for some liquor and delivers an end-of-the-world rant. After the fifth day, when the water doesn't flow in the house, the man and his daughter pack up and go to another small house. End of story. The film is shot in forty long takes in stark black and white. The music is muted, resembles a Bach church piece, and drones on softly throughout the film. This work is for those who were turned on by his previous two films, *Satantango* and *Werckmeister Harmonies*. For sure it will be in the New York Film Festival and will play at the Anthology Film Archives or at one of the two new Lincoln Center theaters. I was hooked by the Bressonian austerity of the film. A few days later, Michel Ciment, the great French film critic, spoke against the film. [It won the Jury Grand Prix (the Silver Bear), and is currently the last narrative feature Tarr has made.]

October *(1928, Sergei Eisenstein, USSR)*

In 2012, we saw this monumental film in the Friedrichstradt-Palast, a magnificent hall with several thousand seats. It was commissioned by the USSR Communist Party to commemorate the tenth anniversary of the 1917 October Revolution. From the Berlinale catalogue:

> Filmed at original locations and featuring veterans of the historical events, the film reconstructs the trajectory of the Russian Revolution and comments on events through the use of suggestive montage and ironic imagery. No sooner was the film premiered at the Bolshoi Theatre on March 14, 1928, than it was withdrawn from cinemas under the pretext of being too "formalist." Eisenstein himself produced a re-edited export version of the film, which was in turn subject to censorship in the various countries where it was shown. For this reason there are many different versions of the film circulating in cinematheques and archives all over the world.

The print we saw is based on a print from the Munich Film Museum. The Party gave Eisenstein tons of money to make this film. The film goes into all the violent events that informed the Revolution. The Berlin Symphony Orchestra performed the music accompanying this silent masterpiece. Before it began Naum Kleiman, the head of the Moscow Cinema Museum, spoke to the audience about the making of the film. Without question, we felt that the showing would be the highlight of the Berlinale. It is truly a monumental work, one of the greatest films in the history of cinema. We were dazzled, smitten by it. We had poor seats because we came on the late side. All I can say is: Wow!

Ulrike Ottinger: Nomad from the Lake *(2012, Brigitte Kramer, Germany)*

An affectionate, accomplished profile of one of Germany's most offbeat filmmakers. Ulrike Ottinger was born to a well-to-do family in a large house on Lake Constance. Her career is traced from the influence growing up by the lake had on her work to the journeys she undertook to make films in Mongolia and Japan. Her films look like no other films—they are extravagant, richly anthropological, laced with multicolored costumes and interesting faces. She is highly regarded in Germany. Unfortunately her films do not travel too well abroad, possibly because of their esoteric nature. Years ago we distributed one of her films, *Taiga*, an eight-hour Mongolian journey. When we saw *Under Snow*, her latest documentary film, also playing in this festival, she greeted us warmly as we entered the theater.

Caesar Must Die *(2012, Paolo and Vittorio Taviani, Italy)*

A powerful prison drama about drama in prison: specifically, about the staging of Shakespeare's *Julius Caesar* with a cast of prisoners from the high-security wing of Rome's Rebibbia jail. The film demonstrates how the universality of Shakespeare's language helps the actors to understand their roles and immerse themselves in the bard's interplay of friendship, betrayal, power, dishonesty, and violence. One of them comments: "Ever since I discovered art this cell has truly become a prison." An unusual, artistic documentary that hovers between learned lines and rehearsal. This is a film unlike any other film I've ever seen. It won the Golden Bear prize.

TORONTO

Bubble *(2005, Steven Soderbergh, USA)*

Produced by Todd Wagner and Mark Cuban, the billionaires who own the Landmark chain of theaters. Their aim is to open the film theatrically on the same day that it comes out in stores in DVD and on television, thereby eliminating the two "windows." Shot in Hi-Def tape on a low budget, the film looks awful on the screen—cheap, little color contrast, often blurry. Set in small-town blue-collar tract houses, depressing bars, low-voltage characters. Two main ones: a young man who lives with his mother and an older fat woman who takes care of the elderly ailing father. They both work in a factory producing rubber dolls. When Rose, an attractive young woman, comes into the factory as a worker, she catches the eye of the young man. Mysteriously, one day Rose is strangled to death. There are no clues or apparent motives. It could serve as a metaphor for the repressed violence of people in America who are trapped by their humdrum lives. I didn't like the film while watching it but the further I get away from it, I think more favorably about it. Will I play it? I don't know. May have to have a second look.

Sketches of Frank Gehry *(2005, Sydney Pollack, USA)*

A charming, incisive, loving, educational portrait of America's top architect. Pollack delves into Gehry's creative processes—such as using cardboard and scissors to come up with the look of buildings as they constantly change shapes. Extensive footage of the Guggenheim Museum in Bilbao and the Walt Disney Concert Hall in Los Angeles, both ravishing buildings. Philip Johnson proclaims Gehry to be America's top architect. The film makes the process of architecture poetic, dramatic, informative. This film is one of my highlights in the festival. I tried to formulate an offer, but John Sloss [of Cinetic Media] is the seller and he uses the Italian lira system, namely, a number with many zeroes attached to it. So I will try to get Michael Barker to spring for it. [Sony Pictures Classics did release the film theatrically in 2006, in advance of its PBS broadcast as part of *American Masters*.]

The Willow Tree *(2005, Majid Majidi, Iran)*

From the director of *The Color of Paradise* and *Baran*. In a tremendous performance, Parviz Parastui plays the role of a renowned professor of Persian poetry at a Tehran university. Blind since early childhood, he leads a full, happy, productive life surrounded by a doting wife and a charming nine-year-old daughter. When a deadly disease strikes, he goes to Paris for a specialist's care. Assured that he is no longer in peril, the doctor tells him he is eligible for a cornea transplant. The operation is a success. He is ecstatic over the recovery of his sight. But back in Tehran, his first delusional experience occurs on a subway train, where he witnesses a pickpocket lifting a wallet from a man's pocket. At home he balks over his wife's "mothering" of him and becomes discontented by a *seen* world in contrast to the world he enjoyed as a blind man. In one episode he covets a beautiful young woman whom he sees at her music school, only then to witness that she is picked up by her boyfriend. He is ultimately reduced to being an unhappy, aggressive man. Sad as this may all seem, the film is well made, so poetic, so imaginative in its exploration of what a seen and unseen life means, that while the tragic downfall of the character is upsetting you walk away from the film with a vision of life you have not encountered before. For us this was the best film we saw in the festival. At the airport, as we were leaving for New York several days later, we encountered the seller and made an offer. He had numerous festival screenings and he admitted that there was only one offer. In today's climate of big money on the table for meretricious films, *The Willow Tree* is a lost soul. My only reservation about the film is its excessively schmaltzy music track. The seller said that is how the Iranian audience likes it. Apparently the film is a big hit in Iran.

Falling *(2006, Barbara Albert, Austria/Germany)*

In a small town, a popular local schoolteacher passes away. Five of his students who are now grown up come back home for the funeral, the first time the former friends have seen each other in fourteen years. Their reunion goes long into the night of the funeral and into the following day as they are all forced to reflect on everything that has changed in the intervening years. A film that explores both character and social comment. I had to leave fifteen minutes before the end to catch another film. I liked what I saw very much, so I'll catch the film at the NYFF. I might be tempted to take on this film. The director has a fresh voice.

Away from Her *(2006, Sarah Polley, Canada)*

Grant (Gordon Pinsent) and Fiona (Julie Christie) have been married for decades. They have been through rough patches, but their lives are inextricably connected, and their relationship seems idyllic. Now retired, they live comfortably in a house in the country, but their contentment is permanently disrupted when Fiona's memory starts to deteriorate. Determined not to saddle Grant with her declining health, she insists on going to a rest home—which shatters Grant. Based on an Alice Munro short story. The film plays like a documentary melodrama. It has some of the best—most moving—acting I've ever seen. Has Academy Award written all over it. Lionsgate bought it for 750K. Bingham Ray quipped: "It's perfect for your senior citizen audience at the Lincoln Plaza.

They'll see it twice because they will have forgotten that they saw the film the first time."

My Best Friend *(2006, Patrice Leconte, France)*

A very funny buddy film. The twist? A buddy is missing. François (French mega-star Daniel Auteuil) is a middle-aged antiques dealer. He has a stylish apartment and a fabulous life, but at a dinner party with a group he considers his dearest acquaintances, he is blindsided by the revelation that none of them likes him. He's arrogant, self-centered, and harsh, and they don't believe he even has a friend. His business partner, Catherine, makes him a bet: if he can produce a *meilleur ami*, she will let him keep the massive Greek vase he acquired that afternoon on the company tab. If not, it's hers. Having accepted the wager, François goes through his address book in search of "my best friend" in vain. Moving through Paris, he runs into a trivia-spouting, magnanimous cabbie named Bruno, brilliantly played by Dany Boon. François, after many false starts, hires Bruno to teach him about learning the "three S's" —being sociable, smiling, and sincere. From there the film takes off like a rocket, with some of the funniest off-the-wall, humane scenes I've seen in many a moon. I think this film is my favorite one in the festival, with the possible exception of Alain Resnais's *Coeurs (Private Fears in Public Places)*, which is pure magic.

Chop Shop *(2007, Ramin Bahrani, USA)*

By the director of *Man Push Cart*, which I haven't seen, the film is set in Willets Point, in the shadow of Shea Stadium. This area of Queens, New York, is known as the Iron Triangle due to a conglomeration of auto repair shops, a nasty enclave where shady deals and hypersalesmanship reign. Twelve-year-old Alejandro gets a job in one of these repair shops, sells M&M's on the subway, steals a woman's purse, participates in shady deals—anything to survive. When his sister, Isamar, shows up, Alejandro moves heaven and earth to provide for her. He finds a place above a repair shop to live. Meanwhile, Isamar earns some money doing blow jobs on truck drivers. . . . The film has the look of actuality, of a speedy documentary, many slices of life. It has energy, heart, grit, humanity. I enjoyed it immensely and hope it gets picked up since I'm ready to play it at LP.

My Winnipeg *(2007, Guy Maddin, Canada)*

A "docu-fantasia" about the director's home town. Riding on a train he fetches up scenes of his life in Winnipeg, growing up with an outspoken unconventional mother who often says shocking things about life, scenes of such well-known events like the Winnipeg General Strike and the loss of the Winnipeg Jets, to scandals like the Golden Boy pageants and a racetrack tragedy that left numerous horses encased in ice for the duration of the winter. Film is wrought in the style of Dziga Vertov. It was my favorite film of the festival. It's also a masterpiece. IFC picked it up.

A Thousand Years of Good Prayers *(2007, Wayne Wang, USA)*

The director, whose first film *Chan Is Missing* (1982) we distributed, returns to low-budget filmmaking. The new film is beautiful, an Ozu-like portrait of an aging caring father who comes from China to visit his daughter. She works as a librarian and is having an affair with a married man. The father is distraught about this, but when he meets an Iranian woman his age and begins a thing with her, he is less annoyed with his daughter. Simply made, no melodramatics, a keen eye for small detail, simple eloquent dialogues. Film would play well at LP.

Cave of Forgotten Dreams *(2010, Werner Herzog, USA/France/ Germany)*

Only Herzog, with his unusual vision of mankind's wonders and hypnotic voice, could capture the beauty and artistic depth of the cave paintings in Chauvet-Pont d'Arc in southern France, created thirty thousand years ago. (Lascaux is roughly as old.) He and his crew descend into the caves with 3-D equipment to capture these exquisite drawings. His philosophical reaction is consistently poetic as he discusses the ability of primitive cavemen to re-create animals and forests. He also interviews a few paleontologists for their thoughts. Herzog continues to cook on all four burners. Film was picked up by IFC.

STANLEY KAUFFMANN
INTERVIEWS DAN TALBOT

(1972, never published; edited for clarity)

SK: Dan, you're in three branches of film endeavor in this country. I think you're the only man, as far as I know, who's in all three at the same time. You run a repertory theater in Manhattan, the New Yorker; you're engaged in very active and, to my mind, important theatrical release and distribution of films; and also run a film library, New Yorker Films, of considerable distinction. Let's take the first part. When and why did you take over the New Yorker? I ought to say for our readers, it's that nice, lovely, cruddy old film theater on upper Broadway.

DT: The New Yorker used to be the Yorktown theater; it was a Brandt house, and they sold it to a friend of mine, Henry Rosenberg, who bought it with the intention of converting it into a Spanish theater.

SK: Tell us the year.

DT: It was in 1960. At that time I'd been back for a brief while after having lived in Europe, needed work, and persuaded him to let me try repertory theater. We started in March of 1960. It was an instant success.

SK: Can you remember your opening bill?

DT: *Henry V* and *The Red Balloon*. It was just one of these fortunate circumstances of having needed work and just having that theater suddenly become available to me—he was very generous and nice about letting me do what I wanted to do. It became so successful that I was able to buy the theater from him a few years later. But that's the genesis of theater itself.

SK: I'm sure you've thought about this a lot—what are your explanations of its immediate success?

DT: I didn't have any formula; I had a notion. Even at that time, I never assumed I was smarter than audiences or knew better what they were looking for. I made an assumption that the audience consisted of my friends and I wanted to show what I wanted to see, and hopefully what they would like to see. This is an ideal way of running a commercial venture, whether it's publishing or film or what have you. It just happened to work out that way. At that time my primary interest was in American repertory, particularly the twenties and thirties, and for about five or six years I pretty much went through a large swath of that period.

SK: Had you felt that that period had been neglected?

DT: Well, it was not just neglected—it didn't exist in theaters. Back in the late forties and early fifties, there were a few theaters, like the Fifth Avenue Cinema and maybe one or two others, that would program very obvious things like Mae West or the Marx Brothers or something like that, but there'd never been a very concerted effort to put together what represented a certain period. And it was extremely successful. I never booked in a program where I thought in advance, *Gee, this is going to make a lot of money.* I just said, *I want to see this film, it would be interesting to see for example what Preston Sturges looks like today,* and I booked him in, played him, and it worked.

SK: Did you go see these films yourself or have them run off for you beforehand, or was it from memory?

DT: No, not at all. A lot of them I had known from my younger years. I also got a lot of tips from Pauline Kael. When I opened the theater, she was operating a twin theater in Berkeley, and we had become friendly and used to exchange a lot of information together, namely things like tracking down a print. She'd call me up and say, "Hey, I know a 35mm print of *Sunset Boulevard*, it's in Los Angeles," then I would confront Paramount in New York and say, "Look, I know there's a 35mm print in Los Angeles, I want to play the show." And I gave her the same kind of information. But I did look at her programming, which I found quite original and startling. She had, I would say, a considerable influence on some of my programming.

SK: Did you use any of her program notes?

DT: No.

SK: Because I know she wrote extensive program notes.

DT: No, I never did use her program notes. As a matter of fact, she frequently sent me critiques of the program notes that I wrote.

SK: Oh, you wrote your own?

DT: Yeah. She'd say, for example, this isn't true, or what a clumsy way of wording it, or something like that. She really carried her whole critical apparatus into the commercial, practical area. Anyway, the point is that what made it interesting for me is that I made a vow that I would never repeat a program. The point of repeating a program is that if you find a successful film or combination and do very big business with it, you obviously want to bring it back within half a year or a year because you have a little secret that other exhibitors don't have, to wit, that this program is a draw, and why not make some money out of it? But I never did that, at least for the first five or six years. Then when I went through that whole period, I got very bored with the theater. With the New Yorker.

SK: Do you think that that theater, that program, that enterprise, would have succeeded the same way five years before? And if not, why not? Or ten years?

DT: Well, I don't know. Let's situate 1960. Let's see, was Eisenhower still president?

SK: Just leaving.

DT: Just leaving. A lot of it had to do perhaps with the political climate. I don't remember if there was much ennui or angst in the air, but I'm sure that had a lot to do with it. For example, you can account for the great success of a book like *On the Road* precisely because of the time it came out. I believe it was published at the beginning of the Eisenhower administration.

SK: Very close to it.

DT: And the whole Beat thing hadn't become a big phenomenon, but it certainly was one of the catalysts for a certain feeling in the air. I think it is clearly a book that only could have been written at that time. I can't imagine a book like *On the Road* having been written during the Kennedy administration or the Roosevelt administration. The same with a film like *Easy Rider*, a film that only could have happened at the time that it did. It played into a certain psychic need and configuration of the society. In the same way, to answer your question about whether the theater would have succeeded five years before, I don't think so. Five years before, we were just emerging from the McCarthy period and there was a depression or recession at that time. It was a two- or three-year period where things were very bad.

SK: The dates of all the recessions were in parallel years.

DT: Right. The point is that in 1960, things were quiet. It was before the civil rights agitation, before the assassinations; nothing really was happening in the culture. Writers were writing and becoming more famous. By then, Mailer and Bellow had pretty much consolidated their positions in the literary world. But there was nothing spectacular going on within the society. That period of quiet allowed for what is essentially—I was going to say frivolous—freer forms of expression. It's not terribly important what I did at that point. I wasn't making a point of forcing the American cinema down people's throats.

SK: I understand. You didn't have any political motivation?

DT: No, none whatsoever.

SK: But isn't it so that in this city, which is still a litmus paper for a lot of things that happen in our country and in the world, a theater starts and presents a repertoire of film for an audience that takes film seriously?

DT: Right.

SK: And it's an immediate success. Now that's not a world-shaking event, socially, sociologically, politically, but culturally, it is.

DT: I suppose you can say that.

SK: Do you think that this has anything to do with a growing attitude of seriousness toward film in general that was going on in this country at that time? Perhaps sparked by the huge success of Agee's film criticism, published in 1958?

DT: Yes, that may have had something to do with it, but it happened to be also at the time that the French New Wave came into being, in 1960, when *Breathless* came out, and film at that time had become a serious subject. There were courses being developed throughout the country. This was the beginning of film being taken seriously and not just as mass entertainment. Certainly, you had the beginning of the art house moment in New York—many theaters were being built. It was the beginning of the East Side being developed, the Village getting a bit fancier and theaters being gussied up there. The atmosphere was right for it, but that said, I'm amazed there weren't more situations like that. If you compare New York, for example, with Paris, the difference is between day and night.

SK: If you look at the history of criticism, for example as I just have, it's a mistake, a very serious mistake to say that there was no serious American film criticism at the beginning . . . there *was*.

DT: Certainly there was that.

SK: The attitude toward serious film criticism was very different in France than the general attitude in the United States. And as you know, there had been many attempts to do, let us call it, repertory in this country before your theater—Cinema 16, various film societies in the thirties, and so on—but they were relatively restricted, while yours was a public operation that was immediately successful and therefore of greater interest.

DT: Obviously there was a felt need for this kind of thing. More people didn't jump into the breach immediately afterward—it did take about six, seven years, and then of course everyone jumped into the breach.

SK: You said, for example, as if it were a casual matter, that you took over this theater and showed just what you liked. But the fact that you wanted to do that and the fact that you had pictures you liked and wanted to show is itself part of the phenomenon. It might not have been true even of you five or ten years before.

DT: Right.

SK: You mentioned that the first five or six years of your enterprise was mostly American films.

DT: Also at that time I was interested in trying to introduce some new films.

SK: Some foreign films?

DT: Foreign films, and some American films. Somewhere I have a list. I launched, up to 1965–66, roughly twenty films, mostly foreign. Among them were Bresson's *Pickpocket* and Kurosawa's *The Idiot*, Antonioni's *Le Amiche*, Buñuel's *The Criminal Life of Archibaldo de la Cruz*, Wajda's *Kanal*, *Pull My Daisy*—that short was one of the early programs at the theater, which I showed with Welles's *The Magnificent Ambersons*.

SK: You're itemizing part of my bill of gratitude to you, and I'm speaking for a lot of people I know, because none of us could have seen those films, certainly as early as that. *Pull My Daisy* leads to another point: Do you have the feeling that—you mentioned Kerouac before—that Kerouac's book was the first salient signal, and the success of your theater was another, of an alternative culture? There was a kind of, call it refuge or avenue that the film world provided—by "film world" I mean all kinds of films. I don't mean dream, I don't mean escapism, I don't mean Joan Crawford on a yacht. The film world provided for young people who were increasingly dissatisfied, and that dissatisfaction was made more horrible by the assassination of Kennedy.

DT: Are you referring now specifically to the independent film movement?

SK: No, audiences.

DT: Or as an alternate medium to the written word?

SK: Yes, a system of quasi-perfections that existed in a very imperfect world.

DT: That's a tough one. The only thing I can speculate is there were a lot of writers in this country and elsewhere who suddenly got very interested in film and felt that through their books they weren't reaching the kind of audience that they'd like to reach. The impulse of an artist is basically an oceanic impulse to want to have everyone wake up the following morning and read what he's delivered before. The fact is that through film you certainly can reach a much wider audience than through books, except for the best-seller. An interesting novelist, if lucky, will have three or four thousand copies of his novel sold; whereas in the analogue of that in film, chances are that it may be seen by as many as fifty or a hundred thousand people. So my only speculation is this desire to want to reach more people.

SK: And you had a long-seated desire to act as a bridge between the film and the audience, because I remember that in the foreword to your anthology *Film*, published in 1959, just before you went into the theater business, you wrote: "The adage that all good art inevitably finds its audience is just not true of movies." Did that line of your own act as a kind of—

DT: Impulse? I think it did. Actually, the line stems from the time I'd been working as a story editor at Warner Brothers and was amazed to see the number of really bright people who had fantastic projects that were very workable. They just weren't able to pull it off, but the end result was that they changed their sights and instead of thinking in terms of making a $2 million picture, somehow they went ahead and made a picture for something like $100,000 or $200,000.

SK: Well, from these films that you've just mentioned, most of which were imports, what encouraged you to import?

DT: Actually, I didn't import them, I just played them. At that time I wasn't in distribution.

SK: Surely no one had *The Idiot* here. You brought that into this country, didn't you?

DT: No, it was owned by a Japanese film company that had offices here, and I arranged for the showing.

SK: Okay, that's a real distinction, but certainly no one I know of made a move toward showing that picture here before you did.

DT: No, no one did make the move. The impulse behind that was simply not wanting to play repertory, American repertory, all year round and wanting to vary it a little with some foreign films that had been neglected. I lost a considerable amount of money on each one of these launchings, and I knew I would lose, but I also knew that I'd recoup the loss by showing repertory programs, which were by and large extremely successful. But as a result of those sporadic showings, I did get very interested in foreign films and independent production in America, and one thing or another led me into distribution. In fact, the film that got me into distribution was Bertolucci's *Before the Revolution*.

SK: That was relatively recently, though.

DT: No, longer ago than that, in 1965.

SK: Of course, I'm sorry.

DT: I was so dazzled by it at the New York Film Festival that I wrote to the Italian producer saying I wanted to open it at the New Yorker. He wrote back and said, "No, I'm not interested in an exhibition deal, but if you make me an offer for distribution then you can have the opportunity of doing what you want with it."

SK: Let's go into this a little more from the point of view of the cultural stream. What in your experience running the New Yorker made you feel that the time was right to do this kind of thing—financially right, or culturally right—to bring these things in? What compelled you to start this work?

DT: Are you talking now about foreign films? Culturally, I think the time wasn't right and it still isn't right—it hasn't gotten any better—it was just some kind of doggedness, persistence on my part, to expose these works.

I mean, the commercial exhibitors wouldn't touch them with a ten-foot pole, there were very few.

SK: You mean the so-called art houses?

DT: Particularly the art houses.

SK: They were doing Brigitte Bardot at the time.

DT: No, Brigitte Bardot was actually in the late fifties, in the early sixties. But by 1965, the art houses in America had been co-opted by the large commercial major studios, and they were showing by and large Hollywood products, as they still do to this day. The so-called art movement started changing around '66, '67 for a variety of reasons.

SK: Changing from what to what?

DT: There was less interest in the offbeat foreign film. I mean, the economics were against it, it was more expensive to launch—now it's just out of the question. The cost is so prohibitive it can't be done. There was simply more money in these commercial films—in the American commercial films or the big Joe Levine kind of foreign film. Nowhere in New York could you see a lesser work by Fellini, for example *Il Bidone*, which was one of the films I launched, or an older Antonioni or an older Kurosawa, or even a *Before the Revolution*. It did show at the New York Film Festival, got some wonderful notices, but died when I opened it and didn't do any business. But that's the genesis of how I got involved in distribution. I showed the film in one or two other cities and then lay low for a while, but then again felt some kind of obligation to get involved in more films. Now I have a library of about 150 films and I'm in it up to here, and am now more interested in distribution than in exhibition because I think we'll be seeing up to five thousand theaters closing within the next five years.

SK: Well, that's why you're so valuable to a lot of people, because you've sensed the inequity of the world flow of film. Ever since American films began pouring out, the flow from America has been very strong to the rest of the world, but the flow has been relatively small the other way. The rest of the world knows a great deal more about American films than this country knows about foreign films.

DT: Absolutely. Why do you think, from a cultural point of view, this is so? Forget about the economic reasons. Do you have any thoughts about that?

SK: I have a couple of ideas. The first is that American films from a long way back were oriented toward world viewing. The world has always been very interested in American subjects—we all know how the western and the gangster are international figures. Even in Uganda and in Thailand. There's always been an ease in the American approach to film that made them digestible around the world. I'm not knocking American proficiency. Hollywood knew how to make films very well just in terms of craft, very well.

DT: But how do you account for the resistance?

SK: But the resistance the other way around, even in the days of silent pictures, was because a German or French or Italian picture was more parochial in its references, and often—let's put this carefully because I don't want to make it sound as if nothing but art was produced abroad—often tried to probe much deeper than American films and was less respectful of the prevailing taboos, not only in censorship boards but also in the mind of the public.

DT: Do you think that maybe—I do, anyway—the basic reason foreign films have never been accepted in this country is because of the profound xenophobic content of American attitudes toward anything foreign? I think this is an extension of the whole line of Babbitt, of the small town, of the dislike of the outsider. How do you feel about that?

SK: There are two possible reasons for that. One is that this is a nation largely of immigrants who wanted to certify their independence from the old country in a certain way, by concentrating on a new country. And second, in the American mind, film has meant the American film, and it was sort of cute or daring or quaint of Sweden to make a film. We're talking, as you know, very roughly. Historically, there's always been a certain amount of import of films into this country. The French were sending us their films in 1908–1909. Italian films like *Quo Vadis?* and *Cabiria* were very big hits the year before the First World War. German films like *The Last Laugh* had a certain variety, a certain success here in the early twenties, and so on. But in general terms what you're saying is absolutely true. And what you did at the New Yorker was to rectify the situation to some small degree, and helped us to see things. I happen to be, as you know, a considerable admirer of Antonioni, and to my knowledge *Le Amiche* has never been shown in this country except when you showed it.

DT: That's true. But you know, there were others who were doing a lot of interesting work. I thank you for your bouquet, but the Museum of Modern

Art was doing, has always been doing, a lot of good work, and Amos Vogel did a lot of good work.

SK: I saw a lot of good things at Cinema 16 that I would not otherwise have seen, but that's, let us call it, a protected society situation, as is the museum, while this is a venture that's out there exposed to the weather.

DT: A lot of my friends think that I have a very strong masochistic streak.

SK: I suppose that's true, but let's hope they're more satisfied.

DT: Also, Don Rugoff did his share, he really did.

SK: Oh, I don't mean to imply that you're the only person who did a good thing for film in this country, and it's typical of you to want to make that perfectly clear to people reading this, but there's still a considerable debt owed to you by people in New York and increasingly around the country for what you've done. Let's take a big jump now to the relative present, and discuss how you feel about what's going on in film production. First let's start in the United States. What do you feel about film? We've been talking largely about audiences up to now.

DT: It's a big subject. I'll tell you that I'm not really—and I'm not saying this out of any modesty—completely equipped to know fully about the production scene here, particularly in detail. Since I've not been looking at many Hollywood films for the last ten years, except for the more obvious ones like *The Godfather* and *The Last Picture Show* and *Easy Rider*, I really don't know.

SK: Why have you not been looking at them?

DT: I've had no interest in what's been put out by Hollywood.

SK: Well, that's a statement.

DT: I mean that there are so many films I saw in the early sixties that were vulgar and imbecilic that I just didn't want to waste my time with it, and then curiously enough, as we got to Vietnam, I just didn't want to see anything being made in this country by Hollywood. I felt angry, like all of us did, that there was such a degree of immorality operating and there were no protests of any significance in Hollywood. Nothing was being turned out that in any way reflected not the war itself but what happened to the society as a result of the war. For the first time in my life, I felt genuinely ashamed of being American and just didn't want to have anything to do with anything that came out of Hollywood. It sounds like I'm putting it in a very simplistic way, with almost a clichéd aspect to it, but I genuinely felt that way. I just couldn't go into a theater and enjoy a $3 million movie made by Hollywood that would inevitably be fluff while Vietnam was taking place. It made me queasy.

SK: And this didn't affect you if you went and saw a piece of fluff that was made in 1935?

DT: No, because what was made in 1935 was before the fact. Just the notion that the stuff could be mass produced while the war was going on I found so immoral. The United States wasn't doing terrible things in 1935 or the thirties. As far as I know, this is the first time they were really getting into something way over their heads in terms of morality.

SK: Well, without pressing the point . . .

DT: All right, let's get into American production. Briefly, here's really what has happened in the last thirty years. In the early thirties and early forties, Hollywood had a production schedule of six hundred pictures a year. Virtually every picture made a minimum of 2,000 percent profit, one of the reasons being that the studios owned all the theaters and they owned the distribution machinery. So you had a situation of such enormous profitability that they could afford to speculate with some of the nuts who came out to Hollywood, like Ben Hecht or Faulkner or Sturges, etc. All right, let him make his little independent picture on the lot. We're not going to worry too much about it because we won't make 5,000 percent profit; we'll make 2,000 percent profit, but at least it will give us a little prestige or something like that. You had the irony of a production being really what amounted to a totally dictatorial, autocratic situation where the head of the studio really was like Hitler, so that the most independent-minded producer or director just couldn't fight the kind of battle for not being interfered with that you've had in the last twenty years. And I find it an irony that under that kind of system, essentially a fascist way of being in the world or making movies, some of the most remarkable films in the history of this country were made. Then what happened was that the independent movie began after the war. The consent decree came along—I think it was in '47 or '48—and divorced the theaters from the studios, and suddenly business started declining because of television. The consent decree plus television plus some other unknown factors to me resulted in the beginning of the decline of audience attendance. And into the breach came the so-called independent movement. At that time, you had Harold Hecht, Burt Lancaster, and Paddy Chayefsky, and they were doing all these films with essentially bank money. That was the beginning of the fight for not being interfered with, having final cut, etc.—and for some reason or other it didn't work. Maybe part of it had to do with the fact that they weren't terribly good movies, on the whole, and they were independent but they still weren't that cheap. They still cost anywhere from $500,000 to $1.5 million. But by then— we're in the fifties now—production schedules had gotten down to less than two hundred a year, from six hundred to two hundred. To me these are all relevant facts because I follow Panofsky's argument that first came technical invention and art afterward, the same way that industrial problems cause movies to move in a certain direction.

SK: Jean Renoir, I heard him saying on television the other night, with respect to painting, that canvases changed when colors became transportable. You could paint outdoors—technology preceded the change in art.

DT: Absolutely. Anyway, then, in the early sixties, less than ninety films a year were produced in America. Mind you, that was at a time when Japan was producing over six hundred a year, France was producing more than ninety pictures a year, India was producing eighty thousand pictures a year as usual. And then began the small independents, the New American Cinema movement.

SK: That's really a whole other life.

DT: Yes. Right. I think that's one of the reasons foreign films became successful here in the early sixties, because there was a market for your Godards and your Truffauts and so forth, for not enough film was being produced in this country. And they caught on, there was a lot that was written about it.

SK: Would you say also it was because the audience was reduced in quantity but the quality was changing? We've all heard the adverse comments about mass university education in this country, but there has to be some effect from it, and there were more college graduates going to films. I put this question to you as a statement rather than as a question: some raising of the intellectual level of the audience recognized that what these better and best foreign directors were doing was not being accomplished or even attempted in this country.

DT: Only in a few major cities, Stanley, only in a few major cities. When you talk about the raising of the level of cultural consciousness you also have to ask who was writing about film at that time. Don't forget that Bosley Crowther was still the critic of the *New York Times*. While he was a "friend of foreign film," basically he was a very provincial critic who really didn't have a feeling for the new and the adventurous. And then some of the other magazines—I don't think you were writing about film at that time.

SK: I began in 1958.

DT: Oh, in the *New Republic*. Well, then you were one of the more serious people around. I don't know who else was around—Andrew Sarris was writing at the time.

SK: Just about the beginning, I think.

DT: He was pretty passionate when he first began. Was Pauline writing at that time?

SK: Yes, but not very widely read. She was broadcasting a great deal, and I heard her on the radio station.

DT: But that's important, you know, because there was nothing that the audiences could bounce off their reactions against. For example, if a critic of any authority made a film seem very interesting and people were impelled to go see it, then you have a relationship. Now, of course, 1972, we have umpteen people writing seriously about them, so it's a changed situation.

SK: But isn't that situation of 1972 something that grew out of what was started in the early sixties?

DT: Oh, absolutely. Out of that and out of the film schools. I mean, just the momentum of all the written material about film as a serious art in the last ten years. The proliferation of books boggles my mind. When I first published my anthology in 1959, there had been virtually nothing written, nothing produced on film. That was one of the early books.

SK: Of the postwar period. There had been some earlier.

DT: Before that, in the thirties. But the critics in the thirties tended to have a Marxist orientation. Paul Goodman was writing . . .

SK: William Troy was writing, very well, for about three years.

DT: William Troy, but it was more political than anything else. Most of the others were hung up on the Soviet cinema. They were saying, Why can't we make films like *Potemkin* and *Alexander Nevsky*, etc.? But anyway, as

far as the situation now, there's a change as a result of the success of directors like Bogdanovich and Friedkin and Coppola and so forth. There's a
change in that suddenly the director has become a star, and you can now
witness a thirty-year-old being given tons of money by the studio to make
any kind of picture that he wants to. Whether it's any good is another matter. But there is a new authority now for younger directors.

SK: I feel—and please argue with this if you feel like it—that this is a result
of the stature and impact of the best foreign films of the sixties. There's
almost a sense of shame on the part of the United States.

DT: I agree, absolutely, I couldn't agree with you more. Suddenly you have Hollywood types who are talking about auteurs. I do think that that's had a
lot to do with it. The fact is that the circus of most American films being
made now in Hollywood and brought on location is virtually as good as
what's being done in Europe. Not the content, though: American movies, from what I can see, just do not deal with what's going on in the
society. They basically never have, except in the thirties.

SK: With exceptions that we all know about.

DT: Yeah. But there's so much happening now. The society is in such a state
of incredible disintegration—just look at the *Times* in the morning. And
I don't know of any [American] films that are dealing with what's happening in any meaningful way. There are no serious films about the
problems of old age, about the new towns and ghettos, about the results of
Vietnam. For example, there must be in this country, I would take a rough
guess, it's a wild guess but maybe a valid one, over ten million victims of
Vietnam, psychic victims. Now this is never reflected in any image that
you see on the screen. There's this incredible malaise stemming from what
this country is doing. I'm sure you know of people who've left the city
because of it, left the country because of it, who've dropped out because of
it. I don't know of any films that even touch on it tangentially. Whereas the
international cinema, the films that are being made in Europe, Africa,
Brazil, etc., really do deal with the felt content of their society.

SK: Just to be clear—*some* of the films that are being made abroad—the majority are still programmed films.

DT: Well, we don't see the bummers, you know, we tend to see only the better
ones, but numerically there's no question in my mind that the foreign
films—and "foreign" now includes Africa and Latin America, etc.—are

dealing with the serious problems, have gotten very, very personal. There's a new kind of film being made in the post-Godard era—films that are so deeply psychological, deeply personal, deeply adventurous in subject matter and narrative techniques, etc., that I must assume that they are still more serious about it, better than we are when it comes to reflecting art, art reflecting the society, etc. I think that there is a numerical disproportion.

SK: There certainly is. I would just like to put in a plug for two honorable exceptions of the past year—I thought that Barbara Loden's film *Wanda* has a real social and psychic dislocation.

DT: I thought that was marvelous. Absolutely. I mean, I don't want to just toss out all American films.

SK: And another film that had a TV stodginess to it but still dealt with the plight of the bourgeoisie as the locus for a lot of the trouble in this country was a film called *Desperate Characters*—I thought it was a genuinely serious picture.

DT: I didn't see it. But I agree with you on *Wanda*, one of the best American films I've seen in ten years.

SK: I quite agree.

DT: I think it's an extraordinary film.

SK: Sloughed off.

DT: Completely sloughed off.

SK: Since you are so enthusiastic, or at least keenly interested in what is happening in these foreign countries, let's talk about that. Which country or countries interests you most as filmmaking goes? Do you want to talk about individuals or countries?

DT: Well, we can do both. I guess we've got to start with Godard and then spring out from there. I have a feeling we don't completely agree on this, but for me Godard is *the* great genius in the history of cinema.

SK: We don't agree on that.

DT: That's okay. I mean, he reinvented the narrative form and is without question in my mind *the* most influential director in terms of *real* influence, that is to say of other young filmmakers wanting to make a film just like that.

SK: Two exceptions to that: one would be D. W. Griffith, whose worldwide influence was tremendous, and then there's Jean Renoir, whose worldwide influence was [also] tremendous. And just to put in the P. S. to your remarks on Godard: we do disagree on a lot of his works—on the sum total of his stature—but I would certainly say that if the truism that the best way to criticize is to make your own work of art [is valid], then without any question Godard is the most effective film critic of the last fifteen years, because his films represent a criticism of the way films were being made.

DT: That's true. I get this feedback. I'm not talking out of my head when I say these things, because I do meet young filmmakers from all over the world. I know many of them personally—some famous, some not so famous—and don't know of one who has not been influenced one way or another by Godard. And a lot of them struggle with the problem of not imitating him. You have someone like Bertolucci, for example, who is profoundly influenced by Godard. *Partner* is a Godardian work.

SK: There are lots of others, I'm not denying that. Makavejev, Tanner, and Lester—they're all outgrowths of Godard.

DT: Now, anyway, what happened was that this guy single-handedly gave us a new cinema, whether one really digs it or not. I don't know any antecedents for it. I could see the roots of his work in maybe ten or fifteen different directors, but I do think he changed the map of film, and as a result of Godard, film did become much more personal and much more adventurous in the sixties. And Truffaut of course was very influential in that suddenly young directors were not intimidated by the technological apparatus of filmmaking, by the monetary intimidations that go into filmmaking, and the net result is an extremely personal cinema.

SK: And a certain elan and freedom.

DT: Elan, yes, and there was no fear of dealing with subject matter in what might seem like an embarrassing psychological way. And then of course Godard went into this whole political thing.

SK: His earlier films, although they're quite wild and rackety, struck me as having a much profounder base of sincerity, of political conviction, than, for example, films like *La Chinoise*.

DT: Well, *La Chinoise* was a turning point for him; that was at a moment when he wasn't quite sure . . . I mean, it reads as a satire on the young Maoists in France, and he has been heavily criticized for not taking them seriously. But by the same token, he said that he did have a lot of sympathy for these young Maoists. I don't know whether he's double-talking there or not, but I don't regard his political films as essentially political. I think that the recent ones, like *Pravda* and *Le Vent d'Est*, are not solely films of his, but I have a basic sympathy toward them and for whatever he does. I find them again trying to do something new in cinema. I think that's all that Godard is about. If he simply regards himself as making films as political guns, I think he's crazy. Because those are films that can be seen by three or four people, and those three or four people may not like them.

SK: They're highly sophisticated and are not going to affect the masses in any notable way.

DT: Not at all. In fact, I had the disquieting experience of being at a screening of *Le Gai Savoir*. Remember that one?

SK: You showed it to me.

DT: Yes. I was sitting with this African director, Sembène, who I think is an extraordinary filmmaker, an extraordinary man, who knows some of the things that are going on in cinema, and he was just so beside himself watching that film. He hated it so much that to me it was interesting to witness a fellow filmmaker reacting like that. It's because Sembène follows kind of an old-fashioned socialist realism tradition and feels there's a moral obligation to tell simple stories in a simple narrative way. He hasn't gone through the ennui of the artist who feels that his work is bourgeois.

SK: And that form has been worn out. There's a theatrical analogue to this: the theatrical counterparts to Sembène in Europe are terribly angry with Peter Handke because his plays are directed at breaches of consciousness rather than at straight-line feeding of new material for new action.

DT: It's true what Godard said, that he regarded everything up to a certain point as show business—period. And I understand that. But for me his political films are not at all political, they're just Godard struggling to do something different with the form, and I'm sure that he's going to go back to making offshoots of some of his greater films, that he's not going to continue to make this kind of film, because he's going to get bored.

SK: To interject a personal note, one of my criticisms with Godard is that he gets visibly bored with what he's making after about twenty minutes of film time, after having started making it. He is, however, inarguably a very, very bright, let's say brilliant man, but he gets terribly bored with what's in hand, in my opinion, in many respects. Let's talk about some other countries. I know you're very interested in Latin America.

DT: Let's go back to France just for a minute, because I think that probably for me the most interesting director working in France now is this fellow Jacques Rivette, who has never really been seen widely over here and may be the most audacious new filmmaker that I know of. One of his films I'm not terribly fond of is his first film, *Paris Belongs to Us*, although the notion of trying to deal with the city making people go paranoid was an interesting one. I'm bringing over, finally, after two years of negotiations, his *L'Amour Fou*—"Mad Love"—which set off a scandal in France when he handed it in at four and a half hours. The producers turned white and they sliced it in half, opened it as a two-hour film, which failed, so then they brought out the four-and-a-half-hour version and it was a big success. He made the film three or four years ago. Since then he's gone on to make a twelve-hour film, and he's most highly regarded . . .

SK: [Let's talk about Japan next.]

DT: About a year and a half ago the opportunity arose to acquire a group of Ozu films. By then I was very deeply involved in distribution. I now have ten Ozu films, I'd say his major works. He made over fifty films, many in the silent era. I do have one silent film of his, a remake of a silent film, *I Was Born, But . . .* , which I'll be launching at some point. [Ozu remade this silent film as *Good Morning* in 1959.] Again, we may have to go back to the question of why certain films catch on at certain times. Why do you think, aside from the fact that *Tokyo Story* is a masterpiece and *Late Spring* a beautiful film, as are his others, that there obviously is some kind of an audience for Ozu?

SK: I have a possibly too sanguine view of the matter—that the film audience in this country has reduced numerically, drastically, but to some degree has improved in quality. The film audience knows much more about film than it ever did, even though there were people going to films two and three times a week lifelong in the twenties and thirties. And a certain amount of refinement of taste—I'm not talking about a nation of esthetes, God forbid—has entered into the filmgoing audience in the major centers, and places where it would enter. You mention distribution. Tell us about your experiences in distribution—how you got into it and how it's working for you, and what responses you've had to it that could tell something qualitative about culture.

DT: I got into it as a result of *Before the Revolution* and then I picked up one or two films subsequently, but for a few years I really didn't do anything. And then about two or three years ago suddenly I had thirty, forty, fifty films, and I had to make a decision as to what to do with them. I owned them for distribution—I had the exclusive license to distribute them—and it was then that I began learning what was involved and what it is to distribute a film, and I got kind of interested in it as my interest in the theater declined.

SK: That is, your own theater, the New Yorker.

DT: My own theater and in the theatrical business in general, because of the enormous decline in theaters in America for the sort of films I was interested in. I started looking for the so-called new outlets that had been explored before, such as by Audio Brandon and Janus Films.

SK: It was a counter-action.

DT: Yeah, and I sort of learned that was where the real market was for this type of film.

SK: What are these places?

DT: Well, by and large they're the universities around the country. Places such as where you teach—Yale, University of Michigan, University of California.

SK: You're talking now about 35mm distribution?

DT: Both: 35 and 16. The bigger and more well-heeled universities have the same facilities as a regular theater. They're funded very heavily so are able to put up a theater for $500,000 in a second, no problem. They have the fanciest equipment.

SK: It's true. The best equipment for theater stages in this country is in the universities.

DT: Exactly. And that's where film courses are being taught and where students have an opportunity to see the films. They no longer go to the downtown theaters. I think the decline of the theater business, as we know it, began with what I think of essentially as the bombing out of cities in America in the last five years. As the racial balances changed in the cities, with urbanites fleeing, people don't go to theaters at night anymore. For example, in Buffalo, a city of over one million people, there's not one motion picture theater open in the downtown area. The last one closed two years ago.

SK: There is a so-called suburban theater?

DT: They're out there—there are suburban theaters going up along highways and in shopping centers. They're showing only *The Godfather, The French Connection*, etc. None of them are showing any foreign films, certainly not. I mean, there's no chance that a film like *La Salamandre* could wind up in one of those suburban theaters. Not a chance.

SK: Since you mentioned that title, the Swiss film *La Salamandre*, to me one of the best films I've seen in many, many months, tell us a little about its commercial history in New York as relevant to what's going on in film.

DT: Well, we have to go back to Paris, and that will give you some insight into what's happening in Paris and New York vis-à-vis theaters. I saw it in Paris last January without subtitles. At that time it was a big hit in Paris—not big by our standards, but it was running in two cinemas simultaneously on the Left Bank. It was in its sixth month—it's still running in that same cinema, incidentally, almost a year later. I decided to take it on: I called Tanner in Geneva and made the arrangements. Then I was faced with the problem of how to open this film and make it work in New York, at just 50 percent of how it worked in Paris. So let's digress for a second and talk about how things are. Again we have to take a leaf out of Panofsky's book, about how things, in this case an industrial situation, affects moviegoing. There were some tax laws passed in Paris about ten years ago that allow investors to build cinemas; though I don't know the exact details, it was the classic tax shelter. The result of that was that multimillionaires were suddenly putting up theaters all over Paris, like crazy, particularly on the Left Bank. They'd buy a building that was run down, renovate, burrow into the ground, put in two or three theaters, and they were off to the races. Whether the theater made money or not, somehow they made money because of this tax shelter. The last time I was in Paris, in June, I saw a six-theater complex somewhere on the Left Bank—they're still going up like mushrooms. This is good, though, for the filmmaker: you have a situation where there are literally over one hundred of what we would call art houses, two-hundred- or three-hundred-seat theaters.

SK: What kind of films?

DT: Everything, everything. They show all the new Hungarian cinema, the new Brazilian cinema, anything being made that's of any remotely interesting cultural value gets shown in Paris as a result of that. And a film like *La Salamandre*, which is head and shoulders above most of the things seen over there, has a chance of running one full year. All right, let's come to New York now, the economics of opening a film like that. There's no mystery or secret: you just have to spend in the vicinity of $25,000 or $35,000 to launch such a picture. The alternate way would be to put it in the New Yorker, open modestly, get a similar set of reviews, but then it wouldn't really go anywhere else. The theory is that if you're in a fancy or prestigious midtown theater and it runs for two or three months, this will result in more sizable commercial bookings around the country. That you could get into what we call an art break. Because after a successful film works in one of these theaters it winds up in twenty or thirty theaters simultaneously—you've seen the ads where they've released *The Conformist* or any successful film. Considering the nature of the reviews, *La Salamandre* did only one-third of what it should have done at the Paris Theater. I mean, it's not a hip theater—they showed *A Man and a Woman* for a year and a half.

SK: It was *Son of a Man and a Woman* by that time.

DT: Yeah. I deliberately chose that theater because, first of all, it had been available to me at the time. I take all the risk when I go in there because I have to guarantee the house and guarantee all the advertising and publicity.

SK: You have to guarantee a certain return.

DT: They take the first X number of dollars of the seats.

SK: But you guarantee that they'll get that.

DT: No. But there's virtually no way that [the Paris Theater] won't gross X number of dollars to reach the guarantee. I mean, just by opening the doors they get that number of people in. But the net is so expensive, considering that one has to spend all that money on advertising, that in order for a picture to work there it has to hit a very high growth. It would have to gross, for argument's sake, $25,000 or $30,000 the first week. It did nowhere near that, maybe a little bit more than a third. Five years ago a film like that easily would have hit those grosses. This has to do with all the things that we've been talking about. What will happen with [*La Salamandre*] . . . I've got it booked now in about ten major cities. It will certainly be a much more commercial film than *Tokyo Story*, but the energy that goes into something like that is enormous, and it's speculative. That's what I don't like about it. I don't like the distribution system in America. It's purely speculative.

SK: As opposed to what?

DT: As opposed to a more cooperative way of getting films distributed in some European countries. The systems are somewhat different. Here's what happens [in America]: someone with a little bit of taste and a bankroll can say, "I'm a foreign film distributor," and he picks a film that he thinks will make him rich. It's a crap shoot. In effect, he's in the stock market. As a result of that, there's a whole mystique about distribution when in fact there is no mystique about distribution. All that distribution is about is moving a print from point A to point B.

SK: The *right* point B.

DT: Yeah, but these are things that are learned, and it exists solely for the purpose of enriching the distributors. It has nothing to do with helping the filmmaker. Most arrangements that are entered into are between the distributor and the producer. By that time the filmmaker has no piece of his film. He's sold his birthright to the producer. I tend to work a little differently. I tend to work mainly with directors.

SK: If they own their films.

DT: Well, in most cases they do, those that I deal with. Because producers of more commercial films tend to sell to richer companies. I always feel a strong moral obligation to the filmmaker. Now part of the terrible thing about film distribution in this country is that there's a very big track record of outright banditry on the part of the distributor. Unlike book publishing, which is honest. But film distribution exists solely for the purpose of making the distributor get rich. And I find this immoral and objectionable. It's changing. There is a newer breed of distributor coming on the scene now, who is more ethical and not interested in being a crook. Finally, being crooked is boring. You have to tie up a lot of psychic energy in two sets of books, in cheating a producer or a filmmaker, and it's a very boring way to spend your time.

SK: An easy way to make a lot of money if all you want is to make a lot of money.

DT: I don't see the social function as a result of a distributor. I'll give you a comparison. There is a setup in France—my friend is the head of it—a kind of distribution, exhibition, and service organization. Here's roughly how it works: this organization is responsible for the programmation of roughly four hundred theaters in France. They more or less decide what gets shown in these theaters. They have an arrangement for the shipping of prints, doing the publicity, in effect assuming some of the functions of a normal distributor, and they get a service fee for this. They don't participate in profits of the film—they just get a straight fee for servicing theaters and producers. So they are an in-between service organization without the built-in greed incentive.

SK: But they are still the doorway.

DT: They are the doorway to the film, but look what this results in. Let's say Filmmaker X, an adventurous, exciting filmmaker, comes along. He has a project he wants to do, with a $100,000 budget. My friend can tell the guy: All right, I like your idea. Go ahead and make the film. We'll guarantee you $50,000; you go to the Centre National du Cinéma, which is a state subsidy organization, and get the other $50,000. What [my friend] will do is take that film when it's finished as a result of the guarantee and put it in four hundred theaters for one week, each theater guaranteeing $1,000. The filmmaker has got his budget before he's begun his film. He doesn't have to go through the process of getting either bank money or speculative money or some horrible producer money or something like that, then making the film, then going through the business of selling it to the distributor, and then worrying about getting it into the theater. He's got it in his guarantee before he even shoots.

SK: A great deal depends, however, on the taste and the imagination of the service organization.

DT: Yes, right. Now, it's not completely perfect because those theaters are not art cinemas, and in order for them to survive they have to do a certain amount of commercial fare. But if they can run successfully for, say, thirty weeks, forty weeks out of the year with commercial stuff, crap, things that none of us are interested in, by virtue of this commercial success—the way they're organized is not meant to enrich the distributor per se—the other twelve weeks that are open will allow twelve interesting films to be made. And we don't have anything remotely resembling that.

SK: That's your fault.

DT: Exactly.

SK: Why don't you get into this kind of work?

DT: I delegate you to introduce me to Rockefeller or Henry Ford. I mean, the only way it could be done in this country is through foundation money. The only way that anything successful in a culturally interesting way can be done is through vast amounts of foundation money. Just as in theater schools, legitimate theater is being supported through foundation money. But to be a successful commercial distributor, I can think of much simpler things to do. It's a very crazy way to earn a living. I think I will beat this game because I'm doing it somewhat differently than the other guys. I'm very cost conscious. I don't have any glorious notions of taking a film and making a big theatrical success out of it, so I minimize the number of 35mm prints that I make, which are costly, and I just order 16mm prints as I need them. I nurse the film, and hopefully it will work. I owe a great deal of money. It's not on a sound financial footing at this point, but I think in two years it's going to work. But I'm not happy about it. You know, four years ago when I wasn't sure whether I wanted to get involved in distribution, I had these thirty films. I went to two other guys who are active in distribution—very active guys, they shall be nameless, who are doing some interesting things—and I said: Look, why are we all competing with one another, why are we involved in doing what is in effect double work? Let's all throw our bones in the kitty and work together. I like to do this kind of thing and you like to do that kind of thing; let's work it cooperatively. They laughed at me. And this is the newer breed of distributor. Because ingrained in these guys' psyches is the idea of this whole competitive thing.

SK: And the big hit.

DT: And the big hit. Stuff like that. And they laughed at me. I was very depressed about it. I'd still like to do something like that; I don't enjoy the financial, commercial rat-race aspect of distribution. I really don't. I would much rather have the time to explore how a wider market could be reached. How to get the films to as many people as possible, in other words, without having to do these survival numbers.

SK: In the middle sixties, I forget the exact year, a group of American film-makers got together and announced a plan—I never knew what happened to it—to do something that vaguely parallels what you describe as this French system. That is, to work up a number of sure bookings. First they were going to get these small guarantees from some universities, and with the capital they could finance low-budget pictures that would be sure of an initial audience. Let's leave out the question of why that didn't go forward. Why couldn't that still be done, with yourself as the head of the project? That wouldn't need foundation money directly in any way.

DT: I don't know.

SK: A hundred universities, which is not a large number, that would guarantee to book, let's put it this way, $5,000 worth of films a year each; you would then have $500,000.

DT: Yes, but what makes you assume that these one hundred universities are going to automatically book in everything that I take on?

SK: That would be part of the year's arrangement.

DT: On their part?

SK: Yes.

DT: They work competitively also. In the bigger universities, the guys that run the film societies and the film programs there are in effect like theater exhibitors. They have their own competition, you know.

SK: Yes, they want to succeed, too.

DT: And they want to succeed for maybe different reasons. Not that the money winds up in their pocket, but it gives them more cachet in their jobs. I mean, there's some direct material reward ultimately for what they're doing. I now have, as a matter of fact, about four or five guys around the country who do almost automatically book in everything that I bring over. I have one in Berkeley who almost sight unseen will book almost everything that I have now. I wish there were more like that. And I do have a few theaters that play a lot of my stuff. I will tell you that now in America there are only four art theaters, legitimate art theaters, what I would call art theaters, that are authentic, that play interesting films.

SK: Will you name them?

DT: Yes. The Bandbox in Philadelphia, the Surf Theatre in San Francisco, the Los Feliz in Los Angeles, and the Orson Welles in Cambridge, Massachusetts. And that's all that you have in America. There's literally nothing else. I'm not exaggerating because I know.

SK: So that if you live anywhere else and you want to see anything other than the programmed fare that comes around, you've got to go to the nearest art house or university or form a film society of your own?

DT: Right. That's where it's at. The universities have very well-known film teachers who are doing very creditable work. Guys like Gerald O'Grady and Charles Samuels up at Williamstown, Massachusetts, they simultaneously do a certain amount of scholarly writing on film and get audiences in their schools very interested in all the new work that's being done, and I've seen many, many difficult films that are being supported by people like that. Gerald O'Grady books in a lot of films that I have, and they are performing a very valuable service, due to the vacuum that has resulted with the closing of all these theaters. You'll see as many as one third of all theaters closing in the next five years.

SK: What is the total now?

DT: Fifteen thousand. *The Godfathers* will get bigger. The blockbusters will get bigger. The big companies will make more money. Look at the irony of this: there's no other period that I can remember as an adult with more interesting, personal films being made around the world. Qualitatively that number is double and triple of ten years ago. And in this country there are no outlets for them, other than the ones we've been talking about. Maybe cable television might jump into this market. That may be a possibility.

SK: It's been discussed, but even then, isn't cable television the competition?

DT: Right. And they'll tend to go commercial. Well, anyway, speaking of distribution, I don't like the system at all. I've played the role as a businessman/speculator in order to survive. First of all, I never take on anything that I don't like. Okay, we're beyond that. Let's say I get something that I do like. I have to make a business judgment as to what I can do with this film in dollars and cents and if I can make it work for the filmmaker, but I hate to have to do this with every film. There are a lot of films I take on that I and ten friends will like and that's it. I have one little film for which I'm in a minority. I've had it now for three years and have had exactly five play dates on it. I'm eager to have people see this film.

SK: That could even happen in an ideal distribution system. There will be ups and downs.

DT: It could. It's a little easier in an ideal distribution system.

SK: The French organization you described.

DT: Yes, that's true.

SK: There would never be 100 percent saturation with everything that you distribute. I know you're sounding a little bit defeated, but that's just the way you talk.

DT: No, I'm very optimistic. Because I think theaters are now irrelevant. They don't serve the same purpose that they used to. Fact of the matter is that by and large, people are afraid to go out in the major cities at night, they don't want to come home at twelve and one in the morning. There is this fear. I mean, what's the point of having a theater if people are afraid to go to it and enjoy what's being shown over there? We have to find an alternate.

SK: And you're in the process of finding it?

DT: And I'm in the process of finding it. I think I have a lot of research to do. I'm interested in the high school market. I'm interested in young people getting to see new works that normally they wouldn't even get to see in a major city.

SK: In your rental business in New York, your 16mm prints particularly, do you have many dealings with high schools?

DT: I'm beginning to now.

SK: We always think in terms of private societies or college and university [film] societies, but it's quite true that anyone who writes film criticism regularly, like myself, gets a great deal of mail from high school people.

DT: Sure. Intellectually the hip kids or the better students are way ahead of the sixteen-year-olds when we were sixteen, and they can handle this kind of thing very easily, no problem. I find some of the schools booking in Ozu and Bresson. Very complex material is being written about these directors, on the highest level, and yet these sixteen-year-old kids are beginning to see this stuff.

SK: A transformation?

DT: I think so. Probably the transformation has taken place in the society, where quite simply it's no longer congenial to have social congress. It isn't how it used to be. Life was physically more congenial twenty years ago, ten years ago. It's less so now. It's no mystery, we know this. With the forms of cultural access changing, you wind up with different systems of distribution, different systems of receiving information, etc. Again I come back to some of the ugly political things that have been going on in this country. There's less of a *joie de l'esprit* in wanting to receive entertainment. Put it this way: when we went to the movies twenty years ago it was by and large an entertainment experience. It wasn't hooked into high art or anything like that. The middlebrow aspect hadn't been operating in film as in other forms of our culture. So there was something very pleasant about going to a neighborhood Loew's theater in an old sweater and seeing a funny movie, or what have you. Then with the beginning of the art house movement in the mid-fifties and the early sixties you got a new kind of theater. A three-hundred- or five-hundred-seat theater done in what I called the Rugoff style, and the force behind that was somehow a psychic intellectual experience—it had nothing to do with entertainment. Then this declined.

SK: The influence it has on the methods of distribution?

DT: Since it's less of a congenial experience being in city centers now, even for an art film—I think you know what my point is.

SK: Yes, yes. Let me ask you one last thing regarding this particular problem. You talk about this disappearance of the moviegoing joy, which all of us have experienced and relished. Anyone who doesn't is a dehydrated fool.

DT: Absolutely.

SK: And that as ambition gets more intense, more intensely occupied with the inner and outer worlds, it's got to sacrifice some of the width of its audience.

DT: I would agree with that. In other words, the more complicated it gets, the less of a wider audience it can hope to reach. Is that what you're saying?

SK: Yes. The way I put it in something I wrote is that there's an interesting historical difference between the history of theater and the history of film. Theater began sacred and then acquired the profane; the film began profane, and there's a very strong effort at the present moment to acquire the sacred, using those terms culturally.

DT: Yes, that's true. That's very apt.

SK: And that we don't make it a grim culture operation, but certainly I think you and I are both willing to see some sacrifices made in order that *some* films reflect things that genuinely concern us.

DT: I went into distribution as the result of a series of accidents. As I remind myself, Sarris once said something very funny, and I have to agree with him: can you imagine a fourteen-year-old boy being asked, "What would you like to do when you grow up?" and that boy saying, "I want to become a foreign film distributor."

SK: I want to be a bookseller.

DT: Well, that's much more legitimate. There's a whole tradition of bookselling that's glorious. But a foreign film distributor? The economic structure is against the film distributor; therefore, a new distributor has to find a new way outside of the existing system, because it's lunatic to traffic in the kind of films that I distribute and think you are going to get them shown widely in theaters. There's no way that it will work anymore. It's the end of an era.

SK: I feel presumptuously that by virtue of the things you've already done, your current obligation is to do more in terms of assisting a new kind of distribution.

DT: Hopefully. I don't know. I'll let you know what happens in three years. I really haven't even begun to do any serious research of it. I'm going to start this fall. I have a couple of ideas that I want to try out, and we'll see what they're all about. All that I've done in the past two years has been to accumulate an enormous library, open films on an ad hoc basis, pray that the reviews would be good, that the response would be good, and that I could get a number of bookings on them—but that's a crazy way of distributing films. There must be about 150 film distributors that open and close shop yearly in New York. Some guy is on a vacation in Sweden, he sees a sex film, he's rich, he says, "Here's $25,000 even. I'm going to make a fortune on it." He brings it over and he goes through the whole process of trying to get the bloody thing launched; then he loses a couple of hundred thousand dollars, and that's the end of his experience.

SK: And if it's an interesting film you want to find three or four years later, there's not a [print] in the United States.

DT: Right. There are a lot of interesting films that have gotten waylaid as a result of these one-shot distributor guys. Of course, some have sold out to the conglomerates, Leo Dratfield's Contemporary Films, etc.—but the ones surviving have been strong for a number of years.

SK: But that's clearly the area that's engaging most of your interest.

DT: At the moment, yes. Because I think, for example, that by the time this gets published, if it gets published, the chances are very strong that I will no longer have the New Yorker. I won't close it down, but the chances are that someone else will have to operate it because there's no way that I can continue to operate it the way it has been going. I've been caught in the inflationary spiral; I can't program the kind of things I want to do over there. I'm not interested in programming commercial or quasi-commercial films.

SK: Or one more Humphrey Bogart festival.

DT: Oh my God, the idea of putting another Humphrey Bogart film in the New Yorker just drives me up a wall. I find that so insanely boring. And yet another situation that's going on in New York: the repertory market is saturated—it's a stupid market, I find it insanely dumb. You have a situation, literally, where two hundred prints are circulating all around New York. It works in the New Yorker so it goes down to the East Village; it works there, then it winds up in the Beekman, the Village, and then three months later it will go to the East Side. What could be more insane than that? It's a mindless kind of exhibition. You know, the moment I stopped uncorking a lot of these prints, we were stuck with an inventory of two hundred films. If you were in a small, economically viable theater like Pauline had in Berkeley and are into that type of programmation, you can do this endlessly. But when she was doing it, she was pretty much alone. When I was doing it, I was pretty much alone. Since then there have been ten other guys doing it. I'm not angry at them, I can't tell them how to run their lives or anything, but I find it so boring. When was the last time that a whole bunch of interesting new films were shown in New York, other than at the Museum of Modern Art? At the American Repertory, for example, I would like to see a lot of Sturges films being shown. Well, the economics of showing these things are crazy because the major distributors have discovered that there's a gold mine in this stuff. The way I used to buy the stuff and program it was relatively simple. Now it's a big deal—it's a lot of money—they say, "Oh well, Preston Sturges, you know that's very big in the revival market, we can't let you have it for $100."

DREAMS ON MY SCREEN

42nd Street (Lloyd Bacon)
Bad Company (Jean Eustache)
Before the Revolution (Bernardo Bertolucci)
Bicycle Thief (Vittorio De Sica)
Black Girl (Ousmane Sembène)
Boudu Saved from Drowning (Jean Renoir)
Breathless (Jean-Luc Godard)
Brief Encounter (David Lean)
Broadway Danny Rose (Woody Allen)
Casque d'Or (Jacques Becker)
Chronicle of Anna Magdalena Bach (Jean-Marie Straub and Danièle Huillet)
City Lights (Charles Chaplin)
Cléo from 5 to 7 (Agnès Varda)
The Conductor (Andrzej Wajda)
Diary of a Country Priest (Robert Bresson)
The Doorway to Hell (Archie Mayo)
Double Indemnity (Billy Wilder)
Dragon Chow (Jan Schütte)
Duck Soup (Leo McCarey)
Easy Living (Mitchell Leisen)
The Fire Within (Louis Malle)
Grand Illusion (Jean Renoir)
Hiroshima Mon Amour (Alain Resnais)

Horse Feathers (Norman Z. McLeod)

The Idiot (Akira Kurosawa)

Ikiru (Akira Kurosawa)

In the White City (Alain Tanner)

It's a Gift (Norman Z. McLeod)

Jazz on a Summer's Day (Bert Stern)

Jeanne Dielman (Chantal Akerman)

Journey to Italy (Roberto Rossellini)

The Koumiko Mystery (Chris Marker)

L'Atalante (Jean Vigo)

La Salamandre (Alain Tanner)

La Strada (Federico Fellini)

Land of Silence and Darkness (Werner Herzog)

Landscape in the Mist (Theo Angelopoulos)

Late Spring (Yasujiro Ozu)

Laughter (Harry d'Abbadie d'Arrast)

Lola (Jacques Demy)

Los Olvidados (Luis Buñuel)

M (Fritz Lang)

The Magnificent Ambersons (Orson Welles)

A Man Escaped (Robert Bresson)

Man of Marble (Andrezj Wajda)

Masculin Féminin (Jean-Luc Godard)

Million Dollar Legs (Edward Cline)

Modern Times (Charles Chaplin)

Mon Oncle Antoine (Claude Jutra)

Mr. Arkadin (Orson Welles)

The Mystery of Kaspar Hauser (Werner Herzog)

The Night of the Shooting Stars (Paolo and Vittorio Taviani)

The Palm Beach Story (Preston Sturges)

Pather Panchali (Satyajit Ray)

Pickpocket (Robert Bresson)

Pull My Daisy (Robert Frank and Alfred Leslie)

The Rules of the Game (Jean Renoir)

Sansho the Bailiff (Kenji Mizoguchi)

Shanghai Express (Josef von Sternberg)

Signs of Life (Werner Herzog)

Singin' in the Rain (Stanley Donen and Gene Kelly)

Six in Paris (Claude Chabrol, Jean Douchet, Jean-Luc Godard, Jean-Daniel Pollet, Éric Rohmer, Jean Rouch)

The Strawberry Blonde (Raoul Walsh)

Stroszek (Werner Herzog)

Sullivan's Travels (Preston Sturges)

Sunset Boulevard (Billy Wilder)

Sweet Smell of Success (Alexander Mackendrick)

Thirty-Two Short Films About Glenn Gould (François Girard)

Tokyo Story (Yasujiro Ozu)

Töni (Jean Renoir)

Top Hat (Mark Sandrich)

Touch of Evil (Orson Welles)

The Treasure of the Sierra Madre (John Huston)

Umberto D. (Vittorio De Sica)

Une Femme Douce (Robert Bresson)

Up to a Certain Point (Tomás Gutiérrez Alea)

Vidas Secas (*Barren Lives*; Nelson Pereira dos Santos)

Viridiana (Luis Buñuel)

Vivre Sa Vie (*My Life to Live*; Jean-Luc Godard)

White Heat (Raoul Walsh)

Woyzeck (Werner Herzog)

Yaaba (Idrissa Ouedraogo)

CREDITS

INDEX